DON'T WAIT FOR
THE NEXT WAR

DON'T WAIT FOR
THE NEXT
WAR

A Strategy for American Growth and Global Leadership

GENERAL (RET.) WESLEY K. CLARK

PUBLICAFFAIRS
New York

Published in the United States by PublicAffairs™,
a Member of the Perseus Books Group

PublicAffairs books are available at special discounts for bulk purchases in the U.S. by
corporations, institutions, and other organizations. For more information, please contact the
Special Markets Department at the Perseus Books Group, 2300 Chestnut Street, Suite 200,
Philadelphia, PA 19103, call (800) 810-4145, ext. 5000, or e-mail special.markets@perseus-
books.com.

Library of Congress Cataloging-in-Publication Data
Clark, Wesley K.
   Don't wait for the next war : a strategy for American growth and global leadership /
Wesley K. Clark.
      pages   cm
   Includes bibliographical references and index.
   ISBN 978-1-61039-433-8 (hardback) — ISBN 978-1-61039-434-5 (e-book)
   1. National security—United States.   2. Strategy—United States.   3. United States—Politics
and government—21st century.   4. United States—Military policy.   5. United States—
Foreign relations.   6. World politics--21st century.   7. Security, International.   I. Title.
II. Title: Rethinking America's global mission.
   UA23.C5588 2014
   355'.033573—dc23

2014024152

First Edition
10 9 8 7 6 5 4 3 2 1

A12006 538759

This book is dedicated to American veterans, who have served both in war and in peace. For more than a century they have borne personally the weight of America's strategy, in its successes and in its failures. In their honor, it is time for the United States to create an effective national strategy before the next war compels us to do so.

CONTENTS

INTRODUCTION

Gathered around a dinner table, sipping their drinks and glancing at the menus, were members of the Syrian opposition: a young businessman from Chicago, a mild-mannered professor from the University of Arkansas, another younger man who had flown in from London, a local associate, and a couple of others. They were in Los Angeles in April 2013 looking for American support—money, friends, influence, and understanding.

Most lived in the United States, some had grown up here; all knew what America stood for: freedom, democracy, opportunity. This was why they, or their families before them, had emigrated here in the first place, and this was precisely what they wanted to take home to Syria. They also knew that America was incredibly strong economically, rich with technology, capital, and promise, and they were very much aware of what our armed forces were capable of. None of them had served in uniform, but they had a profound respect for US military power, and in particular for what our Air Force could do to help their situation at home.

The situation in Syria was, of course, murderous. It was the spring of 2013, and the death toll in that nation had just surpassed 100,000. I was also at the table that night. I had been invited by an associate who had broad business relationships in the Middle East because of my background and general interest in issues of war and diplomacy. Ultimately, while the Syrians wanted support from the US government, they were also looking for friends and whatever forms of assistance might be available outside of government sources.

So we talked about the struggles of a group of brave men and women to resist a tyrannical and brutal regime. The stunning death toll was only the beginning; millions of Syrians had been driven from their homes, and refugees were flooding into neighboring states to escape the fighting. Turkey, Lebanon, and Jordan were all affected. Saudi Arabia, Qatar, and perhaps Turkey were providing the opposition with weapons, but it wasn't enough.

According to the opposition, the regime was directing the Syrian forces to limit the killing to no more than five hundred persons per day in order to temper the international outcry and fend off forcible intervention. It was constantly testing and probing the international community's tolerance. What could Bashar al-Assad's regime get away with? How much brutality could it apply before the world took action? And to complicate things even further, outsiders, including Iran and its political-military arm in the region, Hezbollah, were now involved in the fighting, too.

As the talk around the table continued, I thought about all the representatives of other groups around the world that had looked to America for assistance—people I had known who had undergone similar struggles in their pursuit of freedom.

First, there was Haiti. In 1994, as director of strategic plans and policy for the Joint Chiefs of Staff, I had heard the Haitians talk about the repressive junta led by General Raoul Cédras—on an island, a few murders could be a very effective form of intimidation. I had been among those who had helped then-president Jean-Bertrand Aristide return to government.

Then Bosnia. In 1994–1995 I had met extensively with Bosnian Muslims and Croats. As a member of Richard Holbrooke's diplomatic team charged with ending the conflict, I recalled Haris Silajdžić, then the number-two man in the Bosnian Muslim government, remarking, in the back of a bombed-out building in Mostar, "I can understand why the Serbs would torture a grown man, but a five-year-old boy?" Any torture was shocking and repellant to me. That war finally came to an end when the United States helped to negotiate an agreement in late 1995.

In the late 1990s, as Serb repression in Kosovo grew, I had heard the concerns of leaders in Eastern Europe and the Baltic states as they emerged from Soviet occupation and sought membership in the North Atlantic Treaty Organization (NATO). President Lennart Meri of Estonia told me about the brutal Soviet occupation in Lapland during the 1930s—women had been mutilated and children fed to wild, starving sled dogs as the Laplanders resisted the imposition of communism. I had been shown a picture of an old man with a pistol to his head—he was the last of the Forest Brothers, men who had been executed in Estonia in 1979 by the KGB, after some thirty-five years of resistance. I had met with the Albanians in 1998, and with the Kosovar Albanians in 1998 and 1999, and I had seen the reports of the Serb mortars falling on Kosovo civilians. A whole family—about 60 men, women, and children—had been murdered. I had heard the Kosovar Albanians speak of their fierce determination to break free of the Serbs. Ultimately, NATO fought a war—we called it the Kosovo Air Campaign, to avoid the term "war"—to end Serb ethnic cleansing there.

Even as a retired General Officer (that's what we call ourselves), I was still occasionally contacted and entreated by individuals and groups around the world seeking a better life for themselves and their families. They knew my reputation from my thirty-eight years of service to the United States Army, during which I led NATO's 1999 operations against Serbia as NATO Supreme Allied Commander, and later, my run for the Democratic presidential nomination in 2003–2004. I had spoken with the Iraqi diaspora in 2002–2003, for example, and with parents of

Egyptian protesters in 2011. I had spoken with Libyans working to overthrow Muammar al-Qaddafi, with the members of the People's Mujahedin of Iran (MEK), and now, the Syrians. They were all earnest and brave men and women who wanted a life of freedom and greater opportunity—a life worth fighting for. But they were overmatched, and they wanted our help.

Of course, they were also working our system—to win sympathy, to gain influence, to elicit support, and ultimately, to use America to gain their ends at home. Sure, we were always in danger of being manipulated; but, after all, in the eighteenth century, Benjamin Franklin and Thomas Jefferson had worked Paris in a similar way, during our own Revolutionary War, as they sought allies and resources to give them a leg up in their fight against the British.

It's hard not to be a little flattered when others come to America for assistance. It's a reaffirmation of our country's values and strengths, especially for those of us who served in uniform or in the defense establishment during the Cold War and remember the ideological struggle of those years. Each of us in some small way was part of the system that won the sweetest strategic victory of the past few centuries—a seventy-year-long, worldwide, geostrategic competition and clash of values in which we prevailed without direct conflict. By 1992, people spoke of only one superpower. We had achieved a unipolar international system built around American values.

As I sat at that table in Los Angeles, I was proud that we were still hosting those who admired our values, respected our power, and sought our help in emulating America. Their goal was to attain the political rights and advantages that Americans enjoy.

But I was also concerned. The Assad regime was proving to be a tough nut to crack, and not just because it was so well entrenched. It had strong support from significant minorities and foreign powers.

The United States in 2013 still had 80,000 men and women in Afghanistan as well as bases and fleets throughout the Middle East, not to mention the largest defense budget in US history. And it was still growing. The men and women in uniform had endured almost twelve years of continuous combat, during which time the United States had suffered 40,000 casualties, including over 6,000 dead. We had spent north of $1 trillion. Hundreds of thousands of veterans suffering from varying degrees of posttraumatic stress disorder and traumatic brain injury would need care for years to come, and the American public was getting tired of war and casualty reports. The so-called Arab Spring was quickly turning into winter. Unrest, violence, and rapid, unpredictable political change seemed to be the new normal. The status quo that Western powers had helped to shape during the Cold War was rapidly changing. Many economies in the Middle East were suffering, and even Egypt's domestic oil industry, heavily subsidized, was failing. There was no peace agreement between Israel and the Palestinians, despite decades of American effort, and Iran was on a path to nuclear weapons.

Amid all of this, the United States was engaged in implementing a new policy called "the Pivot to the Pacific." The policy declared that the future of American strategic interest lay in Asia. But the public discussion glossed over what would happen to the regions we were pivoting from.

For twenty years, the US armed forces had maintained a strong focus on the Middle East, beginning in 1990–1991 with the First Gulf War, in which over 500,000 US troops were deployed. After that war the United States fostered partnerships in the region, especially with the members of the Gulf Cooperation Council. We deepened our military relationship with Israel. We strengthened our military presence in the Gulf to deter Saddam Hussein from further aggression. The US Air Force flew Operation Southern Watch from Saudi Arabia, and Northern Watch from Turkey, to maintain pressure on Saddam's regime and to protect the Kurds in northern Iraq. When Saddam refused to permit the reentry of United Nations inspection teams to verify the elimination of his weapons of mass destruction, the United States initiated Operation Desert Fox—four days of strikes against Iraq in December 1998. Subsequently, strikes against Iraq's air defense sites were ordered upon provocation. Throughout this period, the US armed forces and the US Central Command were busy preparing for war. It was, as one very senior US Army leader confided to me in December 1998, "where we wanted to fight."

I had been a participant in much of this—from helping to train and ready the forces that fought the Gulf War, to drawing out the lessons afterward, helping shape deterrent policy toward Saddam, guiding strikes against Iraq, and helping to provide defensive support to Israel in the late 1990s. But for all our effort in the Middle East, what did we have to offer the Syrians by 2013? Had they come to the party too late? Were we through with the region? I didn't have an answer that day in Los Angeles. The meeting ended warmly, but inconclusively.

The next day, the same group met with a US senator. There was another conversation around a dinner table. The senator listened intently as the Syrians described the conditions on the ground in Syria and their needs. But what could actually be done? the senator asked. It was a telling question, one that hinted not only at America's overburdened armed forces but at the lack of a secure, confident strategic platform from which to launch a response.

• • •

Today, the United States stands at a fateful crossroads. After two decades as the world's undisputed superpower, we are facing new realities at home and abroad; it is time to rethink our role and set new objectives and priorities.

Not everything has changed, and yet enough changes have taken place to require a careful reassessment. After more than a decade of frustrating US military engagement, the Middle East remains a region in transition and in turmoil. Deployed US forces are rapidly drawing down. But in the process of pulling back, do we become a nation of passive isolationism, mending ourselves and conserving resources in an effort to address domestic concerns, such as our fading educational superiority and our burgeoning public debt? Or do we remain engaged in the world? Do we maintain our focus on the Middle East—still perhaps the most volatile region in the world and a critical area for the world economy—staying engaged, but with fewer military commitments? Or do we redirect our resources and efforts from the Middle East to Asia in response to growing tensions there? What about the blow-up with Russia in Ukraine that has emerged in the midst of this? And, how should we deal with other significant issues and concerns impacting the United States abroad?

Answering these questions requires that we not overreact to the latest crisis or news story from abroad. America will almost always face acute challenges—including threats, conflicts, and humanitarian crises—and will likely face enough of them to keep our operations centers and the White House Situation Room busy night and day. But our responses to various threats and crises from around the world do not themselves constitute a cohesive national strategy that will bring America together and provide a roadmap to our future.

The fractious nature of political discourse in the United States today suggests that we are deeply at odds with ourselves. The lack of a national sense of purpose seems reflected in the vacuous twenty-four-hour news cycles that capture every nuance of the conduct of minor celebrities, the latest airline crash or lurid horror, but fail to track the major forces and conditions impacting the lives and futures of ordinary Americans. You can sense the need for a new strategy in the faces of the young men and women in uniform today. They travel to and from their assigned duties while facing challenges that no longer seem novel, or even winnable—merely dangerous, dull, and costly.

My objective in this book is to make the case that we need to develop a comprehensive national strategy that addresses the long-term issues confronting the United States at home and abroad. And we need to do so in full awareness that some believe America's power is declining, at least relative to China's. In one of his columns on foreign affairs, Leslie H. Gelb, a former senior government official and president emeritus of the Council on Foreign Relations, wrote that "the real leverage between the United States and China comes down to economic horsepower." Gelb went on to chastise Congress and the Tea Party, quoting old China hand and former US ambassador to China Stapleton Roy, who said, "You talk about getting tough on China. . . . We should first get tough on ourselves."[1]

Crafting and implementing national strategies is more complicated today than it was in the days of Metternich and Bismarck, when Britannia was the balancing power in the concert of Europe. Today, increasingly powerful multinational and international organizations play leading roles on the global stage. These include international governmental organizations (IGOs) like the United Nations, the World Bank, and the African Union as well as influential nongovernmental organizations (NGOs) such as the Bill & Melinda Gates Foundation, or George Soros's Open Society Foundations. Then there are the giant multinational corporations, like Exxon Mobil and General Electric, to name two that are familiar to most Americans. Multinationals may claim a nationality, but often their leadership and perspectives are international—they have little national loyalty and serve no nation's interest, seeking advantages everywhere, maximizing their gains, and minimizing their costs to benefit their shareowners. International security firms can be hired for their expertise, technology, and muscle by any nation, and their sometimes adversaries—nonstate actors like international crime syndicates, drug cartels, and, of course, terrorists—are similarly powerful, fluid, and globalized.

Still, the nation-state remains the fundamental force in world affairs. Nation-states pass and enforce laws and treaties; they tax, regulate, and in many cases support commerce, art, education, and science. States organize, equip, and employ military forces both internally and externally. They have the legal monopoly on the use of violence within their own borders. Absent an international "sovereign" to enforce international law, and despite efforts to provide greater authority to the United Nations to protect populations from abuse and mistreatment within states' borders, states themselves are supreme. Their only restrictions are the rights and authorities they themselves cede and have ceded to international organizations like the United Nations or the European Union.

Strategy, then, is fundamentally about governments' actions, laws, policies, and approaches. But a government's strategies must recognize all the factors in an increasingly complex international environment. For the United States, seeking answers to questions like Syria, and connecting them to larger issues, such as America's vital interests abroad and American prosperity and economic strength, is no simple matter. It's not like Risk, the popular board game, where, to see if you are winning, you simply count "how many countries are in your camp."

Nor is it about popular opinion. Public support is necessary, but it's an unreliable guide. After the First Gulf War, President George H. W. Bush's approval ratings stood at 90 percent for months. But rather than providing an accurate measure of success, the rating reflected a feeling of triumphalism. After Al-Qaeda's strikes against the United States on 9/11, Congress and the American people came together to back our president as we launched into war in Afghanistan, and later in Iraq. It was fear that pulled us together, and the sacrifices of war that held us together for months afterward. But that didn't make our policy choices right or durable. Our decisions may have felt good, but they were no substitute for strategy. So the challenge for the United States is this: At this crucial pivot point, how can the United States find its role in the world without the galvanizing focus of the next war?

CHAPTER 1

The American Strategic Experience

Although its origin is in battle plans, strategy is more than a military concept. It is the way we get things done—how we take and use the resources we have to attain the ends we seek. It applies everywhere, and to every human endeavor, and certainly to almost every successful organization.

Most businesses center their activities around a corporate vision and a strategy—despite being subjected to the buffeting of short-range, quarterly-earnings appraisals by the stock market. Investment decisions usually reflect multiple years of earnings and are built around appraisals of long-term risks and opportunities. Engineering firms plan for the future with elaborate charts and diagrams. States and municipalities normally think strategically about economic development. They do not just trust "the market." Instead they have strategies, creating economic development organizations and planning commissions, holding study sessions, and using other means at their disposal to sift through the challenges and opportunities they face and to propose ways to meet the needs and priorities of the communities they serve. Charities, churches, and nongovernmental organizations all do strategic planning—constructing vision statements, goals, and objectives; adjusting their activities based on self-evaluations; and measuring expenditures against revenues. Good strategies are specific and relatively long-term.

THE NEED FOR A NATIONAL STRATEGY

America, however, does not have a strategy for our nation that the majority of Americans understand and on which they can agree. The experts and academicians fight over it, as do senators, members of Congress, bloggers, and talk-show hosts. *Washington Post* editorial-page editor Jackson Diehl, in November 2010, wrote, "This Administration is notable for its lack of grand strategy." John Mearsheimer, a University of Chicago professor of political science, wrote in the *National Interest*, in January 2011, "America adopted a flawed grand strategy after the Cold War." A month later, British historian Niall Ferguson wrote in *Newsweek* about the Obama administration's "lack of any kind of a coherent grand strategy."[1]

Professor Daniel W. Drezner, a Tufts University professor of international politics, quoting these writers, said that "a grand strategy consists of a clear articulation of national interests married to a set of operational plans for advancing them."[2] But this definition is both too academic and too narrow. In practice, our national strategy has always been built around our political values, our economic interests, and our willingness to use force to defend them. Except among academics or the policy elite, we usually don't lay out the goals and interests with very much specificity, instead acting as though they were just common sense. Ask the average person about America, and he or she will say that America's interests—the purpose of our strategy—have something to do with freedom, opportunities, security, fairness, a good future, and a better, safer, and more prosperous life for our kids. Our interests are our values—or so political candidates often tell us, without ever getting very specific about the conflicts and contradictions inherent in those rather vague concepts.

America is a large, diverse country—but, as Bill Clinton has said many times, what unites us is far greater than what divides us. It's plain to my friends abroad that the interests on which Americans agree are more powerful than those on which we differ, across the political spectrum. However, when it comes to getting there, Americans disagree a lot. For more than a decade, the majority of Americans, in response to public-opinion polls, have said that "the country is headed in the wrong direction." The pattern has been sustained year after year, whether the stock market is up or down, whether we are engaged in warfare or not, and whether we have Democrats or Republicans in office.

Grand strategy is about how nations maneuver to gain their interests abroad. It is in the realm of foreign policy. But that's only a portion of the strategic vision that America needs. President Dwight D. Eisenhower recognized that he couldn't afford to bankrupt America to pay for national defense; similarly, America's strategy today cannot ignore the need for a sustainable vision for economic power at home. The power to maneuver abroad derives not only from our strong military and able diplomats, but also, and even more fundamentally, from our economic power. Economic power is hard power. Just look at how Vladimir Putin has used Russia's natural gas supplies to intimidate Europe and threaten Ukraine.

When I discussed the need for a comprehensive national strategy with a Republican friend, a former high official in the Bush administration, his reaction was, "Wes, that sounds a lot like socialism!" He was only half-joking. When did planning for a stronger, more secure America become socialist? Of course, he knew it was nothing like socialism; but his warning reflected the powerful partisan differences that have filled the void created by the lack of a unifying, forward-looking sense of American purpose. Republicans and Democrats have always seen the balance between private and public interests differently, but we have elevated that difference into a huge political obstacle.

Yes, some parts of the US government bureaucracy do conduct strategic planning. The White House publishes a National Security Strategy Report, for example, that posits a vision for the United States in world affairs, assesses the international environment, and describes how America plans to handle it. This document even deals with a number of economic security issues, such as energy—although it doesn't actually go into detail about the economy itself. The Quadrennial Defense Review, conducted by the Department of Defense, looks at the international situation and projects the forces and other military resources needed to support the nation's foreign policy. These plans form the backbone of the country's National Security Strategy. The State Department has created a Quadrennial Diplomacy and Development Review of foreign policy to strengthen the capacity of civilian government agencies to support the National Security Strategy. The White House also publishes the annual Economic Report of the President, which describes the economy in some detail and discusses US fiscal and monetary policies as well as the global economic environment. The Department of Energy will begin doing a Quadrennial Technology Review, and the General Accounting Office published a broad strategy aimed at reducing America's budget deficit.[3]

What is missing is the big, inclusive picture—a vision that links both our foreign-policy and security issues with our economic power at home, a strategy that is not so completely derived from one administration that it is automatically distrusted by the rival political party. It is a regrettable fact that if we want a unifying political agenda, we have to create it outside of the traditional party structures.

In the United States, most of us believe that that government is best which governs least. A minimalist view of government's function is inherent in the US Constitution and in American political traditions. The fundamental question, though, is what constitutes the acceptable minimalist measures of government. This is the essence of Fourth Amendment issues about privacy, for example, or the "commerce clause" in Article I, and other enduring constitutional questions. Is government only to secure our borders and wage war? Should it intervene in the economy, and if so, for what purposes? These have been recurrent issues in American politics.

One area where we have experienced a linkage of foreign policy and the domestic economy is in free trade agreements, and these efforts illustrate the obstacles we face in trying to create a unified strategy. The first of these, the North American Free Trade Agreement (NAFTA), was highly controversial politically. The arguments in NAFTA's favor were many, ranging from broad support of "free-market principles" to detailed analyses of specific industries. At its signing, President Bill Clinton said, "We have made a decision that will permit us to create an economic order in the world that will promote more growth, more equality, better preservation of the environment, and a greater possibility for world peace. We are on the verge of a global economic expansion sparked by the fact that at this critical moment the United States took a decision that it would compete, not retreat." It took four years for NAFTA to be negotiated and passed by Congress, and it has remained controversial, especially because of its mechanisms for regulating such matters as labor and environmental standards. Still, the agreement has produced significant increases in America's trade and commerce with Mexico and Canada. Later agreements have also occasioned some tough fights, sometimes on issues such as human rights abuses, which tend to be proxies for other, more consequential labor-market issues. And these fights continue today on current efforts with Europe and Asia.

Because national strategies, like free trade agreements, end up picking winners and losers in the domestic economy, they usually need overarching public support. They aren't likely to be developed in the cloistered hallways of academe, expressed in complex formulas understandable only by educated elites, or slipped into legislation unnoticed in the early-morning hours of a holiday weekend. Instead, if they're to be successful, they emerge with powerful simplicity from multiple sources, and often with bumper-sticker clarity.

Creating strategies—even in foreign policy—has been exceptionally difficult for America. As Alexis de Tocqueville, the astute French observer, noted almost two hundred years ago, "foreign policy requires the use of almost none of the qualities that belong to democracy, and, on the contrary, demands the development of nearly all those qualities which it lacks. . . . Only with difficulty can democracy coordinate the details of a great undertaking, settle on one plan, and then follow it stubbornly across all obstacles. It is little capable of devising measures in secret and patiently awaiting their result."

Tocqueville was only partially correct. Although it may be true that the US government was largely incapable of the minuet of intrigue that marked the European politics of Tocqueville's day, the power of America's popular vision gave us a certain constancy and strength in foreign policy that the nondemocratic Europe of his day lacked. We were a nation animated by the idea of the New World and driven by the call of the West. For decades we expanded across the continent, enlarging our nation and pushing against the boundaries of colonial powers to the north, south, and west. That expansion continued despite changes in administrations, political parties, or technology and despite the constraints of treaties with Native Americans or understandings with foreign powers. We had a vision of ourselves—driven by political imagination and hard economics, and implemented by force of arms when necessary—that was large enough to encompass the whole continent and strong enough to carry us through setbacks and challenges.

Thomas Jefferson negotiated the Louisiana Purchase in 1803. Twenty years later, James Monroe warned off the European powers by issuing his Monroe Doctrine. Two decades after that, we were in the Pacific Northwest by the tens of thousands, staking our claim. After another two decades, we completed the first transcontinental railroad and bought Alaska. Decades later, we were still bringing in new states, which were populated by immigrants hungry for land and opportunity. We have described this continental claim as "Manifest Destiny." But in fact it was just a daring, grand project that the vast majority of Americans agreed on. Congress, presidents, governors, businessmen, and ordinary Americans filled in the details, but no amount of private intrigue, or fancy maneuvers by an autocratic government, could have animated the fulfillment of that vision as effectively as American democracy and the free enterprise system did. It was a goal so strong that, ultimately, it triumphed even over the divisive issue of slavery and the less divisive, but no less morally complicated, claims of the Native American peoples.

Usually, we combined idealistic enthusiasm with a clear-eyed prospect of economic gain—as in President Andrew Jackson's machinations to seize Texas, starting in 1829, or in the longing to free Cuba later in the nineteenth century over a time period spanning four US presidents. Strategy wrapped itself in conflict, whether with the Mexicans or with the Spaniards. It was driven by and also drove economic development, including the rapid industrialization of the North during and immediately after the Civil War. Sometimes we weren't successful—we tried twice to take Canada, and failed both times, and negotiated our way out of another fight with Britain over British Columbia. Sometimes we violated standards of conduct that we now enforce vigorously on others—we carried out depredations against Native Americans, inflicted unacceptable brutality in the conflicts against Mexico, and took action on questionable evidence, such as when we launched the Spanish American War. There is no excusing the excesses, crimes, and failures along the way, but nor should those blind us to the success of the overarching purpose that animated the nation—or the value of having such a vision.

Even when we succeeded, we often struggled with the consequences of our actions. The Reconstruction era in the South was followed by decades of internal struggle and lost opportunities. At the dawn of the twentieth century, we freed Cuba after a brief occupation, gave it up, freed the Philippines, and then fought a vicious war there. We engineered Panama's break away from Colombia, built the Panama Canal, and then suffered the need for repeated interventions in Central America and the Caribbean. Some of those interventions would continue throughout the twentieth century, up through the 1989 invasion of Panama to overthrow dictator and former CIA agent Manuel Noriega.

Yes, we made mistakes, but we had a long-term vision, a sometimes fractured consensus of values, overarching agreement on the economic value of expansion westwards, and the military prowess to carry us forward. On balance, looking back, we can see that the rise of the United States to global power was a product of that vision, as well as of the blessings of geography, natural resources, and our remarkable American spirit, and even that it has brought huge benefits to mankind.

Moreover, the US government played a vital part in this strategy, not only in pushing the frontiers, but also in taking measures to encourage commerce and strengthen the tendons of American life. Again and again, government was used by the American people, speaking through Congress and the presidents, to further this vision. Efforts like the Erie Canal, the Homestead Act, and the Land-Grant College Act contributed greatly to the growth of the American heartland. There were preferences for building canals, and of course there was the transcontinental railroad—a decades-long dream finally realized with strong government support. As the great nineteenth-century industrialists—such as Andrew Carnegie and John D. Rockefeller—built their fortunes, they worked closely with government, using it whenever they could, and often to excess.

The economy of nineteenth-century America was driven by scarce labor and cheap land. It became known as the American method: workers in the United States were paid higher wages than their counterparts in Europe, because industry had to compete to attract them against the lure of wide-open lands and other opportunities. We were unlike Europe; there was no call here for unions then, and no talk of "socialism."

By the early twentieth century, as the frontier of the American West closed, America was the world's largest integrated market and its largest industrial power. We had topped Great Britain in iron and steel. We relentlessly invented and mechanized new technologies—telegraph, electricity, light bulbs, telephones, automobiles, tractors and harvesters, and the first airplanes—and were seeing the beginnings of mass production. We had also created new forms of organizations with the corporation and its brainchild, the "trust," or holding company. From this rapid industrialization new political strife arose concerning the proper role of public versus private interests. The Progressive movement emerged to correct some of the excesses of the economy—including monopolistic economic power; dismal, unsafe working conditions; and the exploitation of labor—and other social movements began to soften the heartlessness of rapid industrialization and create a new appreciation of the public good. Throughout much of this period, foreign policy was almost disconnected from domestic strife; it seemed to unfold based on our century-old vision of a Western Hemisphere led and dominated by the United States, and isolated from the quarrels of the Old World in Europe—until World War I.

NATIONAL STRATEGY IN WARTIME

The Great War (1914–1918) marked a new milestone in the emergence of a unified American strategy for action abroad and at home—this was the moment where war became the impetus for strategic consensus. After holding firm on neutrality for two and a half years, and winning his reelection on the promise of keeping the United States out of the war, President Woodrow Wilson bowed to public opinion and led the United States into World War I, siding with Britain, France, and Italy against the Central Powers of Germany, Austria-Hungary, and Turkey. The belligerence contained an avowedly ethical foundation—it would be a war to end all wars, and a peace created along the lines of democratic principles. Wilson mobilized the nation, becoming, in his own words, a "War President."[4]

Partisan fighting diminished in Congress, with congressmen quickly agreeing upon major actions. Taxes were raised, especially taxes on industries that might profit from war. Federal agencies, such as the War Industries Board, coordinated production of war materiel and regulated profits, and prices were fixed for key commodities. Citizens' boards were created to select young men for conscription. A National War Labor Board handled labor issues, opposing wartime strikes that could disrupt production, but advocating an eight-hour workday and equal pay for women; it actually served to promote unionization. An office of propaganda regulated what newspapers could tell the public. Daylight Savings Time was introduced. The federal government took control of the railroads. And all of this was done within a few months.

A new army was raised, and frenetic activity in construction and military industry saw 2 million men organized and deployed to France in less than eighteen months. It was America's first experience in a unified, essentially nonpartisan national strategy, and it came with many mistakes, much confusion, and wasted efforts. Many of Wilson's repressive measures—like the Espionage Act, and later, the Sedition Act, which stifled free speech—were opposed by his strongest supporters.

Despite heroic efforts at home, the US troops in France at the war's end in 1918 were largely equipped and supported by our Allies. A major US industrial effort had been planned to come to fruition in 1920–1921. Yet under the impetus of the Great War, America was attempting something altogether new: an integrated national strategy. By harnessing its economic potential to power its military and foreign policy, America raised the prospect of an overwhelming addition to the Allies' wartime production. This, and the vast flow of American forces to Europe, was decisive in bringing about the early end to the war to end all wars.

War also proved to be a powerful economic engine. The nation's gross domestic product (GDP) rose to $75 billion in 1918, increasing from $60 billion in 1917, and the federal deficit went from $1 billion to $9 billion. Unemployment reached record lows, and women entered the workforce in large numbers.[5]

Not surprisingly, the end of the war saw the end of a unified national strategy. The institutions of wartime industrial mobilization were quickly disestablished, labor unrest deepened, Democrats and Republicans quarreled, and the American economy returned to business as usual. Thus began almost a decade of extraordinary economic expansion fueled by the end of repressed demand at home and abroad, an increase in new technologies and techniques acquired during wartime mobilization, and the peculiar engine of international finance. It was the heyday of laissez-faire economics—the magic of the free, unregulated market—with

America in the driver's seat and a struggling, impoverished Europe. And then it ended in a collapse that was due to a variety of factors at home and abroad—including rampant speculation, excessive debt, income inequality, and loss of an American vision and sense of purpose.

ECONOMIC CRISIS AND TRANSFORMATION

The Great Depression brought to America a second opportunity to create what could have been a unified national strategy, this time focused at home. As stock values plummeted beginning in October 1929, businesses folded and government revenues fell. Conventional thinking demanded further contractions in expenditures and investments in order to reduce debts, but such reflexes made for failing policy. President Herbert Hoover cut public spending. He pursued negotiations for naval treaties to enable the United States to reduce defense expenditures. Yet the Depression deepened. By the summer of 1932, the national unemployment rate stood at 25 percent. Industrial production had fallen by more than half. Prices had collapsed, making debt repayment more difficult. More than 9 percent of farm mortgages were "forced sales" between 1931 and 1933; farm income had fallen by 50 percent from the 1924–1929 averages.[6]

President Franklin Roosevelt, first elected in 1932, used the crisis of the Depression to create what became a transformational change in the US economy. In his famous first Hundred Days, his administration spearheaded legislative proposals dealing with banking, finance and securities, homeowner assistance, agriculture, employment, rural development, and industrial recovery. The government provided immediate assistance to the states to pay for relief, direct job creation (with the Public Works Administration and the Civilian Conservation Corps), aid to farmers, and measures to end the banking crisis and restore the financial system. The Tennessee Valley Authority was established to provide electricity and create economic development in Appalachia. Early measures were followed by other ideas, many of which were championed long after the Depression ended, including labor rights and collective bargaining, rural electrification, contributory pensions for seniors through the Social Security Act, unemployment assistance, and aid to poor families with children. By 1939, the Food Stamp Program had emerged. Roosevelt's programs in this era collectively created millions of jobs, consolidated the National Park System, provided for vast hydroelectric power, electrified homes and farms across America, restored farm income, and funded the construction of roads, highways, and public buildings. It was dramatic proof of the powers of government.

During this same period, Roosevelt used his executive powers and the power of Congress to correct some of the excesses that had contributed to the financial collapse of 1929. The Federal Deposit Insurance Corporation (FDIC) was created to guarantee that small depositors would not lose their money in case of bank failure; solicitation of investment was regulated; and banks were forbidden from making risky investments with the money of small depositors. The distribution of income, which had shifted far toward the most advantaged in society, became more equitable, and so, eventually, did the distribution of wealth. Some efforts failed, such as the efforts of the National Recovery Administration to work with industry and labor to regulate industrial competition and reduce overcapacity. This effort and some others were challenged in court; some were held up, and others were ruled unconstitutional. Roosevelt initially intended to do all of this on a balanced budget, but later his administration ran a deficit simply to get the many programs underway. It was a hodgepodge of programs and efforts, drawn from the ideas of the earlier Progressive era as well as from the US experience in World War I, and lacking solid intellectual coherence. As eminent historian Walt Rostow put it, "Roosevelt released and organized in the New Deal the national gift for action in the face of palpable problems guided by ad hoc theories of limited generality." In other words, Roosevelt was unconcerned with having some grand general theory behind what he was doing; he saw problems, and he took action to solve them, no matter that the solutions were a messy jumble of ideas.[7]

But the Roosevelt era was different from the World War I era in an important way. In World War I, the nation had largely unified itself in pursuit of an external and temporary goal; in the 1930s, after the first few months of Roosevelt's first term, that unity was missing. The strategic effort struck directly against entrenched and powerful economic interests. By the time the midterm elections of 1934 came around, partisanship had returned, and the political infighting was ferocious. A strong conservative coalition emerged in opposition—bankers and financiers, industrialists, anti-immigrant southern democrats, and ideological conservatives. Decades later, my stepfather, who had been a low-level Arkansas bank executive during the 1930s, would complain about "Mr. Roosevelt," and how he had wrecked the American economy (though it didn't prevent him and others of his generation from gratefully accepting their Social Security and Medicare benefits when the time came).

When Roosevelt introduced legislation to alter the ideological balance on the US Supreme Court by adding members, his New Deal coalition in Congress faded away. His extraordinary power then dissipated. Several additional measures were passed, including the Social Security Act, but in 1938 the balance in Congress shifted decisively away from FDR. No one really understood the economy of the day, and Roosevelt now lacked his earlier powers to drive government action. The United States lapsed into recession, and America was left with an unemployment rate that was too high, a medical system that was failing to care for the poor and the elderly, and many of the residual laws and policies that had contributed to the collapse, along with some of the politicians whose work had helped to bring about the very problems they were elected to solve. More importantly, America was left without a national strategic consensus. There was no coherent approach to solving the problems at hand, and no workable coalition of interest groups capable of dealing with the domestic challenges the country faced. The Depression seemed destined to linger on indefinitely.

AMERICA "RESCUED" BY WAR

America's domestic struggles were then once more submerged by threats from abroad. This time, the mobilization was far smoother, thanks to the many studies of industrial mobilization conducted in the aftermath of World War I. The Great Depression vanished: it was driven away by the huge expansion in demand for goods and services as the nation mobilized for war. At first, the United States waited, quietly and secretly assisting Great Britain from the sidelines, with transfers of destroyers under the Lend-Lease program and other efforts. The Japanese attack on Pearl Harbor changed all that. When President Roosevelt spoke of "a day that will live in infamy," the shock of the attack subdued the partisanship of domestic politics and the cringing isolationism that had defined a faction of the Republican Party. Once more war provided the opportunity for a national strategy. Wartime production surged, unemployment disappeared, women were brought into the workforce in large numbers, and everywhere new technologies and new techniques were put into place. In only five years, America was economically and socially transformed.

At the end of the war, as the institutions of the wartime economy were dismantled, some became concerned that the demobilization of the industrial workforce and the return of 10 million Americans in uniform to civilian life would throw the economy back into isolationism and depression. But that's not what happened. The GI Bill soaked up manpower in higher education, and the new federal-backed Federal Housing Administration, coupled with benefits for veterans' home-buying, sparked a residential construction boom. Moreover, America's leaders realized that the nation could no longer withdraw from its engagement and responsibilities in the world. As a result, new international institutions, such as the United Nations, the International Monetary Fund, and the World Bank, as well as the Bretton Woods agreement on currency exchange, were implemented.

NO REST FROM CHALLENGES

Soviet leader Joseph Stalin's ambitions in Europe initiated a series of continuing crises in postwar Europe. Subversion began immediately in Eastern Europe. Noncommunist parliamentarians and potential leaders were harassed and intimidated, and the power of noncommunist elements progressively declined. The Red Army and Communist takeovers of the internal police were instrumental in these efforts in Poland, Czechoslovakia, and other East European countries. The Soviet Union tried but failed to isolate and drive out the US, British, and French occupation of Berlin and Greece. The Chinese Communist defeat of the Chinese Nationalists, and the Soviets' test of their first A-bomb, ended any illusion of postwar international harmony. Fear of an enemy abroad once more proved to be the most potent motivating force in American politics.

George Kennan, who in 1946 was serving as the chargé d'affaires of the US embassy in Moscow, wrote a long policy proposal and sent it back to the State Department. Subsequently expanded into a 1947 article for the journal *Foreign Affairs*, it served as the seminal piece in a new US strategy. Kennan explained that the Soviet leadership saw an innate antagonism between their system and the West. We could expect, he continued, that the Soviets would be difficult to deal with, always pushing and probing, shifting tactically, but implacably hostile strategically. Kennan recommended that "the main element of any United States policy toward the Soviet Union must be long term"; we must pursue, he said, "patient but firm and vigilant containment of Russian expansionist tendencies." Soviet pressure had to be contained by "the adroit and vigilant application of counterforce at a series of constantly shifting geographical and political points, corresponding to the shifts and maneuvers of Soviet policy." Kennan suggested that perhaps the seeds of its own decay were already present and bearing fruit in the Soviet Union. The United States, he said, should pull together for the long-term challenge, contrasting our values and successes against the Soviet Union's, and, by our successes, further increase the Soviet Union's difficulties. These were the key insights needed, and Kennan's views provided the foundation for a foreign policy consensus that would last for over forty years.[8]

In 1947, President Harry S. Truman announced that the United States would support Greece and Turkey with economic and military assistance to prevent them from falling under Soviet domination. In the same year, the Marshall Plan was announced, and it was in operation, delivering economic assistance to Western European governments, by 1948. In 1949, the North Atlantic Treaty Organization was created by the United States and Britain to bring together the nations of Western Europe for the purpose of deterring a possible Soviet military invasion of their territory. By early 1950, the United States had decided that a major expansion of peacetime military expenditures and capabilities was necessary—but it had excluded South Korea from the American defense perimeter. In June of that year North Korean

forces attacked across the 38th parallel, the boundary line between North and South Korea. Surprising some, the United States
almost immediately deployed ground forces from Japan, sent
additional forces from the United States, and mobilized the
United Nations to resist North Korean aggression, all the while
aware that the real threat was in Europe, where the Soviet Union
had massed major ground forces. So the Truman administration
interpreted containment.

For more than two years, the battles raged in Korea. At first it
seemed that a US defeat was imminent, but then a near-miraculous
recovery was sparked by a risky amphibious landing far behind
enemy lines at Inchon, followed by a march north to the Chinese
border, and then massive Chinese intervention and a series of see-
saw battles. There was much fighting, but without decisive results,
and America was frustrated. Then, in mid-1952, General Dwight
D. Eisenhower, the world-renowned World War II military leader,
left his post as NATO's first commander, returned to the United
States to run for president on the Republican ticket, promising to
"go to Korea," and won.

Modern American strategy really begins with Eisenhower.
Building on Kennan's prescription and the efforts of the Truman
administration, Ike created a politically supported, unified national strategy using the Cold War—not a hot war—as the motivating force. This strategy was not just about actions abroad; it
was also about building strength at home. Gaining the Republican nomination, he defeated the party insiders who sought to return the United States to an isolationist policy abroad; he was
then able to apply the lessons and experiences of his military service, as well as his stint as president of Columbia University, to
the broadest challenges facing America. In his First Inaugural Address on January 20, 1953, Eisenhower laid the conceptual foundation for his presidency: "The world and we have passed the
midpoint of a century of continuing challenges. We sense with all

our faculties that the forces of good and evil are massed and armed and opposed as never before."

Ike built his remarks that day upon powerful moral and emotional themes. "How far have we come in mankind's long pilgrimage from darkness into light? Are we nearing the light—a day of peace and prosperity for mankind? Or are the shadows of another night closing in upon us?" It was a strategy resting on a foundation of fear, but also claiming for the United States the moral "high ground" of saving mankind.

And then the clincher: "Great as are the preoccupations absorbing us at home, concerned as we are with matters that deeply affect our livelihood today and our vision for the future, each of these domestic problems is dwarfed by, and often even created by, this question that involves all mankind."

Ike's intent was to persuade all Americans that they must work together at home in order to overcome civilization-threatening challenges from abroad. This message was the essence of his national strategy. He used the leverage of profound challenges abroad to gain domestic political cooperation between the parties. It was a remarkably prescient way of framing the future and guiding the nation forward.

Ike was a Republican; he was no friend of the New Deal, no social reformer, and no ally of unions. He believed that America was built upon the strength of our economy—manufacturing and agriculture. His aim was to maintain America's national security without bankrupting the American economy. He sought minimal defense expenditures and lower taxes. Nevertheless, he left in place, and even expanded, the social safety net that Roosevelt had created. His appointments to the Supreme Court made school segregation illegal and broadly attacked all forms of discrimination. As a twelve-year-old in Little Rock, I saw the troopers of the 101st Airborne Division arrive to enforce the Supreme Court's historic *Brown v. Board of Education* ruling—an exercise of federal power that would seem almost unimaginable in today's heated political environment.

Ike's defense strategy was called the New Look. He built a force of long-range bombers to deter Soviet expansionism by using the threat of massive nuclear retaliation. He favored the Air Force over the Army's ground troops—so much so that Army Chief of Staff Maxwell Taylor retired and wrote a book highly critical of the defense policies of his old boss. But Eisenhower saw that defense spending had to be balanced against other needs.

Meanwhile, he sought to roll back the Communist grip in Eastern Europe covertly by inserting CIA agents and organizers, all recent émigrés from Eastern Europe, back into their home countries to organize resistance to Soviet domination. Most Americans knew nothing of this program. Visiting Romania in 1998 as NATO Supreme Allied Commander, Europe, I was riding along a country highway with Romanian President Emil Constantinescu when he described the program to me. "That mountain there," he said, pointing to the massive hills rising to the north, "is where your CIA used to drop its agents in the 1950s." Sadly, these men, inserted throughout Eastern Europe, were all compromised, captured, and eventually executed. Ike's rollback policy didn't work.

While trying to keep the Soviets off-balance, Ike avoided major war. He ended the war in Korea. He refused to put US troops on the ground in support of the French in Southeast Asia. He blocked the British and the French in their invasion of Egypt to capture and hold the Suez Canal. He did not send in US troops to assist the brave Hungarian Freedom Fighters when they revolted against Soviet domination in 1956, though he did dispatch troops into Lebanon in 1958 to stabilize a situation that appeared to open the door to a Communist takeover there. It was, in short, an implementation of the very grand strategy of containment first prescribed by George Kennan—though Kennan himself may have preferred to rely less on military and more on diplomatic and economic measures.

Meanwhile, Ike used government to develop the national means to support his strategy. Eisenhower supported the funding and building of the Interstate Highway System, which fundamentally transformed the American economy. The original plan called for 41,000 miles of road, and it was proclaimed complete in 1992. The cost has been estimated at over $400 billion in 2006 dollars, making it the largest public works project ever undertaken in the United States. Some 90 percent of the costs were paid by the federal government. This enormous project provided millions of jobs, enabled a vast expansion of the economy to take place, and solidified America's reliance on the automobile.

Ike also believed in technology, and he was the beneficiary of the transformative World War II investments in science and technology that had been led by Roosevelt's science adviser, Vannevar Bush. Basic and applied research, together with major investments in manufacturing, allowed firms like Boeing, Lockheed, Grumman, Fairchild, and dozens of others to form the basis for a peacetime military-industrial complex centered around the jet engine. For example, Boeing took the defense investment in the B-47 jet bomber and turned it into the world's first and most successful jet passenger aircraft, the Boeing 707. It revolutionized air travel.

Under Eisenhower the military-industrial complex found its peacetime footing and its enduring influence. The complex was broadly based in academic research, policy analysis, and manufacturing. Universities and their scientists became dependent on government-funded research; think tanks like RAND emerged that could relate military hardware and threats to broader foreign policy issues; and aerospace companies advanced year by year in both commercial and military manufacturing, sometimes expanding into more mundane shipbuilding, and eventually growing into large systems-integrators. This growth touched basic economic sectors such as communications and materials, with the demands for electronics creating new firms, shaping new industries, and opening up demands for titanium, rare earths, and other exotic materials that have found uses well beyond the defense sector.

But it was Sputnik—the first Earth-satellite—launched by the Soviets in October 1957, that truly energized the military-industrial complex. It spurred military research and development tax credits, special assistance for schools and teacher education in science and math, a broader interest in technology, and a flood of defense-related research and development. Year after year this attention produced technology breakthroughs, new possibilities, and new products, which found their way not only to the defense sector but also to the broader economy. Advances in computers, microminiaturized electronics, lasers, aviation electronics and radios, communications satellites, navigational systems, manufacturing processes (including chipmaking and ceramics), jet engines, new materials, weather forecasting, medical technologies, and even the Internet emerged from the steady stream of defense dollars invested in risky ideas far beyond what the commercial world could have pursued on its own. Even after the post–Vietnam War downturn in investment in defense research and development (R&D) and other national hard-science pursuits, the civilian and commercial applications of earlier investments continued to appear in the commercial marketplace. It has been a dramatic illustration of the power of government to drive technology and economic growth.

As defense firms grew and consolidated, they built public and political influence. And in this respect they found able partners with the armed forces, especially the US Air Force. By the 1990s the system of influence was well-anchored and broadly understood. In 1991, when I visited the headquarters of the Strategic Air Command in Omaha, Nebraska, with a group of other newly appointed brigadier generals, I listened closely as a senior Air Force officer proudly explained that parts of the B-2 bomber were to be manufactured in forty-nine of the fifty states; this plan, of course, was intended to provide political insurance against funding cuts during the procurement process. And it succeeded.

Even as President Eisenhower worked to manage the economy and muster America's strength to deal with the threat of communism, he foresaw the risk in this new nexus of political and economic power. It was this risk that he warned against in his Farewell Address in 1961:

> This conjunction of a military establishment and a large arms industry is new in the American experience. The total influence—economic, political, even spiritual—is felt in every city, every State house, every office of the Federal government. We recognize the imperative need for this development. Yet we must not fail to recognize its grave implications. Our toil, resources and livelihood are all involved; so is the very structure of our society.
>
> In the councils of government, we must guard against the acquisition of unwarranted influence, whether sought or unsought, by the military/industrial complex. . . .
>
> We must never let the weight of this combination endanger our liberties or democratic processes.

Yes, Eisenhower was concerned about the changes he had wrought in the US economy and their political consequences; but they were changes driven by vision and necessity. His basic idea was that America had to pull together and shape its efforts at home to deal with long-term challenges abroad. This was the central idea behind his national strategy. At the time, it was a strategy so simple and obvious that Americans, in adopting it, hardly recognized it as strategic at all.

There were three corollaries to Ike's strategy as well. The first was that, in spite of being built around fear, it sought not to wage war and strike out, but to avoid war and move mankind forward. It was essentially values-based, long-term, and defensive in nature. Second, it recognized that America's greatest strengths were in its economy, and not its armed forces, and that overinvestment in defense could itself become a threat to national security. Finally, even in peacetime, the power of government must impact and shape the economy in order to deal with the existential challenge from abroad.

Over the next three decades, each American president who came into office was able to draw on the strategic framework laid down by Eisenhower. During this period the United States was rocked by profound social and political changes—civil rights, the sexual revolution, women in the workforce, a population increase of almost 40 percent, a tripling of the GDP, successive waves of immigration, the construction of the interstate highways, and an explosion of travel and tourism—as well as the long shadow cast by the lost war in Vietnam. Nevertheless, Ike's framing of the national strategy held together. For three decades after Ike, the United States worked to deter Soviet aggression and to contain Soviet expansionism. We lived out Ike's strategy. Democrats and Republicans disagreed at times, and each sought to gain political strength from their respective interpretations of the relative priorities embedded within the strategy; but Ike's strategy, motivated by an existential threat, saw us safely through his two terms as president and another thirty years beyond.

NOT THE END OF HISTORY, BUT THE END OF A STRATEGY

The era of Ike's strategy ended when the Soviet Union disintegrated. We had won the Cold War, but we had lost some things, too: we had lost both our adversary and a well-understood, publicly accepted strategic vision for how America should face the world, and, in so doing, we had lost a major impetus for cooperative politics.

Historian and former State Department planner Francis Fukuyama wrote in *The National Interest* in the summer of 1989 that "what we may be witnessing is not just the end of the Cold War, or the passing of a particular period of postwar history, but the end of history as such: that is, the end point of mankind's ideological evolution and the universalization of Western liberal democracy as the final form of human government." It was a powerful and controversial analysis, whose title ("The End of History?") seemed to foretell a new era of American domination, though Fukuyama warned that both religion and nationalism could still provoke passionate challenges to a liberal democratic world order. Both President George H. W. Bush and his Democratic rivals made much of the "peace dividend," which they believed would reduce defense expenditures and allow funds to be reallocated to domestic priorities. Soviet leader Mikhail Gorbachev and President Bush spoke of a new world order, but Gorbachev was soon gone and the Soviet Union with him. Suddenly it seemed as if we didn't need a strategy, and we took a strategic vacation.[9]

I came to the Pentagon in April 1994. I had just been promoted to lieutenant general and had been appointed as director of strategic plans and policy for the Joint Chiefs of Staff, and I found myself asking—and being asked—what is our strategy? The question arose often because of the collapse of the Soviet Union. When I had worked for General Alexander Haig, the NATO Supreme Allied Commander in the late 1970s, I had observed that he always used the external threat to justify and explain the US defense posture and our commitment to our allies. It was in his every speech: "The relentless growth of Soviet military power, year-in, and year-out, far in excess of any defensive needs . . . "

he would say. Our strategy was "threat-oriented." In 1994, we were missing this rationale. Inside the Pentagon we tried fervently to explain and justify our force structure of thirteen Army divisions, eleven carrier battle groups, and fourteen tactical fighter wings. Perhaps this was exactly the kind of Pentagon resistance to change that President Eisenhower had warned against in his Farewell Address in 1961—but we saw it as our duty to look out for the nation's defense, and to do so by resisting any further deepening of the "peace dividend." It was puzzling—we were representing our duty as we saw it, but the overall political consensus driven by the Cold War was gone.

As the Joint Staff director of strategic plans and policy, I had a broad overview of virtually everything we were doing within the Defense Department. My boss, General John Shalikashvili, chairman of the Joint Chiefs of Staff, told me my job was "to drive" the staff—to recommend to him the priorities, highlight the risks, and support him in working the critical national and strategic issues where military power and foreign policy met. It was a heady assignment. I worked on the Nuclear Posture Review, which examined whether we should retain or restructure our nuclear force, and how we should go about achieving these things if we were going to pursue them. Behind the scenes we were planning and developing strategies against potential threats from Iraq, North Korea, and Iran. We were investigating new challenges, too, such as cyber-war, and developing new technologies carried forth from their origins in the Cold War, albeit with a reduced budget. But there was no existential threat upon which to anchor US strategy. We were the unrivaled superpower—adrift in the world without an agreed-upon national strategy—but with everyone else's crises laid at our doorstep.

Every weekend in Washington in the spring of 1994 there were frantic White House Situation Room meetings. My first Sunday on the job, I was in the Situation Room for three hours, backing up the vice chairman of the Joint Chiefs, Admiral Bill Owens, as the Principals Committee considered the air mission over Bosnia, Operation Deny Flight. What constitutes a threat? When can our pilots shoot? At what point can a pilot legally preempt an attack? In the room were lawyers, policy analysts, military officers, and university professors—including the national security adviser and his deputy, the secretary of state, the secretary of defense, the UN ambassador, the vice president's national security adviser, and the vice chairman of the Joint Chiefs of Staff—all gesturing and wagging their hands like fighter pilots as they wrestled with the intellectual challenge of providing sound, effective, and legally acceptable guidance to pilots 4,000 miles away over the Adriatic Sea. It was grueling work just to listen to the fine points of discussion, knowing that each of us would have to return to work that Sunday evening and that Monday morning would come all too soon. It seemed that we were actually too busy wrestling with imminent crises to think about a bigger picture.

Meanwhile, the regional commanders in Europe and the Pacific were quick to promote "peacetime engagement," a way of deploying forces to demonstrate presence and interest by the United States and to further strengthen relationships with host governments. We repurposed Cold War implements. Military leaders articulated and defended the approach, including General George Joulwan, the NATO commander in Europe; General J. H. Binford Peay III, the commander of US Central Command; General Barry McCaffrey, in the Southern Command; Admiral Paul David Miller and Marine General John J. (Jack) Sheehan of the Atlantic Command; and Admiral Joe Prueher, Pacific Command. We set up military-funded and -led schools in Europe, Africa, and Asia to promote democracy, human rights, and civilian control of the military. Joint exercises with scores of countries designed to build military-to-military relationships and to expand beyond the Cold War were set up also. In the Middle East, we strengthened long-standing exercises with partners in the region and even helped broker the emergence of cooperative organizations in the Gulf. We developed closer security cooperation with Israel. And the Pentagon became the "go-to" agency for a decade of crisis activities, restoring President Aristide to power in Haiti, delivering relief to Rwandans, helping implement the Dayton Peace Agreement in Bosnia, and culminating in the NATO bombing campaign against Serbia in 1999 and the subsequent NATO-led occupation of Kosovo.

In response to congressional demands for a national security strategy, the Clinton administration promised and labored to devise one, but more than a year into the new administration there was still no strategy document. The administration did eventually produce a national security strategy (*A National Security Strategy of Engagement and Enlargement*).[10] Although principally written by the National Security Council staff, the Departments of State and Defense also had their say. I was proud to have a piece of the Pentagon responsibility for editing and commenting, along with principal Pentagon authors Edward (Ted) L. Warner III, the Defense Department's assistant secretary for strategy and requirements, and Walter B. Slocombe, undersecretary of defense for policy. It was written—well-written, we believed—and published, but it never really commanded the attention of the American people. It wasn't "existential-threat-driven." It didn't transcend foreign policy to reorganize domestic politics or priorities. Indeed, the threat wasn't there, as we saw the world—the United States had emerged as the sole superpower. New opportunities presented themselves, and new challenges—challenges such as regional instability and nuclear proliferation, transnational threats like terrorism and organized crime, and the threat of a resurgent Russia. Prescient? Yes. But an existential threat? No. Fear? No again.

In foreign policy, President Clinton was able to use adroit diplomacy and the leftover tools of the Cold War to advance American values and interests abroad, even in the absence of public understanding and support. In none of his major international efforts did he ever command a majority of popular support up front, however—not in restoring democracy to Haiti, or in bailing out Mexico's financial system, halting the war in Bosnia, or intervening to halt ethnic cleansing in Kosovo. Executive-branch action led and shaped public support, but it seldom won actual endorsement before execution—just conditional acquiescence. It was successful foreign policy—but pragmatic and improvisational, guided by President Clinton himself, and resisted by his partisan opponents in Congress. As one US senator candidly asked me, "You don't want to go fight Clinton's wars in the Balkans, do you?" So, in the post–Cold War period, at the very zenith of American power, the US government had no unified strategy for pulling America together. Instead, amid the new ideas afoot— globalism, NAFTA, the World Trade Organization (WTO), environmentalism, the dawning of a new era of world peace, the rise of nonstate actors such as Al-Qaeda—there was only a beleaguered executive branch, led by a brilliant president and supported by some congressional allies, threading its way through a minefield of competing priorities and partisan criticism.

Meanwhile, the US economy reaped a rich harvest from four decades of patient government investment in defense as that technology migrated to the private sector. This new technology, including personal computers, the Internet, and cellphones, seemed to be transforming the economic and political landscapes. Raising taxes and outmaneuvering an opposing Congress, President Clinton moved toward a balanced budget. In the process America grew at a prodigious rate, creating 22 million new jobs, maintaining low inflation, and bypassing Japan and Germany to become the driving force in the world economy.

When I stood on the field at my retirement at Fort Myer, Virginia, in June 2000, the men and women in uniform who were present in ranks before me stood tall and straight, and no one doubted that they represented the finest armed forces in the world. I could hardly wait to try my hand in innovation and leadership in the private sector. America's investment bankers were the envy of the world, the Internet explosion was producing overnight wealth, and thousands of Europeans were in New York and Silicon Valley, studying American business methods. American movies and culture were everywhere, and nations in Eastern Europe were clamoring to join us in NATO. What a moment it was! Who cared about a "national strategy" in the bright summer sunshine of America's triumph?

Shortly after retirement, I was speaking to a technology convention at Lake Tahoe about US foreign policy, NATO, and international challenges. During the speech, one of the businessmen in the back of the room remarked to my wife Gert, "Good speech, but, really, we're businessmen. Why is he talking to us about this? We don't have time to worry about foreign policy; that's what we have professionals like your husband for."

It was into this vacuum of American strategy that Al-Qaeda struck: tragic and terrible, yet to some in government, no doubt, a rare opportunity to refocus America. In the late summer of 2001, the new administration of President George W. Bush was already seen to be drifting. *Time* magazine portrayed General Colin Powell, the new secretary of state, as the "odd man out" in an internal struggle carried over from the earlier administration of President George H. W. Bush, and a president who was bored and out of his depth. That changed with 9/11. The iconic picture of President Bush with the first responders and others at the site of the World Trade Center, wearing his hard hat and proclaiming American determination and courage, set a new tone and gave awesome power to his administration. As Colin Powell said, the strikes on America were an act of war. And in wartime, America comes together. Karl Rove, who was senior adviser to the president, was reported to have remarked that they would position Bush to run in 2004 as a "war president," implying significant advantages in his quest for reelection.

As President George W. Bush addressed Congress in the wake of the terrorist strikes, the TV camera panned the faces of Democratic legislators. Along with the patriotism, you could also see the dawning recognition that President Bush held the trump cards: there would be a bipartisan approach, driven, once again, by war. Journalist Anne Applebaum, writing in Slate on the tenth anniversary of 9/11, put it like this: "In the wake of al-Qaida's attack on New York and Washington, an organizing principle suddenly presented itself. Like the 'Cold War,' the new 'war on terror,' as it instantly became known, clearly defined America's friends, enemies, and priorities. . . . [It] appealed both to American realism and American idealism. . . . The speed with which we all adopted this new paradigm was impressive, if somewhat alarming."[11]

In short order, the United States bombed Afghanistan, and, with the on-the ground leadership of a few hundred Special Forces soldiers, overthrew the Taliban regime. In the process, we missed capturing Osama bin Laden and would have to proceed to search for him until the dramatic operation of May 2011 that ended in his death. In the meantime, we worked vigorously to plan, prepare, and invade Iraq, overthrowing Saddam Hussein and his Baathist regime. To make the strategy work, the administration hiked military expenditures and increased the size of the armed forces. On the domestic side, a Department of Homeland Security was created. The Bush administration cut taxes, squeezed domestic discretionary expenditures, loosened regulations, and lowered interest rates, seeking domestic prosperity in the midst of war—ballooning the national debt in the process. Was it, perhaps, a lesson learned from the "guns-vs.-butter" debate of the Lyndon B. Johnson years, in which excessive government spending on defense drove domestic inflation? No, unfortunately, it was just the opposite. Ignoring the lessons of recent history, the administration was simply following through on campaign pledges to take advantage of the budget surpluses it had inherited—it was "guns *and* butter!" In the end, the Bush administration led us into a deepening crisis in Afghanistan, began uneasy preparations for departure from Iraq, deepened US budget deficits, and set in motion the circumstances that led to the financial crisis and the most severe recession in seventy years. No future administrations would be likely to want to follow this lead.

ENOUGH BLAME TO GO AROUND

It would be unfair to lay on the Bush administration all the blame for the myopia that emerged in the wake of 9/11. Democrats were surely part of it, drawn along by the organizing power of a genuine threat, and concerned by the awesome shift in public opinion and the newfound power of the president, which in turn had come about in part because many Democrats seemed to lack much appreciation for national security. In a small meeting of the Democratic Leadership Council in Washington to which I was invited in December 2001, several Democrats complained that they and their party knew little about national security. They seemed to have forgotten that Woodrow Wilson, Franklin Roosevelt, and Harry Truman were all Democrats, and had performed quite well as wartime leaders. Many of the top leaders of the Democratic Party supported the congressional resolution authorizing the invasion of Iraq. Contrary voices, like those of Senator Bob Graham of Florida, chair of the Senate Intelligence Committee at the time, were drowned out. Mounting an effective political opposition was difficult. Resisting the Bush tax cuts was also exceedingly hard. It was only in 2006 that public opinion turned decisively against the war, enabling Barack Obama, who was then a senator from Illinois, to receive the Democratic nomination and subsequently win the 2008 presidential election.

If it was even debatable earlier, it is now clear that the Bush-era foreign policy was a costly failure. Our actions released Iran's power in the region; provided Al-Qaeda with recruiting tools, making it a magnet for extremists; expended vast resources, distracting attention from other real challenges at home and abroad; and sparked the emergence of a Sunni-Shia power struggle in Iraq, which is now infecting the region with wider, more destructive warfare—we failed to replace Saddam's government with a stable, Western-oriented structure. The neoconservatives, or neocons, who pushed for the invasion of Iraq were simply wrong; our military power was not going to successfully transform the Middle East into a bastion of Western democracy. Liberating Iraq in 2003 was not like liberating France in 1944. But, more fundamentally, the policy wasn't sufficiently broad enough to recognize and enhance the true sources of American power and to protect vital American interests elsewhere. In that sense, its failure was even more profound.

President Obama worked to more effectively prosecute the original intent of dismantling Al-Qaeda. He completed the withdrawal of US forces from Iraq. After a surge of US forces into Afghanistan, he reduced American military deployments in the region and used other, less conventional means to continue the fight against Al-Qaeda. He was forceful in his decision to act upon the available intelligence to take down Osama bin Laden, and in so doing, exposed Pakistan's double-dealing policy of allying itself with the United States while simultaneously training and directing the Taliban (and assorted other jihadists) in their efforts to defeat NATO and the government of Afghanistan. In his 2010 national defense strategy, President Obama recognized US security interests elsewhere, and even announced, by 2011, a "pivot" to Asia, with a pending deployment of a Marine unit to northern Australia.

But despite the rhetoric and continuing efforts, the United States still seemed to lack a consensus-based national sense of purpose that was understood by all, that bridged the partisan divides, and that provided a reasonable way forward to deal with the most substantial challenges we faced. In September 2013, the Atlantic Council, a nonpartisan think tank, noted the lack of strategic vision toward Arab transitions. In December, experts at a congressional hearing bemoaned the lack of a US strategy toward China. By January 2014, Obama's Republican opponents were blaming the administration for the resurgence of Al-Qaeda in Iraq and clamoring for US military assistance to Iraq, air strikes, and possibly the reintroduction of US forces on the ground. Russian leader Vladimir Putin was drawing Ukraine back in toward its historical relationship to Russia by May 2014, cleverly masking his use of force by inserting special forces to incite disorder and calls for Russian help to justify a military seizure—a strategy whose outcome was not yet determined as this book went to press—and in Syria, the opposition and rebel forces were still battling Bashar al-Assad and seeking outside support. In June 2014, as I was putting the last thoughts into this book, ISIL (the Islamic State of Iraq and the Levant) and a collection of other terrorists were turning their power upon the Shiite-dominated government of Iraq, overrunning the Iraqi military, conducting summary executions, and threatening to seize Baghdad. So what were we to do next?[12]

CHAPTER 2

How America Ended Up
in the Middle East

One of the most famously asked questions in the game of golf is, "Which shot is the most important?" And the answer, which every golfer knows, is, "The next one."

For the United States, there are several "next shots" to anticipate presently. Commentators and analysts each have their own favorites. One will say it is nuclear proliferation in Iran; for another, it's "loose nukes in Pakistan." Yet another will warn of a North Korean implosion, or war by accident on the Korean Peninsula, or, with an eye on the Ukraine crisis with Russia, a restart of the Cold War. The National Intelligence Council's *Global Trends 2030* report listed several potential "Black Swan events"—events considered unlikely, but which would have a severe impact.[1] These included a severe pandemic, much more rapid climate change, collapse of the euro or the European Union itself, a reformed Iran, a democratic or collapsed China, nuclear war, and more powerful solar geomagnetic storms. The world is full of potential disasters. But Americans have been conditioned by events over the past two decades to think of the Middle East as the region most deserving of our critical foreign policy attention.

The United States historically has had ties to Israel, dating from Israel's war for independence in 1948, and every American president since that time has said that Israel's survival is a vital American interest. We have worked to prevent terrorism and nuclear proliferation in the region. But our interest in the Middle East has been driven by one other factor that we do not admit so publicly: oil.

The oil in Saudi Arabia, Iraq, and other places in the Middle East is plentiful and cheap. Oil production costs there are the lowest in the world. Saudi Arabia and Iran, both US friends and allies at the time, helped to form the Organization of the Petroleum Exporting Countries (OPEC) in 1960. It was a cartel—precisely the kind of cartel that the United States had historically opposed. But in this case it originated with US friends and allies, countries vital to holding the line against Soviet penetration of the region. The United States assented to its formation—and then, years later, as US oil production declined and consumption rose, we became one of the oil-importing countries that OPEC's price increases could target. Oil supplies tightened and prices began to rise in 1973. Then, in October 1973, as the United States assisted Israel with emergency defense equipment and ammunition replenishment during the Yom Kippur War, Arab oil producers refused to sell to the United States. Prices jumped, and a new vital national security interest was created—secure access to petroleum.

As a captain teaching at West Point, I was sent on temporary duty to the US Army Staff in the Pentagon during the summer of 1973, where I wrote the first Army studies on the energy crisis and its implications. At the time, the Army was engaged in recovering from the Vietnam War—some elements were still deployed there—as well as facing up to the modernized Soviet threat to Europe and transitioning to the all-volunteer force. The last thing the Army wanted was to be told it might have future missions in the Persian Gulf—but that was what the studies showed. Britain had withdrawn from the Middle East in the late 1960s, so if there was trouble, it would be the United States that would be called upon to intervene.

The United States strengthened its relationship with Saudi Arabia after the fall of the shah of Iran in 1979. A new US regional military command was formed to support allies and anchor US defenses in the area. In 1990, when Iraq invaded and seized Kuwait, the United States responded by deploying more than a half million soldiers, sailors, airmen, and Marines, creating a global coalition to protect Saudi Arabia and its oilfields, and, subsequently, striking to eject Iraqi forces and to restore Kuwait's independence.

The Gulf War—or as it is now called, the First Gulf War—was perceived as a magnificent military victory. New technologies were employed, our armed forces triumphed with minimal casualties, the Iraqi enemy was defeated, and our Kuwaiti friends were liberated. To a large degree, America finally threw off the "Vietnam syndrome": it was a clear-cut military victory. Our technology was validated, and our president, George H. W. Bush, was lionized, with a massive surge in his popularity. The United States was fully launched into the post–Cold War world as the sole superpower. What was our strategy?

FOREIGN POLICY MEETS DOMESTIC POLITICS

At this point, US domestic politics strongly impacted America's perception of the global challenges and opportunities we faced. I saw it firsthand, and in an eerie foretaste of problems to come, it began with a split within the Republican Party that would have vast consequences for US policy in the Middle East.

On a lazy Friday afternoon in Washington, DC, in late May 1991, warm and sunny, I went in to see my former boss, General Colin Powell, who at that time was chairman of the Joint Chiefs of Staff. As always, General Powell was open to seeing old friends. Washington and the Pentagon seemed relaxed. The nation's leaders were getting back their stride after winning the biggest military victory for American forces since World War II: the First Gulf War, with forty-four days of bombing, four days of ground action, which included a magnificent armored maneuver, and fewer than three hundred killed on our side. Kuwait was free. Troops were being redeployed, and talk of a victory parade was in the air.

I walked into the big E-ring office in the Pentagon, a little intimidated. "Sir, I'm in town for the Capstone Course, and just wanted to stop by and say hello. And say congratulations for everything that was done in the Gulf War," I opened. General Powell was in his element, four stars on his shoulders, beaming broadly, and warmly welcoming. He was reveling in a job universally acknowledged as well done.

We'd first served together at Fort Carson, Colorado, in 1981, where he had been a brigadier general, the assistant division commander for operations and training, and I had been a lieutenant colonel, commanding the 1st Battalion, 77th Armor. Then, in 1983, when he was a two-star, he headed up the transition program for incoming Army Chief of Staff John Wickham, and he had invited me to work with him. Since then our contacts had been friendly, but he was moving upward rapidly.

After a few minutes with Powell, I decided to visit Paul Wolfowitz, undersecretary of defense for policy. As the commanding general at the Army's National Training Center (NTC) deep in the Mojave Desert, I had had to escort the most prominent visitors, such as the undersecretary, who had spent a couple of days there earlier that year. He was about my age, a formidable defense intellectual, and I had actually been at one or two conferences with him over the years. We had hit it off during his visit, and he had invited me to come see him when I came to Washington next. Well, I thought, why not?

I knocked on his office door, and one of his assistants opened it. "Sure, come on back," he said. I walked in and saw the undersecretary sitting behind his desk, thoughtful, and perhaps a bit distracted.

"Good afternoon, Mr. Secretary," I opened. I paused. It felt a little awkward as he looked up at me. I thought I better put it in context. "Sir, when you visited us out at the NTC in January, you said I should stop by to say hello when I got back to the Pentagon." I paused. No reaction. I tried again. "Well, I just wanted to stop by and say congratulations for all that was done overseas. You must be very proud of the operation and the troops."

I wasn't one of those troops, and, sure, that was a little disappointing. I'd been held in position at the National Training Center during the war to continue the training activities for our mobilizing National Guard forces. But I was so proud of what our team and the Army had accomplished.

Now Wolfowitz was engaged. He looked up at me intently. "Yes," he said, "of course. . . . But, we didn't get Saddam Hussein. President Bush says his own people will take him out. . . . Maybe, but I doubt it."

I knew there was a rebellion underway as the Shiites in southern Iraq took advantage of Saddam's defeat to rise up against his control, and I had read there was some argument as to whether or not President Bush had flinched and called a halt too soon, or should have ordered General Norman Schwarzkopf Jr. to Baghdad. But I wasn't prepared with an opinion one way or the other on Saddam's future.

"Still, we did learn one thing," Wolfowitz continued. "We learned that we can intervene militarily in the region with impunity, and the Soviets won't do a thing to stop us."

Throughout my military career, the Soviets had been *the* factor—our major concern and potential adversary. Everything we did was measured against the Soviets. It was a huge shift, I thought, if they were no longer a factor.

"And," Wolfowitz continued, "we've got about five to ten years to take out these old Soviet 'surrogate' regimes—Iraq, Syria, and the rest—before the next superpower comes along to challenge us in the region."

Here was a BIG IDEA. "You mean, use force? Attack?" I asked.

"Well, if necessary," he said.

"And only five to ten years?" I probed. Wolfowitz was making it sound as if we were going to war again, soon.

"Well, no one knows, maybe more than that," he offered.

"And the next superpower, you're thinking, China?" I wanted to draw him out some more.

"Could be . . . " he replied. And after a few personal pleasantries the conversation trailed off. I excused myself and walked out.

Wolfowitz had revealed in those few words a significant strategic idea: American forces would no longer be used just as a deterrent, but offensively to reshape the Middle East. That would be the focus: the Middle East, and, possibly, war.

Left unspoken was the great distinction between America's role in the Cold War—essentially deterrent and defensive, and this new vision of an American strategic "offense" with all the risks, costs, and moral quandaries that implied.

In those two meetings with Powell and Wolfowitz, I had stumbled upon the split in the Republican Party, a split between the hardline, anti-Soviet conservatives—who later emerged as the neocons—and the more moderate wing of the party, led by the first President Bush and represented in national security affairs by his adviser, Brent Scowcroft, a retired Air Force lieutenant general. The error in Iraq, according to the hardliners, was that the United States had not marched on into Iraq and eliminated Saddam Hussein.

Paul Wolfowitz and Defense Secretary Dick Cheney took the germ of the concept that Wolfowitz had articulated to me—preventing another power from dominating the region—along with several other concepts, and crafted a new national security strategy for the post–Cold War era. It was written into the Defense Planning Guidance, a document outlining Defense Department goals, in draft form, and apparently taken to the White House in 1992, though it may not have been approved. After the Republicans lost the presidency that year, Wolfowitz and others took the idea back into civilian life, and it eventually seemed to become the key concept driving the policies and approach that took the United States to war in Iraq in 2003.

This approach was not actually a response to an urgent threat—but rather an expression of American "triumphalism" that sought to "sweep the board" of old potential adversaries. As such, it appealed to several constituencies, including Americans who favored deeper military engagement to protect Israel. And thereby it offered a partisan pathway into disrupting the traditional alignment of Israel and the Democrats. A study by the Institute for Advanced Strategic and Political Studies, done for Israeli Prime Minister Benjamin Netanyahu, advocated a new approach to Israel's peace and security in the region, and this plan included seeking regime change in Iraq.[2] The call for "regime change" then emerged, as a response to Saddam's refusal to cooperate with the onerous UN weapons inspections. The aim of regime change in Iraq was adopted in the Iraq Liberation Act (HR 4655), which was passed by Congress in 1998. Although President Clinton signed the bill, he did not act upon it.

But taking on Saddam became an urgent priority for the administration of George W. Bush from the time Bush took office.[3]

The terrorist strikes of 9/11 provided the *casus belli*, the justification for war. And war had once more provided the impetus and opportunity to unify America and create a strategy.

Within a few days of 9/11, a preliminary determination had apparently been made to attack Iraq—not a formal decision, written up with courses of action, advantages, and disadvantages, but a determination to begin the work to invade Iraq. One participant in the Camp David meeting that took place the weekend after 9/11 recounted to me how President George W. Bush had confided, as he bid him farewell, "Don't worry about Saddam, we'll get him." A few days later, when I visited the Pentagon, I was called in by a general on the Joint Staff and told that the decision had been made to invade Iraq. "But why?" I asked. The general replied that he didn't know, but, he speculated, "Maybe the administration doesn't know what else to do. We're not very good at fighting terrorists." A few weeks later, he informed me about a memo originating in the Office of the Secretary of Defense outlining a concept of going after seven states in five years, using military action to effect regime change, beginning with Iraq and Syria. The "new" strategy seemed to come straight from the old Wolfowitz concept from 1991, I reckoned.

For more than a decade afterward, there were many reasons put forward for the invasion of Iraq: halting the proliferation of nuclear weapons, making the Middle East safer, showing Al-Qaeda the real capabilities of the US military, deterring future attacks, preparing the way for an Israeli-Palestinian agreement, securing access to oil, spreading democracy, and even settling an old score against the Bush family. Deputy Secretary of Defense Wolfowitz, in a series of interviews with Sam Tannenhaus for *Vanity Fair* in 2003, explained it this way: "For reasons that have a lot to do with the U.S. government bureaucracy, we settled on the one issue that everyone could agree on which was weapons of mass destruction as the core reason. But . . . there have always been three fundamental concerns. One is weapons of mass destruction, the second is support for terrorism, the third is the criminal treatment of the Iraqi people." Robert Gates, who served as secretary of defense from 2006 to 2011 and earlier had held posts in the CIA, wrote about the Iraq and Afghanistan wars in his 2014 book *Duty*. He quotes then National Security Adviser Condoleezza Rice as writing, years later, "The fact is, we invaded Iraq because we had run out of other options. The sanctions were not working, the inspections were unsatisfactory, and we could not get Saddam to leave by other means." Gates wryly notes, "Particularly later, as the war dragged on, fewer and fewer people accepted that logic."[4]

I always felt that the underlying rationale behind the invasion was more strategic. It was really about the neoconservative agenda sketched out that day in May 1991, in Undersecretary of Defense Paul Wolfowitz's office, and reflected in that 2001 Pentagon memo—to drive out the old Soviet surrogate leaders, institute democratic reform in the Middle East, maintain dominance in the region, and control access by our rivals and potential adversaries to the region's oil resources. It would prove to be a policy of historic overreach.

Throughout 2001 and 2002, the Bush administration angled to plan, prepare, and justify the invasion. Even as the Taliban government in Afghanistan was collapsing in the fall of 2001 under the weight of the American offensive, Secretary of Defense Donald Rumsfeld was distracting the US Central Command by tasking them to present the plan for invading Iraq. In his State of the Union speech in January 2002, President Bush paved the way to war, emphasizing that we would prevent the "worst weapons from falling into the hands of the worst people." An "axis of evil" was designated, consisting of Iraq, North Korea, and Iran. So now the move against Saddam could be described as a necessary preventive war. Intelligence assets were quickly displaced from Afghanistan to begin preparation for the invasion. Several iterations of the invasion plan were prepared, briefed, and critiqued.

Washington was alive with rumors and discussions. Secrets were in the air. In March 2002, I went in to see Senator John Kerry, citing the rumors, expressing concern, and predicting the approximate invasion date of March 2003. In April 2002, British Special Air Service (SAS) officers, seeing me in an airport, said hello and explained they were going to Tampa for "planning—wink, wink!" Later that month, I was invited to speak on the likely invasion and consequences to the Goldman-Sachs investment committee. I predicted a three-week campaign and said that seizing Baghdad would probably not prove to be difficult. However, I warned about the challenges of what would happen afterward.

I could never see the urgency of attacking Iraq, and I tried to warn against it while respecting the possibility that some new intelligence might exist to which I was not privy. I tried to limit my remarks to those which should reasonably be within the purview of a retired military officer. Secretary Rumsfeld briefed several of us privately in his conference room, trying to use us to shape the public dialogue. Meanwhile, I kept trying to ask, discreetly, whether there was some new, compelling, urgent information that could explain these plans. Had Saddam revived his nuclear program, or did he have some weapons that we didn't know about? Deep in my gut I just didn't want to be against the US drive to invade, but I was, nevertheless.

My information from my recent command in Europe was that there were a few Scud missiles unaccounted for, perhaps some precursors for chemical weapons, and maybe a couple of tons of growth medium for bioweapons, but that these programs had been essentially eliminated. And in every case, I was told by people who should have been in a position to know: "No, nothing new." There was no compelling reason to attack at this time.

Beyond the puzzle over intelligence, the Bush administration's myopic public focus on Iraq was a poor strategic notion to begin with, not only because we also had troops in Afghanistan, but also because the major threat cited—weapons of mass destruction—was hardly unique to Iraq. The administration was doing its best to ignore the other "outlaw" state that already had chemical and biological weapons, and also had a near-term, effective means of getting nuclear weaponry: North Korea. If one really wanted to halt nuclear proliferation, the focus should have been on North Korea, but, as later information showed, the Bush administration had seemed to suppress information in 2002 that North Korea was well on its way to developing a nuclear weapon. Iran also had chemical and probably biological weapons, as well as some kind of nuclear program. And if one really wanted to punish those who had attacked the United States, and prevent future attacks, the first focus should have been on Al-Qaeda, in its refuges in Afghanistan and Pakistan. In addition, it was clear that Saddam's military was much weaker in 2003 than it had been when he invaded Kuwait in 1990. We were also overflying Iraq on a daily basis, and by the summer of 2002, actively bombing key targets under the justification of the earlier operations Northern Watch and Southern Watch.

Nevertheless, the invasion of Iraq was a popular cause in the United States. A large majority of the American people believed in it, in part because many believed Iraq was somehow connected to 9/11. Many in the American news media favored the war, and embedding reporters with the troops would assure that journalistic skepticism would be held in check by support-our-troops patriotism. Even though Europeans were skeptical, most nations in the region supported us—for varying reasons. One British newspaper publisher explained to his European friends, some of whom were doubtful about the war, at the World Economic Forum in Davos, Switzerland, in January 2003: "The road to Jerusalem runs through Baghdad"; in other words, striking Saddam would pave the way for peace between Israel and the Palestinians. For the Saudis, attacking Iraq was continuing payback to Saddam for his threat to the Saudi kingdom in 1990–1991. For the Israelis, the elimination of a dictator who had fired Scud missiles at Israel and posed a substantial threat would be a boon. For some others, it was more a matter of going along with a US decision rather than resisting it. For Iran, Syria, Libya, and others aligned against the United States, it was a time of anxiety and uncertainty.

The 2003 invasion of Iraq caught no one by surprise, except perhaps for Saddam himself, who reportedly never really believed the Americans would actually invade. Some insider talk indicated that he had turned down a $2 billion offer from the Saudis to abdicate a few weeks before the invasion. Unlike 1991, this time there was no prolonged bombing campaign. The invasion did indeed last just three weeks, beginning with the so-called "shock and awe" of precision bombing and ending with the occupation of Baghdad. It provided compelling imagery of new weaponry, disciplined soldiers, and rapid, bold action.

THE "POTTERY BARN" RULE

What followed the invasion was the oldest and most thankless of military duties—occupying a hostile country. Almost every successful army in history has done it: Alexander the Great's Macedonians, Rome's legions, the Crusaders, the Normans after invading England, and even the Americans, in Germany and Japan after World War II. Occupation is onerous, boring, and critically important.

The United States prepared for the occupation of Germany after World War II by creating and training special military government units. As it turned out, these units ended up relying on many of the same local authorities used by Adolf Hitler, despite an intense desire to denazify Germany. The Soviets were cunning, ruthless occupiers in Europe; when they occupied eastern Poland in 1939, they arrived fully prepared with linguists, exiled Communists from each region, and lists of sympathizers and adversaries. They cleverly declared that laws wouldn't be enforced for several days, urging the population to seek revenge against the upper-class landlords and the Polish nobility through murder and arson. The Soviet occupation of Eastern Europe after World War II was aided by indigenous Communist groups and buttressed by Soviet military and military intelligence units—it was not left to chance. General Douglas MacArthur, in post–World War II Japan, was careful to cultivate a relationship with the Japanese emperor and to use his legitimacy to buttress the authority obtained through the legal documents of surrender. Everyone had an angle when it came to occupation.

Sadly, the American occupation of Iraq was a fiasco. In late 2002, I made a brief call on the current director of strategic plans and policy for the Joint Chiefs of Staff, who would have been responsible for coordinating postwar planning. When I had held the position, post-conflict planning was my specialty, and we had worked it especially for the planned invasion of Haiti. But on this particular day, when I asked the incumbent, "How are we doing with post-conflict planning?" he looked up at the ceiling (his office was one floor directly below the offices of the secretary and deputy secretary of defense), pointed upward, and said, "They won't let me do it." When the State Department, under the leadership of General Colin Powell, offered its postwar assessment, it was rejected by the Pentagon civilian leadership. Powell was later quoted as warning the president about the consequences of invasion using the so-called Pottery Barn rule: you break it, you own it.

The top US commander, General Tommy Franks, retired a few months after the invasion, having completed a remarkable military career by leading the military forces that had invaded and overthrown two governments. He had expected that as the fighting concluded, the forces would quickly be withdrawn, just as had happened in 1991, and just as his boss, Secretary Rumsfeld, wanted. But, amid the chaos and confusion, withdrawal wasn't in the cards. If anything, our troops needed to be reinforced.

Franks was replaced by his deputy. Astute, experienced, and fluent in Arabic, General John Abizaid brought with him the exact set of skills and judgment needed for the job. He saw the deteriorating security situation, and he was the first to call it guerrilla warfare. But Abizaid was responsible for the entire theater, including Afghanistan, problems with Iran, the Gulf States, and even Sudan and the Horn of Africa. He had to rely on his Iraq commander in-country, newly promoted Lieutenant General Ricardo Sanchez. Sanchez was elevated from a two-star division commander to a three-star corps commander. During the aftermath of the invasion, he was initially put in charge of retrograding the troops out of Iraq, only to discover instead that he was commanding a theater-level occupation of a country without the specific staff assistance, policy guidance, and specialized units necessary. It would have been a difficult position for any combat leader, but he was dealing with a complete change of plans, and he was not supported adequately by higher headquarters, including the policymakers in the Office of the Secretary of Defense and the White House. Without that support he and his headquarters were virtually incapable of effectively controlling or even staying abreast of a rapidly evolving situation on the ground.

Fundamentally, the force level was simply inadequate to occupy the country in the immediate aftermath of combat. I knew this even before the invasion began, as did other military leaders, and we pointed it out publicly. The lack of adequate force was compounded by several immediate mistakes directed by US civilian leaders—tolerance of looting, dismissal of the existing Iraqi

Army, the decision to forbid participation of Baathist Party members in public life, and a complete lack of the kind of political-military finesse that other successful occupying powers have shown throughout history.

During the summer of 2003, the US military quickly transitioned from preparation to retrograde into occupation activities, combating increasingly organized armed resistance. Under General Sanchez's leadership, Saddam Hussein was eventually captured—a moment of triumph—and the search for the missing weapons of mass destruction was concluded, with nothing found; week after week, month after month, the searches continued until it became undeniable that this justification for the invasion was based on an error. On the civilian side, Paul Bremer, who was Sanchez's boss in theater, appointed an advisory council, organized an electoral process, and began preparing to transition to Iraqi rule under US occupation authority. It was his responsibility to put the high-flying rhetoric that President Bush had used in envisioning a postwar democratic Iraq into effect.

However, the situation continued to deteriorate. The Iranians had gone from fear and respect of US power to a dawning recognition of how ill-informed and ineffective the on-the-ground implementation of US policy was. Using various Shia groups and their own Quds Force, a unit of the Iranian Revolutionary Guards, they quickly penetrated Shia organizations, built influence, and strengthened the indigenous Shia militias to oppose former Baathists and also some US occupation efforts. US forces largely stayed away from the Sadr City slum in Baghdad, where Moqtada al-Sadr, an influential Iraqi leader opposing coalition forces, had strong support. (Sadr City was informally named after his father, a famous Shia cleric.) Meanwhile, the ex-Baathists were joined by an infusion of Sunni terrorists, and by April 2004 they had begun a fierce resistance against US forces in Anbar Province, west of Baghdad. During this same period, the pictures of Iraqi prisoners undergoing humiliating treatment in prison also became public, further inciting Iraqi opposition.

Recognizing the need to beef up the leadership on the ground, the United States replaced three-star general Sanchez with four-star general George Casey, an experienced Joint Staff officer and former vice chief of staff of the Army. Casey was undoubtedly the right man for the job, by virtue of his recent assignments, his skills, and his temperament. He had even served a tour in the Sinai with UN forces as a junior officer. By the time he took command in the late summer of 2004, there was no denying that an insurgency was underway, led by former Baathists. Violence was rampant, and US forces were put to a severe test of urban warfare in the town of Ramadi, and later in Fallujah. Before Casey left Washington to take command, he called and we discussed one of the oldest lessons in warfare: when force is used, use it decisively—no more Ramadi-like, slow, agonizing, casualty-laden assaults.

Casey knew he had to use force, and he proved he knew how to use it effectively. In Fallujah, US Marine and then US Army units eliminated a stubborn Shia extremist defense. But the angry rebellion of former Baathists and displaced officers opened the window for a more insidious invasion. Sunni extremists affiliated with Al-Qaeda used the presence of US forces as a recruiting incentive to rally would-be terrorists and combatants from throughout the Islamic world. Iraq may not have had many terrorists when the United States invaded, but two years later, the Al-Qaeda-led conflict against the Americans was raging full force, coupled with an intra-Iraqi conflict between Sunnis, supercharged by Al-Qaeda terrorists, and Shia militias that were supported by Iran.

As the situation worsened, there was some presidential rhetoric about sustained commitments. But we had made few preparations for a long-term struggle: we had virtually no US officer or noncommissioned officer (NCO) training programs in Arabic; cultural familiarization was rudimentary; detailed understanding of local conditions, political leaders, rivalries, and factions was missing; and we lacked the organizational infrastructure for the kind of civic-action projects needed to win and maintain support from the local population. These were all elements that had been created during our Vietnam experience in the 1960s, but they had been neglected here. Casey, and his deputy who ran the ground operations, Lieutenant General Peter Chiarelli, recognized the needs and worked hard to fix all this when they got on the ground. But we had invaded with the assumption that we would win and withdraw, and when that proved not to be the case, inadequate US forces found themselves unprepared in the middle of an insurgency and an active civil war, fighting against both Iranian-backed Shia extremists and Sunni extremists, with the civilian population terrorized in between. It was everything that informed observers of the region had feared and predicted—and even worse, it opened the door to growing Iranian influence.

In addition to a lack of troops and poor preparations for the occupation itself, there was another major problem: the strategic and regional diplomacy to accompany the military operation was poorly conceived and ineffective. Military action should always be used to leverage diplomacy. While use of force is an extreme expression of national will, its greatest value often comes not from destruction or occupation but from the weight it gives to US diplomacy. When I traveled to visit the Gulf states and meet with the leadership there in 2004 and 2005, as part of my work with a major investment bank, there was a universal sense that the Bush administration didn't consult, it dictated. It didn't listen to its Middle Eastern allies; instead it tended to alienate them. Criticism from Qatar was especially candid: "We told you Americans that Iraq is a tribal country. Why did you not listen?"

IN SEARCH OF A MIDDLE EAST STRATEGY

When the failure to find weapons of mass destruction began to undercut, on a strategic and political level, the major rationale for the invasion of Iraq, President Bush began to emphasize another rationale: the spread of freedom and democracy across the region. Starting late 2003, and then in his Second Inaugural Address and in his State of the Union speech in January 2005, the president rolled out what he called a "forward" policy—what some commentators saw as an "aggressive" foreign policy.

Bush explained in a speech at the National Endowment for Democracy, in October 2005, that he likened the "murderous ideology of the Islamic radicals" to the "ideology of communism," and said that, in addition to preventing attacks, the United States wanted to "deny weapons of mass destruction to outlaw regimes," prevent sanctuary for radical groups, and prevent militants from occupying and controlling a country. But even more fundamentally, the United States wanted "to deny the militants future recruits by replacing hatred and resentment with democracy and hope." It seemed as though the more difficult the going in Iraq became, the more the president emphasized the values of freedom and democracy. It was also a canny domestic political approach that crossed party lines. It was difficult for Democrats to argue against their own ideals of human rights and democratic values.

I tried out the idea of democracy and human rights on the prime minister of Lebanon at the time, Rafic Hariri, at a conference in Marrakech, Morocco, in 2004. "We used human rights to undercut the Soviet surrogate regimes in Eastern Europe," I said. "They had signed the Helsinki Accords—the same statements that we as know-it-all Army officers had considered woolly-headed idealism when we first heard of it—and the regimes simply crumbled when repeatedly confronted with the deep inconsistencies between what they had agreed on and what their actions really were . . . "

Hariri waved his hand and cut me off with a smile. "That won't work here," he said. "In this region you can't insist on political rights first—there is no tradition of democracy. You have to start with economic rights, and put in place systems of commercial law which enable all citizens to have economic opportunity." It was obvious that he was right.

One of the first examples of this error was US support for direct elections in the Palestinian territories in 2006. It ended badly. As one European statesman explained to me, "We told [Secretary of State] Condi [Rice] not to insist on elections, that Hamas would surely win. But she insisted, and now they have won. She called me the next day, shocked, and asked, 'What are we going to do now?'" The result was increased militancy in Gaza, followed by an Israeli invasion of Gaza in 2009, and an opening for Iran to reach out to strengthen Hamas, just as it had strengthened Hezbollah after the Israeli military action in Lebanon in 2006.

Meanwhile, with the US military deployed in Iraq, we were limited in our ability to extract concessions by the threat, or implicit threat, of military action against other potential adversaries, such as Iran. Earlier, the buildup and initial exercise of US power in the invasion had apparently shocked the Iranian political leadership; an opening for dialogue appeared in 2002–2003, expressed through representatives in Switzerland, but was ignored by the Bush administration. It was as though the political leaders and analysts in the US national security system imagined that they were leading an invasion of Nazi Germany and pressing for unconditional surrender, or that any effective use of diplomacy might be interpreted as a weakness. Sure enough, once the Iranians saw the clumsy and under-resourced American occupation effort, they switched from accommodating US power to using the United States as a foil to strengthen their own influence in the region.

By 2005, the Saudis were telling many of us privately that they viewed the United States as a failure in the region. The Saudis replaced their ambassador to the United States, and then, according to foreign sources, engaged in a billion-dollar covert operation to back the Sunnis in Iraq, paying off tribal sheikhs to cooperate with the Americans, and even paying and arming certain Sunni elements in Lebanon to resist Shia encroachments there. It was a dangerous game, but the Saudi effort in Iraq's Anbar Province and other Sunni areas was effective in restraining Sunni cooperation with Al-Qaeda terrorists in Iraq—the American media read this strictly as a function of "the surge," but, reportedly, Saudi payoff money provided the foundation. The simultaneous Saudi effort in Lebanon misfired, and ended up creating a brief armed conflict with the Lebanese armed forces.

DOUBLING DOWN

As interethnic violence escalated in Iraq in 2006, it became clear that it was too late to rely on the conventional tools of counterinsurgency, such as civic-action programs. The United States faced a make-or-break decision: withdraw or escalate. President Bush appointed an Iraq Study Group and courageously decided that he would reinforce our troops rather than withdraw. General David Petraeus, one of the Army's most talented officers, replaced outgoing General George Casey, and he soon became the face of President George W. Bush's decision to initiate the surge.

With the Sunnis in Anbar Province swinging from opposition to cooperation with the US forces, General Petraeus was able to concentrate on Baghdad itself. He deployed troops in smaller packets, isolated Shia and Sunni fighters in specific neighborhoods, brought in intensive and effective small-unit tactics, and eliminated, bit by bit, the death squads and opposing fighters. All of this was accompanied by a renewed effort to field small teams combining social, economic, cultural, and medical personnel who could actually help to promote economic recovery and social healing. Commanders were given civic-action funds that they themselves could commit to small projects. Within months, the impact was obvious, and by 2008 US casualties, as well as the incessant car bombings, kidnappings, and murders, had been greatly reduced. Although it did not bring a final victory, the surge was highly successful in reversing what was shaping up to be a military defeat and providing a space in which democracy could possibly emerge. There was hope that the Iraqi economy could be rebuilt and that the United States might be able to make a dignified withdrawal.

The surge was an Iraq-only military phenomenon and it was apparently not connected to broadened US diplomacy in the region. No significant diplomatic concessions were extracted from Iran, and little from Syria. Indeed, relations with longtime US and NATO ally Turkey were repaired with great difficulty. Only in Libya had the diplomatic leverage of the US military commitment in the Gulf been successfully applied. Thanks principally to British Prime Minister Tony Blair, Libyan strongman Muammar al-Qaddafi gave up his program to create nuclear and chemical weapons, turning all the materials over to the West in 2005. Qaddafi exposed the nuclear proliferation activities of Pakistan's chief scientist, Abdul Qadeer Khan (who remains in house arrest today, without interrogation or punishment). Libya began to be reintegrated into the world community. Eventually, payments were made to the relatives of the families of those killed in the Pan Am 103 flight that exploded over Lockerbie. Sanctions were lifted, diplomatic relations were restored, and Libya was opened for business again with the West.

When I visited Libya in 2009, Western business was much in evidence, with a bevy of energy-sector deals underway and new construction. As I made my way through the lobby of Tripoli's only modernized hotel, a middle-aged Western executive came up to me and introduced himself. "Sir, as a lieutenant, I worked for you when you were in Bamberg, Germany, in 1976," he said. Now he was running the operations in Libya for a major international oilfield services firm, and they were building a new city in Libya's south to get at the oil there. It was a token benefit for the catastrophe in Iraq. But this boon to the United States and its allies was to be short-lived.

Diplomatic opportunities had been missed during the early years of the action in Iraq, certainly with Iran, possibly with Syria as well. There had been no invasion of these countries, but concessions could certainly have been extracted when the overwhelming military power of the United States was evident, before US limitations and weaknesses in the occupation phase had been exposed. The Iranian nuclear program could possibly have been curtailed, and perhaps the linkage with Hezbollah, also. The great strategists of the neoconservative movement thought too narrowly, not too grandly, and they limited their reach to the force of American arms rather than taking advantage of the diplomatic power that military action generated.

By the time US forces withdrew from Iraq at the end of 2011, although it appeared that Al-Qaeda in Iraq had been eliminated as an effective force, reconciliation between Sunni and Shia seemed a distant probability. The real winner in the region seemed to be Iran, which had gained wholesale access to Iraq, and through Iraq, to its expanding efforts in Lebanon and the Palestinian territories.

In January 2011, the "Arab Spring" arrived in Egypt, driven by years of corruption and repression, as well as rising expectations among the young and educated. Perhaps years of "freedom and democracy" rhetoric from US presidents and diplomats played a role as well. Tahrir Square became a symbol of protest. The demonstrations there were initially led by westernized, and in some cases, Western-educated, middle-class young Egyptians. But as they continued, the cautious and long-suppressed Muslim Brotherhood began to come forward. Suddenly, it was not so ob-

vious what the United States should do: after a period of consul-
tations in Washington, President Obama withdrew his support
from Egyptian President Hosni Mubarak.

I asked a well-known Egyptian journalist, whose son had
taken part in the demonstrations, what he thought about the
prospect of early elections. "Too soon," he said. "Only the Muslim Brotherhood is organized. They will win." He said it with a
shrug; it was Egypt, and expectations were low among those who
really understood what is required for democracy.

The parliamentary elections held in Egypt in the autumn of
2011 did result in a win by the Muslim Brotherhood and even
more extreme Salafist parties. The military slowly withdrew from
its protective role. A highly conservative constitution was drafted
by the Islamist majority, and in 2012 a new president was elected,
a man with decades in the Muslim Brotherhood, whose views had
been hardened by imprisonment and repression. He implemented
the new constitution by presidential decree, without popular consent. Egypt was headed toward a democratically elected, ultra-
conservative Islamist government. The United States felt bound to
support a democratically elected government, but by 2013 Egypt
was a mess: prices had risen, subsidies for bread and fuel had
been reduced, a major quarrel with the International Monetary
Fund had made the Egyptian pound unconvertible into hard currency, tourism and foreign direct investment were drying up, the
oil industry was collapsing, unemployment—always a problem—
was rising, and the uneasy social compact by which Egypt's government had maintained its minimalist legitimacy with the
Egyptian people was clearly broken. Elections hadn't brought
freedom; they had brought a different kind of authoritarianism.

In Libya, meanwhile, the Arab Spring had undone the benefit
the United States had received from a more compliant Colonel
Qaddafi. Some tribal forces were against Qaddafi, and members
of the old ruling family that had been displaced by Qaddafi were

quiet publicly, but privately were calling for him to be over-thrown. On American television there was outspoken support for US intervention from the same neoconservatives who had urged the US invasion of Iraq. Washington dithered. Soon Qaddafi's threat to crush the revolutionaries in Benghazi succeeded in pro-voking Western intervention in support of the rebels. President Obama called for Qaddafi's departure.

Soon thereafter, through a contact in Oman, Qaddafi's team reached out to me for advice. I immediately contacted the State Department and was encouraged to meet with them. Saif al-Islam al-Qaddafi, one of Muammar al-Qaddafi's sons and his political heir-apparent, sent his chief of staff to see me during my visit to Istanbul in April 2011. With the permission of the State Depart-ment, I warned him that NATO governments would isolate Qadd-afi from reinforcement, strengthen the rebels, pound his forces from the air, and relentlessly pursue him. He had best surrender, I said, or he would eventually be pulled from a hole in the ground, just like Saddam Hussein. Qaddafi and his people received similar advice from a number of other interlocutors.

By July 2011, the Qaddafi regime was on the run, and the same group called me again. With the assistant secretary of state listening in, I warned again that they should surrender before it was too late. They quibbled. A few weeks later, on October 20, Muammar al-Qaddafi was pulled from a culvert and murdered.

The Libyan turmoil continues to this day. In September 2012, the US consulate in Benghazi was stormed by an Islamist militia pre-sumably affiliated with Al-Qaeda, and Ambassador J. Christopher Stevens was killed. Weapons from Libya have spread all over North Africa and, reportedly, back into the Middle East. Saif al-Islam al-Qaddafi was captured and as of this writing is in confinement awaiting trial. His extradition to an international court has been re-fused by the Libyan government. Private reports, unverified, say that he has been heavily tortured. The eastern portion of Libya, centered around Benghazi, remains largely beyond government control. If US leverage over Libya had benefited briefly from the invasion of Iraq, by 2011 any benefits had disappeared. By 2014, almost three years into post-Qaddafi Libya, the government was fractured and ineffective, the eastern part of the country remained beyond government control, and US policy was in strategic limbo there.

There were also major difficulties in Syria. By 2012, the country was convulsed by rebellion. But rather than a revolt against tyranny, this rebellion was becoming an extension of the deeper sectarian struggles throughout the region that had taken center stage during the American occupation of Iraq. Alawites, the sect of the Assad family, Christians, and secular Sunnis were struggling against Sunni extremists. Refugees were seeking sanctuary in Turkey, Lebanon, and Jordan. Saudi Arabia, Turkey, and Qatar were arming the rebels, and the Qataris were reportedly providing weapons carelessly to Sunni extremists, even those potentially affiliated with Al-Qaeda, so long as they would fight against Bashar al-Assad. It had become a Wahhabi vs. Wahhabi struggle, with the Qataris and Saudis each competing with the other for influence within the rebel groups.

For more than a year, the United States provided limited support for Syrian refugees and engaged behind the scenes to assess the nature and strength of various opposition groups. Although President Obama called on Bashar al-Assad to give up power, the United States did little openly. Russia and China conspired to block a UN Security Council resolution authorizing action against Assad. Initially, the Syrian opposition lacked a unified political face or voice; Syrian exiles in France and elsewhere seemed to have little influence on the ground; and there were literally hundreds of quasi-independent Syrian armed efforts. Some of the most effective fighters were those associated with known terrorist organizations, such as the Al-Nusra Front. Meanwhile, Iran also engaged its proxy, Hezbollah, in the fighting to reinforce its ally, Assad, and sent weapons and members of the Iranian Presidential

Guard to Syria through Iraq. By the summer of 2013, there were reports of Iraqi Shias fighting against the Sunnis in Syria.

Syria posed a tougher case for Western intervention than Libya had. Its armed forces were stronger, it possessed chemical and probably biological weapons, and it had an active, ongoing Russian presence. Seeking to contain the risks, President Obama specified that his "red line," the line which Assad must not cross, was the use of chemical weapons, and yet by April 2013 that line had been crossed, according to French, British, and ultimately, US sources. When Secretary of State John Kerry decreed that the United States would provide non-lethal assistance to the rebels, and tried to use this leverage to call for a peace conference of the parties, Russia trumped the American red line by persuading Assad to renounce his chemical weapons, forestalling US airstrikes and enabling Assad to continue to tighten his grip against the rebel groups. Strategically, the United States had been outmaneuvered—there would be no air strikes against chemical weapons facilities to assist the opposition fighters. By the late spring of 2014, the tide of battle had turned against the Syrian opposition supported by the United States, with consequences not only in Syria but also worldwide, as friends, allies, and potential adversaries took stock of American resolve.

AIMING FOR THE MIDEAST

President Bush had used war to unify the country, at least temporarily, just as his predecessors Wilson, Roosevelt, and Truman had done. Yet the results were inconclusive. Each and every action in the Middle East seemed to beget more requirements. There was no clean ending anywhere—not in an increasingly tortuous Iraq, not with the escalation of pressure against Iran, not in what some termed the "long war" against Al-Qaeda, not in Afghanistan, and not in relations with the United States' tenuous and double-dealing ally, nuclear-armed Pakistan. In many cases, the US engagements, however effective they may have been in dealing with acute problems, abetted longer-term concerns.

American power seemed to be more the power to strike than to build. Neither military force nor appeals to democracy were adequate to address the challenges of rising expectations and seething anti-Western sentiment. US actions in the Middle East, particularly in Iraq, had contributed to violence and instability, providing a recruiting and training ground for terrorists. Our efforts were designed to advance US interests in the region, and we had been successful in assuring the survival of Israel, beating down Al-Qaeda—or at least its centralized leadership—and protecting the flow of oil. But the gains came at tremendous cost in lives and resources and dealt a substantial blow to our values (preventive war and torture are not values to which we have historically subscribed). By 2014 America seemed to be riding a "bucking bronco" of change and instability with implications far beyond the region.

US men and women in uniform have paid a heavy price. There were never enough of them. The volunteer force served a country that, far from generally mobilizing, had actually promoted consumption and tax cuts during the conflict. Repetitive tours, family disruptions, profound emotional disturbances for several hundred thousand troops—all of these things reflected the burden that was inequitably placed on the military as an institution. And as a result of the "guns-and-butter" approach, along with the impact of the financial crisis on the US budget deficit, the men and women in the armed forces are facing possible cuts in pay increases and benefits, reductions in family and support programs, and cutbacks in military manpower. Veterans and retirees who served in earlier wars face cuts in benefits as well. All of this is quite different from the victory parade down Pennsylvania Avenue that greeted our troops during their 1991 homecoming.

More than twenty-two years after I heard the Big Idea that the United States should move to dominate the region, we see the results. Who then could have imagined its awful impact? The thousands of deaths, including almost 6,000 Americans? The millions of refugees, the trillions of dollars, and continuing and deepening struggles across the Middle East? Our military actions on top of an already conflict-torn, rapidly modernizing region succeeded in deposing Saddam Hussein and taking down Osama bin Laden, but at a price far greater than most of us would have anticipated.

Some will want to write off our decade-long effort in the region, conceding that despite this massive commitment of resources and national effort, surprisingly little has been accomplished. But we still have vital interests in the region—we need access to oil, and we want nuclear nonproliferation and the security of Israel. Even if these interests are becoming less prominent relative to other rising challenges facing the United States, they are important.

Since oil is priced on a world-market basis, any risks to supplies in the volatile Middle East still have an immediate impact here at home. The emerging Sunni-Shia sectarian struggle, which is spreading from Iraq to Syria and into Lebanon, and involves both Saudi Arabia and Iran, certainly threatens stability in the oil markets. And the Strait of Hormuz, at the east end of the Persian Gulf, remains a key chokepoint for shipments of much of the world's oil.

Iran's nuclear ambitions remain a point of contention. For years, every American president has said that "all options remain on the table" if Iran persists in its apparent aim of developing a nuclear weapon. Along with the Shia-Sunni sectarian conflicts, Iran's reach for regional hegemony has continued to pull the United States into the region.

One country that looks stronger than most in the Middle East, both militarily and economically, is Israel. In part this is because it has suffered none of the disastrous destabilizations that have afflicted its neighbors. Its economy, led by its tech sector, has produced a decade of solid achievement and substantial economic growth. Israel is quickly going to find itself becoming a significant energy producer, possibly an oil and gas exporting country, and very wealthy indeed. The security fence separating Israel from the West Bank, controversial at the time of its construction, has yielded increasing safety and security from suicide bombings and terrorist activities within Israel.

With the success of the fence, Israel's relative security position in the region is far stronger today than it was a few years ago. Israel retains the capability to defend its borders against any combination of potentially hostile powers; diplomatically, it has maintained excellent security relations with Egypt to its west and Jordan to its east. Its antiballistic missile capabilities can not only blunt small rocket attacks from Lebanon or Gaza, but also defend against intermediate-range missile strikes originating in Iran. Of course, this military balance is dynamic. But Israel has first-rate military technology, sometimes even better than that deployed by the United States, such as its short-range anti-missile defense, called Iron Dome, and a strong economy to back it up. Israel will remain a vital interest of the United States, but this interest can be satisfied by existing and projected US forces and capabilities. Israel doesn't need excessive US military support.

We have many friends and partners in the region, and we have interests in their social, economic, and political well-being and progress. Countries such as Saudi Arabia, Kuwait, Qatar, the United Arab Emirates, Jordan, and Egypt have been of great help in enabling our policies over the years. We have worked extensively with Oman and Yemen; we have long-standing arrangements with Morocco, and we have attempted to help Libya and Tunisia through current difficulties. No doubt the United States will remain committed to continuing our work to secure a lasting peace agreement between Israel and the Palestinians, when the opportunity is present, and to the security and survival of Israel.

Working through the issues in the region will take years of sustained effort. The region's energy resources will keep it in the front ranks of economic significance; its security and governance challenges will provide a decade or more of "political risk" for businesses and economies excessively reliant upon the region. The United States will be affected by the outcomes of these matters and therefore needs to be engaged appropriately.

But others have now begun to assert themselves more strongly into the region. With Russian forces on the ground, Russian diplomacy active in Syria and Iran, and Russia chafing to grip Egypt, and with the Russian Mediterranean force at its greatest strength ever, we may have reached the end of the window described by Wolfowitz and others, twenty-odd years ago, in which we could use force with impunity. China is deeply invested in Iran and is building an infrastructure by which to capture Iran's exported hydrocarbons. So the apparent aim of the hardliners in the Republican Party of the early 1990s—a restructuring of the regimes and relationships in the region by US force—is no longer feasible.

Not only did the US invasion of Iraq contribute to instabilities in the region, we also opened the door for the rising power of Iran. China was also a "winner," deepening its regional relationships at our expense. Even more significantly, the war in Iraq anesthetized us to some of the other, more strategic challenges we are facing today. Iraq has dominated the news cycle for years, has consumed precious resources, and has wasted lives and distracted our leadership and our elected representatives. It seemed that the only urgent problems we faced were in the Middle East, because that was where our troops were dying. Strategy, in the minds of the public and decisionmakers, almost seemed synonymous with the military and with warfare.

For the United States, it is past time for us to look more widely at the international environment and the challenges and opportunities we face elsewhere.

CHAPTER 3

Five Challenges for a New National Strategy

While the United States was deeply engaged in the Middle East, the Asia-Pacific region became the new center of economic power, diplomatic maneuver, and growing risk.

Half of mankind's 7 billion people live in the region stretching from India in the west through China and Japan in the east. The region is home to the world's second- and third-largest economies (China and Japan), its largest Muslim nation (Indonesia), the United States' largest creditor and trading partner (China), and some of the world's greatest emitters of greenhouse gases (China, India, and Japan).

The region also is beset by a number of unresolved territorial issues. While the United States was spending its blood and treasure in the Middle East—and accumulating some $14 trillion in new US public debt—East Asian economies were growing rapidly: not only China, but also India, Indonesia, Vietnam, and the Philippines. Asia is also home to the most rapid buildup of military power today, and it is a hotbed of tensions caused by China's economic clout and growing assertiveness. During the decade of our preoccupation in the Middle East, the East Asian Summit meetings began—without the participation of the president of the United States. The Shanghai Cooperation Council, to which the United States was invited as an observer but declined, has grown into an increasingly robust framework for Chinese and Russian military exercises and the concert of diplomatic measures throughout Central Asia. The pivot to Asia was long overdue.

But it won't be enough to transfer the focus of our attention, our diplomacy, or our military forces to another part of the world, though that is certainly part of what we must do. More fundamentally, we need to pivot "qualitatively" to face a new class of challenges that are multinational in scope, interrelated in character, and growing in significance, and that require a long-term perspective. These challenges will not go away by themselves; nor will we outgrow them. Each has multiple dimensions—political, cultural, and economic, as well as military or security broadly defined; a "single-axis" approach to analyzing the problem will not capture its complexity or depth. None of these problems can be understood (or resolved) by "leaving it up to the market." Each has originated through a combination of government and private-sector actions, and dealing with each one effectively will require a combination of public and private efforts, in the United States and abroad. Finally, each of these problems impacts the others, and their solutions are also intertwined. The combination of these characteristics means that the sum of these challenges differs qualitatively and in significance from anything the United States has faced before.

These challenges should be distinguished from the immediate and acute crises that arise in the course of executing US foreign policy—a coup attempt here, a currency collapse there, a missile launching, a threat of war, a requirement to intervene to thwart aggression or enforce a peace agreement. Those are the normal everyday challenges a superpower must face.

But these immediate crises must be viewed and dealt with in the context of the long-term, strategic challenges we face: terrorism, which disrupts governments, wrecks economies, destroys lives, and potentially could shake the foundations of our global civilization; cybersecurity, because our global economy is increasingly dependent on packets of information that are scattered, and then reassembled, over open communications lines that we call the Internet; the US financial system, because its health and stability is not only fundamental in the global economy, but far more fragile than we have typically understood; China, because its rapid rise and ambitions could spark conflict and undercut global institutions; and, most fundamentally, climate change, which probably poses the most dangerous long-term risks to our nation and to mankind as a whole.

If we can come to understand these deeper, more strategic challenges correctly and can frame a national strategy to deal with them, we will have the foundation from which to handle the acute crises that erupt from time to time.

CHALLENGE ONE: TERRORISM

Terrorism against chiefly civilian targets is a form of asymmetric warfare against governments, and sometimes is directed against the United States. We began working against terrorists in the 1980s, when Iranian-sponsored terrorists blew up the Marine barracks in Beirut and Palestinian groups began kidnapping and killing Americans. Then, we and our friends and allies thought we had largely defeated it. When General Wayne Downing, one of the original leaders in the US Army Special Forces, was preparing to take command of the US Joint Special Operations Command in 1989, he asked, "What are we going to do with our Special Forces if there are no terrorists to fight?" Downing and the rest of us learned that his question wouldn't need to be answered anytime soon.

The first bombing of the World Trade Center in 1993 was a wake-up call to a new threat, and by the mid-1990s the United States had identified Osama bin Laden as an important terrorist and asked for his extradition. Following the bombings of the US embassies in Kenya and Tanzania, the United States targeted Osama bin Laden with a cruise missile strike. Only excessive military caution kept President Clinton from ordering a Special Forces strike against him at the time, which might have forestalled the destruction of 9/11. The United States may have had sufficient information—pocketed away in agencies or neglected in reports that had not been thoroughly digested—during the summer of 2001 to have prevented Osama bin Laden's terrorist strike, if only the top leadership at the White House had realized the dangers and focused the various agencies of the federal government on the threat.

It has been more than a decade since that time, and the terrorist threat has transformed and migrated, but the threat remains significant. Although their capabilities are not yet—and perhaps never will be—sufficient to be considered "existential" to the United States, the various Islamist terrorist groups can wreak political and economic havoc abroad, and they could stage attacks that would have significant consequences for the United States. Their old targets remain favorites—the commercial air travel system and public infrastructure. US airlines continue to register incidents indicative of vulnerabilities. Passenger screening beyond the United States still varies significantly, despite years of effort, and it is still a challenge to be certain the screeners are doing enough to catch people like the "underwear bomber," Abdul Farouk Abdulmutallab, who was arrested on Christmas Day 2009 following his failed attempt to detonate a plastic explosive on an international flight.

But the most daunting threat to commercial aviation is probably the surface-to-air missile. In 2002, terrorists tried to shoot down an airliner with surface-to-air missiles in Kenya. But their training was poor, and the missiles were first-generation, hand-held devices. The aircraft survived, but the attack still called attention to the need for more sophisticated self-protection systems for commercial aircraft. Recently, it has been suggested that terrorists may be gaining access to more sophisticated surface-to-air weapons. The third-generation Russian SA-18, for example, has sufficient advanced guidance to see through some kinds of countermeasures, and can strike aircraft flying at well over 15,000 feet. The loss of sophisticated weaponry as the Qaddafi regime fell in Libya in 2011 was rumored to be significant; estimates of the number of missing surface-to-air missiles run from four hundred to several thousand. Qatar, Saudi Arabia, and Turkey have been supplying lethal weaponry to rebel groups in Syria since 2012, including perhaps some surface-to-air missiles.

These weapons could be lethal to airliners and devastating to air travel and international commerce. Strikes at other targets—malls, public transportation, and other specific targets, such as military recruiting stations—have reminded us that the terrorist threat can inflict damage in other ways, too. Certain elements of infrastructure whose destruction would be especially damaging—petrochemical plants, tunnels, the electrical power grid, and the water infrastructure, for example—also remain vulnerable. Finally, there is also the danger that nuclear proliferation will lead to terrorist acquisition of a nuclear weapon or "dirty bomb."

Terrorist technologies and skills have become increasingly sophisticated over time. New means of communication, new travel and training networks, and new explosive technologies are constantly under development. There are continuing worries about "detection-proof" bombs. In February 2014, the United States issued a warning against a new "shoe-bomb" threat, apparently originating from a terrorist cell in Yemen. Despite the loss of so much of its core leadership, Al-Qaeda and its affiliates have proved remarkably resilient and dangerous.

Estimates of the significance of the threat vary, but US government reports have noted that Al-Qaeda-affiliated cells exist in seventy countries. Annually some thousands of new recruits are estimated to be drawn into the terrorist campaigns against the West and against targeted regional governments. The situation in Syria is especially dangerous in this regard; literally thousands of new recruits have been drawn into the terrorist training network as a result of this conflict. These young men, from many different countries, including Russia and Western nations, gain firsthand training and experience by fighting in Syria and become radicalized there. As many as 7,000 may have been recruited by Syrian rebel groups from outside of Syria, with perhaps 1,000 or more drawn from Europe. Some have reportedly come from the United States. Many will be able to return home, or relocate elsewhere in the West, bringing their new battlefield skills with them. In May 2014, former NSA Director General Keith Alexander confirmed that, based on evidence he has seen, the threat of terrorist attacks in the United States is growing.[1]

"Self-radicalization" has also become more pronounced, in which otherwise peaceful members of society become alienated, angry, and vengeful and conduct "lone-wolf" attacks. The attack perpetrated by US Army psychiatrist Major Nidal Hassan killed 13 people at Fort Hood, Texas, in November 2009; the attack at the Boston marathon in 2013 killed 3 people, and 260 were injured. For our friends and allies abroad, who for now are bearing the brunt of the fighting, the September 2013 attack on the Westgate Mall in Kenya is a foretaste of the potential dangers ahead as Al-Qaeda transforms into more localized terrorist organizations capable of hideous atrocities. The impact of such actions goes well beyond the immediate casualties and damages inflicted, of course.

At home, the terrorist threat has led to the creation of an entire "terrorist-industrial complex" (as General Colin Powell termed it). Others have used the term "security-industrial complex." The quest for security has drawn billions of dollars and created a vast, Washington-centric matrix of highly paid analysts, technologists, and contractors whose work is cloaked in secrecy—and the scale of their work has impacted the region economically. According to a *Washington Post* investigation, this field now includes perhaps 1,200 government organizations, 1,900 companies, and 854,000 people with security clearances (not counting members of the armed forces). The Department of Homeland Security has become the third-largest agency of government, behind the Defense Department and the Veterans Administration. Billions of dollars of assistance have been disbursed to state and local agencies, creating a much tighter integration of local, state, and federal law-enforcement authorities than ever existed previously. New technologies, some fresh off the battlefields of Iraq and Afghanistan, have been deployed at home, along with new organizations, procedures, and personnel, and increasingly, organizations such as the FBI have moved beyond law enforcement and into preventive counterterrorist actions.[2]

The security-industrial complex has grown so rapidly not only because of the desire to prevent the next attack, but also because of the fear of political backlash should prevention fail. Although more than 60,000 Americans die violently each year, either from gunshots or automobile accidents, the acceptable standard for terrorist events in the United States is zero. Each incident finds political leaders seeking to commit greater resources to the task and to place greater impositions on Americans' privacy and liberties. Reversing this trend has proved difficult, partly because the nature of the threat raises the old Cold War question of "how much is enough." How much security, on a daily basis, is enough to protect us? And these costs are imposed not only on the government—via new intelligence methods, new analysis centers, enhanced counterterrorist striking power, new embassies abroad, critical infrastructure protection, airline security, border security, and the like—but also on the private sector. The costs imposed run into the hundreds of billions of dollars annually.

The terrorist threat has impacted our political culture and psyche, too. Americans have accepted inconveniences and intrusions that have given the US government much greater access to and potential control over our private lives. Monitoring and surveillance have increased. Revelations that the National Security Agency can monitor anything and everything, and may be doing so already, initially raised surprisingly little public concern. Centralized coordination of security forces has improved law enforcement's grip, and police forces have become both more militarized and less localized in their capabilities, attitudes, and concerns. New technologies, such as security cameras with facial recognition, radically change the assumption of anonymity in public, and hence the sense of personal privacy and liberty. The potential for abuse has grown correspondingly. The security network is also a duplicative, inefficient hybrid of overlapping departmental fiefdoms.

The roots of all these issues were easy to see in the weeks and months after 9/11. The problem of how to detect and track terrorists received much attention at the Defense Advanced Research Projects Agency (DARPA), under the auspices of John Poindexter, a retired US Navy rear admiral who had joined DARPA after becoming senior vice president of a technology firm. He and his team were creating the Total Information Awareness (TIA) program, assembling, collating, and analyzing data to improve the nation's ability to detect, track, and prevent terrorist activities. Various companies already collected data, and much of it was available and processed in real time. Cellphone metadata—that is, the phone numbers associated with incoming and outgoing calls, along with the time and duration of the calls and the locations of the cellphones when the calls were made—was already being tracked for billing and network operation purposes, though the actual conversations themselves were not being recorded, so far as we knew. The metadata from cellphone calls would be useful in following suspected terrorists in real time as well as in tracing out networks of possible accomplices and supporters who might not otherwise have been identified. Credit-card purchases were also reported electronically in real time, and these records could be used to track suspects and their activities. Moreover, credit cards were issued upon the basis of substantial personal and financial information, which was useful as well. It was only logical to those concerned with antiterrorist activities and presidential protection that this data should be able to be synthesized in real time, whether or not a specific individual was on a watch list. Who could know when a new threat might emerge?

Working as a consultant to an Arkansas-based data company, I attended meetings at DARPA in early 2002, when all of this was being discussed. The Total Information Awareness program became a target of civil libertarians and was ended, along with Poindexter's position, in the spring of 2003. But the logic and framework stuck; it would be only a short step to integrate satel-lite imagery, or streaming video from Unmanned Aerial Vehicles, with a nationwide database of security cameras (UK intelligence had a substantial lead in these methods), and even with facial recognition software and audio coverage of selected locations. In the years after 9/11, every major metropolitan area began to es-tablish its own operations center with video and audio coverage of key facilities, road and rail networks, and even crime-prone neighborhoods. On-street video surveillance was visible and often alarmed to signal gunshots or other critical events to remote oper-ators. Meanwhile, former military personnel were busy setting up

SWAT teams and incident-response training, bringing to the domestic security scene all the hard-won lessons from three decades of post–Vietnam War training technologies and methods.

These intrusions have sparked serious debate about our constitutional right to privacy, but there is no dispute at the political level that the first function of government is to protect its citizens. The idea that some of these international terrorists are US-born only intensifies pressures to strengthen domestic surveillance. And these worries, in turn, have created the opportunity for a far greater concentration of power in the hands of the government than Americans have traditionally experienced—or found acceptable. Indeed, the idea that the US military is involved on a continuing, daily basis in working with domestic law enforcement, transferring methodologies and training as well as specific information, revealed in *Washington Post* reporter Dana Priest's book *Top Secret America*, represents a level of military involvement at home not seen since the American Civil War. This new role deeply threatens traditional American concepts of civil-military relations and the distribution of power between the federal government and state and local authorities.

The revelations of Edward Snowden beginning in the spring of 2013 triggered a deeper discussion of these dangers. But the information that Snowden leaked went well beyond the domestic realm to include details about US spying on foreign governments and leaders. As American privacy advocates reacted strongly at home, key US allies reacted even more strongly abroad. German Chancellor Angela Merkel was especially incensed that her mobile phone, and those of some of her close associates, had been monitored. Foreign reaction was, of course, highly hypocritical. It may well be that US methods of interception, decryption, and data processing are far more advanced than the kinds of technologies available to other nations. But it is certain that every nation is doing what it can to provide sensitive information to its leaders, and in some cases to its leading industries, and that most of them have far less public accountability or safeguards than the United States does.

In December 2013, President Obama's Review Group on Intelligence and Communications Technology, an advisory panel, recommended a series of measures to roll back the authorities of the National Security Agency. The panel recommended changes in the methods used to store telephone metadata and suggested additional restraints and oversights on domestic and foreign surveillance. Some in Congress and the security field called for the recommendations to be rejected, saying they constituted "unilateral US cyber-disarmament." But even if some of these recommendations are adopted—reportedly much of the NSA collection has not yielded anything substantial—such collection will be restored the moment the next terrorist threat emerges. It is the nature of "terrorism" to raise fears out of proportion to the danger to any one individual, and hence to compel governments to take measures far out of proportion to the actual threat in order to protect the public and secure its own legitimacy.[3]

The characteristics of the terrorist problem are symptomatic of the broader range of national security issues the United States faces in the century ahead: problems that are long-term; widely distributed across many countries; and multidimensional, affecting security, economic opportunities, and American values and standards. And these challenges have arisen asymmetrically, despite—perhaps because of—the overwhelming diplomatic, military, and economic strength of the United States over the past two decades.

CHALLENGE TWO: CYBERSECURITY

Closely associated with terrorism is the threat of cyber-attacks and intrusions, which can be associated with either espionage or theft. In the popular usage, "cyber" refers to anything connected with the Internet. The Internet has totally infiltrated American life. By its design, it is open to everyone; it is controlled by no government, charges no fees, and is regulated by no one. And because we are all connected, we are all vulnerable. The United States is probably the most vulnerable nation in the world in terms of cyber-threats because our economy and infrastructure are so deeply connected to the Internet. A recent survey found that some 500,000 infrastructure-related "targets" are available for attack.[4]

Identity theft—the use of stolen Social Security numbers, credit-card numbers, and other identifying data to steal money or goods—is an increasing danger. Individual personal data can be taken electronically online and used for illicit purposes. Perhaps fifteen years ago, identity theft may have been the work of lone hackers, but today it is increasingly the work of major crime. One of the companies I advise has a system that can detect searches of the peer-to-peer space; its technical experts daily find personal identity information floating in the open, waiting to be stolen and exploited. In other cases, bulk personal and account information is lifted. The Target credit breach in December 2013, exposing millions of consumers to data theft, and the Heartbleed security flaw that came to light in April 2014 were only the latest of these problems to emerge.

Typically, stolen individual information is used for illicit financial gain. Information stolen in bulk is usually sold onward. In some cases, batches of stolen credit-card numbers are sold to groups of thieves who attempt to make fraudulent purchases online. In other cases, criminals use the data to withdraw money from accounts, through bank transfers or ATM withdrawals. Estimates of losses range into the hundreds of millions of dollars per year worldwide. But because there is no system to accurately capture and tally the losses, no one really knows.

Law-enforcement efforts have tied much of the criminal activity to organized crime gangs operating from Russia and Eastern Europe. They have found sophisticated groups of criminals, often specializing in distinct aspects of the crime, and sometimes connected indirectly to governments.

Beyond the theft of money, however, it is the theft of data that poses even larger problems. Businesses live on privacy to guide their investments, marketing, bidding, and production. Industrial firms invest in design and engineering, some of it cutting edge, especially in the aerospace industry, but also in the energy and power sectors. Theft of this data constitutes economic and industrial espionage. While some theft of economic data has always occurred, the Internet enables corporations to be penetrated and looted without any physical trace; truckloads of data can be electronically carted off.

The oil industry has been a principal target of organized cyber-attack. Other major efforts have targeted defense firms like Lockheed Martin, Northrup Grumman, and BAE Systems, which reportedly lost reams of data on America's state-of-the-art F-35 Joint Strike Fighter. According to the *Wall Street Journal*, the fighter program was broken into repeatedly, possibly as early as 2007, with the spies encrypting the technology as it was stolen. Investigators reportedly traced the intrusions back to China, where, presumably, the data could accelerate Chinese aircraft design, or reveal flaws or characteristics in the US design that could be exploited. But there is also the real possibility that access to data storage inside such firms provides the opportunity to insert malicious and destructive code that could delay production or even compromise the performance of aircraft or other weapons systems under certain conditions. The threat of cyber-theft raises the specter of enemy hackers circumventing years of careful control of communications, aerospace, nuclear, and other national-security-sensitive technologies and undercutting a host of US and US-sponsored nonproliferation efforts.[5]

These threats are of course a threat to business and to sensitive US national security programs. But, systemically, these efforts also pose a major threat to the US economy itself. Our economic advantages in technology, research, and development—advantages for which the United States spends tens of billions of dollars each year—are being stolen. This is our national treasure, the sum of millions of hours of work and billions of dollars, directly paid for or indirectly supported by the US taxpayer, flowing out of the country. The flow is sometimes invisible, usually cannot be traced, and often goes unreported. In our economy, we rely on markets—stock markets, commodity markets, futures markets—and cyber-espionage provides vast opportunities for insider information to be used for private profit and ultimately for the destruction of the market systems fundamental to the US economy.

It is possible for criminals and rogue actors to use the Internet to degrade, disrupt, and destroy an economy that is "wired," as ours is. Anything that can be accessed through the Internet is potentially vulnerable to being entered electronically, and anything that can be entered and is controlled by software can be made to malfunction, turn itself off, or even destroy itself as a result of skillful exploitation of the vulnerabilities of computer programs and networks. Today, the US economy has made use of Internet connectivity in remote data collection and controls for virtually everything. Everything is connected—electric generators, transformers, and other utility-related infrastructure; banks and other financial institutions; rail and highway dispatch; wholesale and retail suppliers of food, clothing, appliances, and automobiles; newspapers and other media; and municipal governments and their agencies, including fire, police, paramedics, hospitals, and even street lights.

Much of it is not only connected, but is also accessed, tasked, and controlled remotely, over the Internet. Bank account numbers could be altered, financial flows disrupted, electrical power grids shut down, generators destroyed, radars and air-traffic control systems altered, media turned off, rail shipments and logistics schedules disrupted, and perhaps commercial jets disabled in flight (most modern planes rely on electronic instrumentation and maintain broadband connectivity to the ground). And even if the actual destruction could be limited in such attacks, the disruptions could cause the collapse of public confidence in some of the pillars of the US economy.

In 1994, when I was director for strategic plans and policy for Joint Chiefs of Staff, I was called down to the office of the Joint Chiefs vice chairman to participate in an extremely sensitive discussion of how future warfare could use cyber-attacks instead of bombs to destroy specific elements or sectors of an adversary's economy. It was known that viruses and other specialized programs could be inserted from abroad through the Internet or through other means, and that hardware, such as chips, could have "backdoors" accessible from abroad, and so forth. It wasn't necessary to take out whole factories or power stations or facilities physically with weaponry—just find the critical nodes and disrupt them with cyber. Measures were being put in place across various government agencies to explore and prepare capabilities for just these kinds of operations. And they have obviously borne fruit.

It turns out that the US Joint Staff may have been barely keeping pace with the Chinese, who began earnestly reexamining warfare in the aftermath of Desert Storm in 1991. By the time two Chinese colonels released a book called *Unrestricted Warfare* in 1999, it was clear that we had been in an intellectual arms race. They describe using network warfare to take down all classes of targets. Nothing is to be off limits.

Today, cyber-attack is not a US monopoly. It has actually been employed against us and our allies on numerous occasions, and with increasing sophistication. Perhaps the first incident was the Chinese cyber-response to NATO after we mistakenly bombed their embassy in Belgrade during the Kosovo campaign in 1999; NATO websites were besieged with a flood of spurious emails originating from China. In 2007, in retaliation for what was seen as an anti-Russian decision, the government of Estonia was viciously attacked; institutions and commercial transactions were blocked by what has now become known as a Distributed Denial of Service Attack (DDOS). The crescendo of emails was even more effective against Georgia in the brief Russian-Georgian conflict of 2008. In March 2013, North Korea apparently attacked South Korean TV stations and banks, blocking transactions, and in one case erasing files. In June 2013, North Korea attacked the South Korean president's website as well as other government sites.

In 2007, several US departments, including Defense, State, Homeland Security, and Commerce, all suffered major cyber-intrusions. Information was lost, websites were taken down, emails were restricted, and National Aeronautics and Space Administration (NASA) technology was compromised. In 2012, Saudi oil activities and US banks and financial institutions were hit with continuous waves of cyber-attacks believed to be from Iran; the attacks, continuing in 2013, were described as sophisticated distributed denial of service attacks (DDOS) and forced online banks to be shut down temporarily. US utility companies continue to acknowledge thousands of attacks and probes each day. In the 2014 Ukraine crisis, the Ukrainian government was hit by repeated cyber-attacks, apparently originating in Russia.

Authorities believe that our power grid, a prime target, has been effectively compromised with cyber-inserted software that could devastate our electric power systems in a crisis. They also believe that our most sensitive communications are likely penetrated and untrustworthy in a crisis. And it is believed that much of US critical infrastructure is vulnerable to sophisticated attack.[6]

A 2013 study by the Mandiant Corporation identified a Chinese military unit with large facilities in Shanghai and supported by large bandwidth connectivity through China Telecom. Mandiant believes the unit is augmented by hundreds of operators, as well as by skilled linguists. Other studies have identified particular universities affiliated with China's cyber-activities, as well as semiofficial "militia" groups that are participating in cyber-warfare activities. Economic espionage is ideally suited to advancing the effectiveness of state-owned enterprises in the natural resources, in aerospace development, and in satellite and telecommunications technologies. In May 2014, the US government filed criminal charges against five Chinese military officers, charging them with cyber-theft of business secrets of US companies.[7]

But China may also be preparing for the execution of actual operations, should it deem them necessary. According to the Mandiant study, the Chinese unit practices long-term penetration of a target's servers, inserting code and withdrawing data over a period of many months. These are the kinds of attacks that often are not detected, because the hackers are able to turn off alarms; in some cases they succeed in concealing the penetration for some time.[8]

Chinese writers have emphasized, however, that computer network defense is China's highest priority. In this regard, China has advantages over the United States. By virtue of the Chinese government's control of cyberspace, its operatives can see, regulate, and, if necessary, control every site. In a crisis, the Chinese government could literally shut off China's entire Internet from outside access. And because China's infrastructure is neither as modernized nor as efficiency-conscious as ours, the country probably retains manual backups for many of its key systems.

Individual business enterprises cannot track the evolving threats and devise detection and countermeasures in an efficient manner. For years, businesses have been buying firewalls and antivirus software, such as Norton Internet Security, and allowing these specialized companies to take the lead in providing protection. But the scale of cyber-development simply exceeds the capacity of private companies to keep up. Like physical security, cybersecurity is a cost of doing business that businesses would like to avoid, if possible. In addition, admission of cybersecurity failures could destroy business reputations and contribute to substantial additional losses.

It isn't that the US government is unaware of the problem. In fact, the government and its agencies have been concerned with information security and computer vulnerabilities for over twenty years. In 1994, the Joint Security Commission, set up by the Pentagon and the intelligence community, assessed the risks of networked information. After the Oklahoma City bombing in 1995, President Clinton established a Presidential Commission on Critical Infrastructure Protection. By 2000, there was a US national plan on this issue. By 2008, President Bush had directed a Comprehensive National Cybersecurity Initiative and initiated it through National Security Presidential Directive 54. Although the specifics have never been released, these initiatives obviously failed to tackle the tough job of protecting the private sector and American corporations.[9]

The Center for Strategic and International Studies authored a study on cyberspace security in 2008, and the National Academy of Sciences addressed the cybersecurity problem in 2009. When President Obama took office, he initiated his own review of the cyber-threat and reissued the Comprehensive National Cybersecurity Initiative in his own name. However, it is largely directed at cybersecurity for the federal government and its agencies, and looks at the private and corporate sectors only through R&D efforts. This leaves corporate America and our critical infrastructure exceedingly vulnerable to attack.[10]

Unfortunately, US private industry hasn't wanted to be regulated and restricted by government directives and requirements concerning cybersecurity. There were intense lobbying campaigns by industry groups in 2011 and 2012 to forestall cyber-defense legislation. Consequently, the US Congress has continued to vote down such legislation. The Cyber Intelligence Sharing and Protection Act would enable the US Cyber Command to extend its protection to private enterprises, at a cost to those enterprises, but as of this writing had not been approved by both houses of Congress.

In early 2013, President Obama released an executive order on "Improving Critical Infrastructure Security" that sought to strengthen government's partnership with private industry. Simultaneously the president signed a presidential policy directive on "Critical Infrastructure Protection and Resilience" that is designed to strengthen the government's ability to address the implications of a cyber-incident. Various infrastructure providers were directed to take steps to secure their systems.

But these are small steps to address an overwhelming national security problem. America's wealth is being drawn out in huge troves of data; our entire economy is open to penetration, theft, and destruction from a system that, ironically, was created and engineered by our own technological wizards and that has often been hailed as one of America's greatest contributions to the world.

CHALLENGE THREE:
THE US FINANCIAL SYSTEM

The financial system figures prominently as a potential target of cyber-strikes, but it poses unique vulnerabilities of its own beyond cyber-attacks. The impact of the Great Recession of 2008, which originated from within the US financial system, has been so severe that it has impacted US national security.

The immediate impact was both economic and political. Some 8.8 million jobs were lost. The US unemployment rate increased from 5 percent to over 10 percent, and the Dow Jones Industrial Average (DJIA) dropped by more than 50 percent from its 2007 high to its low in 2009 (14,198 to 6,547). The S&P 500 declined from almost 1,496 to 808 between the fourth quarter of 2007 and the first quarter of 2009. The average home price in twenty metropolitan areas dropped 34 percent from highs in 2006 to early 2009. Nearly $11 trillion of household wealth vanished, according to the Financial Crisis Inquiry Commission. It is estimated that the Great Recession has cost the United States between $6 trillion and $14 trillion of GDP that would have been created in the absence of the financial crisis. All of this robbed the government of vital resources.[11]

In fact, six years after the onset of the Great Recession, there is increasing recognition that the economy seems fundamentally different from in its prerecession days; the economic system seems less sound, and our future less secure. The recovery has been prolonged and painful, and economic growth has been far below the normal growth that has occurred after other recessions. Job creation has been anemic—the almost 9 million jobs lost were not recovered until May 2014, and on balance, the new jobs were not as good as the old ones. Many large companies have focused on reducing expenses—in terms of both employment and investment—rather than on developing new products and markets or new streams of revenue, and they have done so quite successfully for their bottom line.[12]

Corporate profits as a percentage of the US GDP grew from 4 percent in 2001 to over 10 percent in 2011. But corporations have been reluctant to invest their earnings; instead, stock buybacks are in favor. Meanwhile, the median family income in the United States has declined in real terms. According to Emmanuel Saez, an economist at the University of California at Berkeley, between 2009 and 2012 inflation-adjusted family income across America climbed 6 percent, but 95 percent of this increase went to those in the top 1 percent. In 2012, the richest 10 percent received more than half of all income generated in the United States, the largest share since recordkeeping began in the United States in 1917. According to a 2013 study by the Organization for Economic Cooperation and Development (OECD), the level of income inequality in the United States is far above the average; it is exceeded only by Turkey, Mexico, and Chile. In addition, the extraordinarily low interest rates implemented by the Federal Reserve have penalized the elderly and other savers to the tune of some $758 billion since the Great Recession, according to one study, constituting essentially a transfer payment to the financial system.[13]

Out of this recession—the job losses, the foreclosures, and the loss of household wealth—was born the extreme anger that has boiled over into politics in the form of the Tea Party and other ultraconservatives. As former president Theodore Roosevelt observed a century ago, "when the average man loses his money, he is simply like a wounded snake and strikes right and left at anything, innocent or the reverse, that presents itself as conspicuous in his mind."[14] Since its emergence during the 2010 election cycle, the Tea Party has stood for doctrinaire antigovernment policies that have hindered appropriate responses to the Great Recession. These elements have used control within the Republican Party to block or delay routine government actions such as raising the debt ceiling, or combining increasing tax revenues with entitlement reform and other federal spending reduction methods. These periodic crises of performance by the federal government have shaken confidence abroad in the stability of the US economy, imperiled business activities such as investment and hiring, and reduced the power and influence of the United States abroad.

If we want to prevent a recurrence of the Great Recession, then we have to look to the causes of the crisis. The congressionally mandated 2011 *Financial Crisis Inquiry Report* summarized the origins in this way:

> While the vulnerabilities that caused the crisis were years in the making, it was the collapse of the housing bubble—

fueled by low interest rates, easy and available credit, scant regulation, and toxic mortgages—that was the spark that ignited a string of events which led to a full-blown crisis in the fall of 2008. Trillions of dollars in risky mortgages had become embedded throughout the financial system, as mortgage-related securities were packaged, repackaged, and sold to investors around the world. When the bubble burst, hundreds of billions of dollars in losses in mortgages and mortgage-related securities shook markets as well as financial institutions that had significant exposures to these mortgages and borrowed heavily against them. . . . The losses were magnified by derivatives."[15]

Many of us saw bits and pieces of the housing bubble as it developed: rapidly rising home prices, new types of mortgages, lots of people taking out "home-equity loans" based on the inflating value of their homes, and increasing enthusiasm for investments. But it was hard to put the whole picture together. One day in July 2007, one of my colleagues at Goldman Sachs, where I consulted for their Private Equity Group, called to say that they wouldn't be making any more investments through the private-equity funds for a while—the banks were refusing to agree to loans because they couldn't repackage and sell them onward. It tuned out that the overnight commercial paper market had frozen, just on fear—one bank's lack of confidence in another's. A banker would look at his own holdings and say, "What we've got looks bad. But if ours is bad, theirs must be worse; don't loan." And so the markets froze. Prompt action by the Federal Reserve unlocked the markets, and by October 2007, the financial system seemed almost normal again.

In early 2008 I visited with the "risk manager" at Goldman Sachs, a former Federal Reserve banker, to ask about the crisis. "We are in the sixth inning of a nine-inning game," he said. This was about two months before the first of the major institutions to go, Bear Stearns, failed and had to be sold. A few months later, Lehman Brothers, a larger institution, was allowed to fail. Recently released minutes of the Federal Reserve Board's deliberations show that even the Fed didn't see it coming, and when the bubble burst, had trouble reacting with the appropriate degree of power.[16]

Actually, when stripped down to its essential causes, the financial crisis of 2008 was like almost every other financial crisis—it was rooted in an expansion of debt, until that debt reached the point that confidence in its repayment was lost.

It was a familiar pattern in early America. There were bank crises in 1819, 1837, 1857, 1873, 1884, 1893, and again in 1907, and finally, in 1929, with the Great Depression. According to family legend, my great-grandfather, Thomas Wesley Reynolds, lost his assets in the financial panic of 1893, which began in New York, but impacted his small engineering company in Arkansas. The collapse of the stock market in October 1929 precipitated a general business collapse for years in the United States, including massive bank failures, a decline in America's industrial output and employment, and a 50 percent decline in farm income.

As a result of the 1930s' Depression, measures were put in place to regulate the securities industry (including the Securities Act of 1933 and the Investment Advisors Act of 1940) and reform of the banking sector (including strengthening the role of the Federal Reserve). Some of these laws formed the foundation for lasting progress and revered institutions. Others lapsed when they were no longer needed. And some were systematically weakened until they were finally revoked altogether. Nevertheless, for decades they provided a framework of regulation that largely stabilized the financial sector and prevented the recurrence of financial crises in the United States.

However, these restrictive laws opened the way for a shadow banking sector—lending by financial institutions that were not banks—that rivaled the banks in scale and competed effectively against them. This sector was largely unregulated. US banks were also being impacted by competition from foreign banks, which were not subject to the same restrictions. In struggling to meet that competition and to enhance their own earnings, the banking sector engaged in a concerted, long-term effort over many years to be released from the Depression-era restraints.

Restrictions on intrastate branch banking were lifted in many states. Usury laws were amended or repealed to enable the growth of the credit-card industry and other financial services. Step by step, the restrictive provisions of the Banking Act of 1933, nicknamed the Glass-Steagall Act, were lifted, making it possible for banks to issue "commercial paper," to allow automatic withdrawals to purchase securities, and to securitize and sell onward the mortgages they had been holding. Banks could even engage in credit default swaps. Nationwide, banking laws were further amended in 1994 by the Riegle-Neal Interstate Banking and Branching Efficiency Act. In 1999, after decades of epic struggle, the Glass-Steagall Act was finally repealed. In 2000, the regulation of derivatives was forbidden by law—the market was to be entirely entrusted to self-regulation. Further efforts were underway to restrain regulatory agencies through concerted political action. According to data collected by the Financial Crisis Inquiry Commission, between 1999 and 2008 the financial services sector spent $2.8 billion on lobbying, through political action committees alone giving more than $1 billion in campaign contributions.[17]

All of that effort paid off—for a while. The US financial sector, which includes the banking sector, investment banking, fixed income and derivatives trading, and other elements of the so-called shadow banking system, grew rapidly—at a much faster rate than the economy itself—for thirty-five years, and its growth was based on its use of debt. The Financial Crisis Inquiry Commission summarized the problem:

From 1978 to 2007 the amount of debt held by the financial sector soared from $3 trillion to $36 trillion, more than doubling as a share of Gross Domestic Product. The very nature of many Wall Street firms changed, from relatively staid private partnerships to publicly traded corporations taking greater and more diverse kind of risks. By 2005 the 10 largest U.S. commercial banks held 55% of the industry's assets, more than double the level held in 1990. On the eve of the crisis in 2006, financial sector profits constituted 27% of all corporate profits in the United States, up from 15% in 1980.[18]

Banks make money when they originate debt. They can loan money themselves, they can structure loans and sell them to others, or they can sell wagers on such debt, as to whether it will be repaid or not. So it was in the interests of the banking system to increase debts. Debt is priced by risk, and risk is evaluated by ratings agencies, and ratings agencies made money rating mortgage-backed securities. The higher the rating they could award, the more they would be asked to rate. The Financial Crisis Inquiry Commission found that rating agencies were not only rating more products than they could effectively analyze, but that their ratings were entirely too high. Simply put, these ratings agencies—Standard and Poor's, Fitch, and Moody's—were incentivized to underweight risk. So they did not fulfill their function in safeguarding the nation.

The Financial Crisis Inquiry Commission saw these and other systemic problems and explained how they had contributed to the crisis. In the words of the commission members, "We conclude this financial crisis was avoidable. The crisis was the result of human action and inaction. . . . We conclude widespread failures in financial regulation and supervision proved devastating to the stability of the nation's financial markets."[19]

Much has been done to repair the damage done by the financial crisis, but the root causes of the crisis, and our vulnerability to further financial shocks, have not been entirely corrected. Some progress has been made. Reserves have been increased, off-balance-sheet transactions have been reduced, and new regulatory agencies, such as the Financial Stability Oversight Council and the Consumer Financial Protection Bureau, have been created. But the Dodd-Frank Act,[20] which was to have corrected the problems, remains to be fully implemented. Many of its provisions have been bogged down in the regulatory-writing phase. Intense lobbying by the financial industry has continued, and many of the most restrictive provisions have been watered down. For example, the controversial Volcker Rule, which would have limited the ability of bank holding companies to trade for their own accounts (so-called proprietary trading), has been greatly weakened, in part because the prospect of detailed tough regulation was just too difficult.

Trading in over-the-counter derivatives, such as "naked swaps"—unbacked by any collateral—remains unregulated. The rating agencies are essentially unreformed. And the large banks are even larger, and more interwoven, than before the crisis. Therefore, we may be only a step away—an economic crash somewhere, a bank failure, a euro crisis—from another crisis of confidence and the potential collapse of the financial system. This time, with the nation's finances already burdened by debt, the danger is high. The Fed is holding some $3.6 trillion in debt now, up from less than $1 trillion before the crisis, and the US national debt has become larger than the US GDP for the first time ever. With a huge financial sector, large debt in derivatives unsecured by collateral, and all the vicissitudes of the global economy, the potential for a more dangerous economic collapse is on the horizon, but the financial means to stabilize and recover from it are much weaker than before.

Moreover, the sprawling growth of the financial sector is likely connected to a number of other problems that have beset the US economy in recent years. Among these are the low rate of job creation, persistent unemployment, and rising income and wealth inequality. Representative of the trends is a recent Brookings Institution study on business, concluding that "business dynamism and entrepreneurship are experiencing a troubling secular decline in the United States." These trends all spell trouble for a society that prides itself on hard work, rugged individualism, economic opportunity, entrepreneurship, social mobility, and rags-to-riches stories every bit as much as on its commitment to fairness and public-spiritedness. These are the values of the American dream; they legitimate the society and the traditions upon which our political system is based. They also exert a powerful attraction abroad, providing the ideals legitimating America's military and economic power.[21]

And as economists such as Nobel Prize winner Joseph Stiglitz point out, managing the economy through excessive reliance on monetary instruments has meant lowering interest rates to stimulate aggregate demand. "Cheap money" actually distorts economic growth by fueling "bubbles." The bubbles may feed the growth of the financial sector, but they also lead to rising inequality, declines in macroeconomic performance, and increased economic instability. Other economists have gone even further. They have examined changes in the principles underlying corporations and the economy and suggested that the concept of "maximizing shareholder value" is itself at the root of much of our economic challenge today. This principle teaches that corporations exist only to serve the interests of their shareholders—not the managers, the workers, the community, or the nation. So it follows, according to this notion, that these other "stakeholders" don't matter intrinsically—only insofar as displeasing them could reduce the returns to shareholders. This school of thought believes that the idea of maximizing shareholder value as it is now expressed is very much related to the short-term thinking, reluctance to invest and take risks, and excessive reliance on debt that characterize today's business environment in the United States.[22]

When I taught economics at West Point in the early 1970s, we taught our students that corporations should be good "corporate citizens," and that the economy benefited from the "countervailing" power of unions and corporations. When I began work in the private sector, one of my friends in the private equity business at Goldman explained the new thinking: "We give the CEOs of these companies we buy as much of their compensation as possible in stock, so their interests and the shareholders' interests are as closely aligned as possible." It sounded smart, and even benign, but according to some, this is the motivating force behind the short-term thinking, stock buybacks, lack of investment in R&D, lack of loyalty to employees, and other ailments in the American economy. They are all connected to an excessive emphasis on "financial engineering," and often associated with excessive reliance on debt.

The impact of the expansive growth of the US financial system, and the financial crisis that resulted, has been twofold. First, it has put the nation into a longer-term low-growth scenario, with higher risks and fewer disposable resources to deal with the other challenges we face, such as national security, education, health care, poverty, and the environment. Second, if not remedied, weaknesses and vulnerabilities in the financial system will lead to even greater volatility and risks in the future. These are systemic risks that undercut the most fundamental elements of American national security: the power of our economy.

CHALLENGE FOUR: CHINA

One factor that looms large in terms of systemic risk is China, the largest foreign holder of US debt, the world's second-largest economic power behind the United States, and the most populous nation, with more than 1.3 billion people. China's middle class is larger than the entire population of the United States. Its GDP is $8.2 trillion; according to recent calculations it has already over-taken the United States in "purchasing power," and it could over-take the United States in nominal GDP as the world's largest economy sometime between 2020 and 2030. It is already the world's largest steel and cement producer and trading nation. It is the largest market for automobiles, cellphones, and, by 2020, may be the largest market for luxury items. China's demand for raw materials as well as for goods and services has been driving the world economy, especially since the financial collapse of 2008. When China booms, world economic growth spurts; when China slows, world economic growth stumbles.[23]

China is not a free-market-oriented, laissez-faire-style, capital-ist economy, however, with investors seeking the greatest returns, or with free movement of capital and labor, and it does not have what we like to call "consumer sovereignty." Nor is it guided by what the economist Adam Smith called "the invisible hand" of the market. While China's economy may appear to reflect some of these elements, it is the Chinese Communist Party that is instead the forceful directing hand behind both the state and the econ-omy. Communist Party cells exist in most businesses, whether they are private companies or state-owned enterprises. The identity and activities of the party are state secrets that are not divulged to foreigners. But, normally, the CEO of the firm is not the final authority—the party boss is. The CEO typically defers to the party leader on all strategic and many personnel decisions. The network of party leadership across various business lines gives the econ-omy uniquely strong strategic direction and resilience.[24]

And for this reason, standard signs of economic distress—such as too much outstanding credit, an excessive "shadow-banking" sector (which is in some respects following the pattern of the

US financial services sector), high ratios of nonperforming loans, overbuilding of residential real estate, or overinvestment in key industries, all of which are to be found in China—are likely to be more manageable in China than in traditional market-driven economies like that of the United States. Moreover, there is a distinctive Chinese way of doing business in which there is greater reliance than in the West on trusted personal connections and general agreements—and less reliance on specific legal agreements and hard-and-fast accounting—that invites state and party influence at every level.

China itself faces distinct risks as it moves its economy forward. Like other developing economies, China began its growth spurt by using its low-cost labor to produce goods for export. As wages rise in China, these early manufacturing efforts have become less competitive relative to even lower wage-cost nations elsewhere in Asia. China must transition its manufacturing and job creation into other industries, sectors, and regions that are more appropriate to its rising wage and cost levels. In addition, China has, by Western standards, overinvested in some types of infrastructure, such as housing and heavy industry, including steel, and even some renewable energy production, such as photovoltaic cell manufacturing. Looked at in gross terms, China's economy seems to be yielding less macroeconomic growth per unit of investment, and per unit of debt, than in the past. These are typically signs that an economy is maturing; but these choices may also result in recessionary stumbles in times of economic growth and credit crises in debt markets.[25]

Finally, the institution of the Communist Party raises questions. Official Chinese sources note that some 182,000 officials in state-owned enterprises and government agencies had been removed for "corruption." The costs of corruption, the economic impact of dealing with it, and the risks associated with these efforts are also factors bearing on China's future growth.[26]

Still, given China's enormous resources and strong leadership, its announced target growth rate of 7.5 percent per year seems achievable. But it is not simply systemic financial and economic risk that makes China of particular concern. Rather, it is China's long-term national strategy, and in particular, whether as one of two leading global powers, China will rise and ascend peacefully within the international diplomatic, legal, and security structures present today—or will instead push, shove, intimidate, fight, and ultimately wreck and seek to rebuild global systems into the structures, processes, and powers that best suit its own heritage, culture, and self-interests. China's demonstrated single-minded determination and effectiveness, the same qualities that have yielded such spectacular economic results over three decades, force us to face this deeper question.

In 1983—my first visit to China—the country was still shivering under the possible threat from the Soviet Union, which had been acutely felt in the late 1960s and 1970s. It was engaged in a sharp conflict on its southern border against Vietnam, which was supported by the Soviet Union. There was a strategic convergence between America's and China's concerns, and an opportunity for a broad strategic partnership to form in order to manage the Soviet threat—although, as our Chinese hosts explained, under the "Four Modernizations," national defense was the lowest priority (coming after agriculture, industry, and science and technology). China's strategy was to grow by permitting private farming and marketing, an aim that included releasing its agricultural sector from some of the most restrictive Communist practices, and by restarting its educational system.

By 1988, my second visit, China had moved away from the idea of pursuing a strategic partnership with the United States. Senior Chinese leaders were happy to listen to our analysis of the Soviet threat, and especially to learn of our weapons systems and training technologies, but they were reluctant to reveal much about their own. By then they saw no threat from the Soviet Union, and meanwhile, their economy was booming. The second modernization, industry, was in full swing. Heavy industries, such as steel, oil, and coal, were favored initially. China surpassed the United States in coal production in 1985. By 1996, it had surpassed the United States in steel production. Today, China's coal production is almost four times that of the United States, and its steel production is about eight times greater. Its aluminum production is roughly five times greater, and its titanium production is more than double that of the United States.[27]

The third modernization, science and technology, has been a continuing focus. For more than two decades, US and foreign leaders have approached China offering "gifts" in the form of economic cooperation—assisting in building industries, promoting trade, and encouraging educational and cultural exchange. It is a policy often called "constructive engagement." Some of these investments and cooperative programs were strategic, while others simply reflected commercial interests. As a Japanese general visiting the Pentagon in 1994 explained, "Japan is investing $100 billion in China in an effort to control it." As a result of these efforts, automotive manufacturing was an early leader in China, with Japanese companies such as Toyota and Honda, followed by American and European companies, first building parts and conducting assembly there and then moving on to full-scale manufacturing. Walmart's investments in China provided the stimulus and example for modernizing Chinese logistics capabilities, while big US companies like General Electric and Boeing transferred valuable aerospace technologies. In 2011, GE formed a joint venture with China's avionics industry leader, Aviation Industry Corporation of China, or AVIC, to enable GE avionics technology to reach wider markets. Today, a majority of the Fortune 500 companies, including major companies such as Microsoft, GE, and Apple, have some or a large portion of their research—not just their manufacturing—done in China. Unlike the rationale cited by the Japanese officer, US investments in China have been simply good business—and have been approved by US political leaders aiming to strengthen the US economy through trade and investment abroad. But, as one of my Chinese "friends" explained last year, "we know everything." This technology transfer is the result of a major strategic effort by China.

Another element of China's emphasis on science and technology has been to rapidly expand its university system in order to facilitate the development of its own technologies. China currently has the largest system of higher education in the world, with perhaps 25 million students currently enrolled. Between 1998 and 2008, China created approximately one hundred new research universities, taking advantage of US assistance wherever possible. As the president of Cornell University explained in 2005, "We have excellent relations with several Chinese universities; we host their scholars here, and teach them our research methods." China has augmented its own efforts to educate students by sending hundreds of thousands of Chinese students to the United States to attend universities here; tens of thousands have participated in research, including government-sponsored research in the United States, gaining specific knowledge and skills to take back to China. These exchanges not only accelerate China's development, but also can provide a basis for greater long-term understanding and cooperation between China and the United States.[28]

In fact, the outlines of China's long-term strategy are clearly visible, but the impact of that strategy has been largely underestimated in the West. The strategy has been consistent for decades— seek education, capital, and technology from the West; manufacture goods at the lowest cost for export, incorporating Western technologies; amass foreign exchange to secure long-term access to critical resources, such as oil, iron ore, and bauxite; keep the value of the renminbi low; be humble and compliant; and work for the long term, aiming high. As China's reformist leader Deng Xiaoping said, in his famous "24 Character Strategy," "Observe calmly; secure our position; cope with affairs calmly; hide our capacities and bide our time, be good at maintaining a low profile; and never claim leadership."[29]

Visiting China on business in 2005, I had a friendly, informal conversation with a young banker, a Communist Party member who had been one of President Hu Jintao's top youth advisers. He had learned English, and had spent a year at the John F. Kennedy School of Government at Harvard, so we enjoyed talking. "China is now a great power," he said. "It will never again suffer the humiliation of its neighbors. But we know you Americans were friends of Britain, and they gave you leadership of the world. China wants to be a friend of the United States, so that you will give us leadership of the world." Americans often chuckled complacently when I related the conversation, patronizing China's naïve ambition to rival America, but welcoming the intended friendship.

China is now shifting into what seems to be a second phase of its strategy. It is more confident, more assertive, and also more closed. It is raising its profile, asserting its authority in its region and in global affairs. When the West was reeling from the economic crisis of 2008, brought on by the crash of the mortgage-backed securities markets, China countered the financial crisis with a muscular stimulus program that sustained a high level of growth in the Chinese economy. It has celebrated its progress with a space program, which in December 2013 landed a rover vehicle on the moon. The space program has military as well as civilian purposes: it is a major part of China's defense activities and has the capacity to shoot down satellites and operate its own equivalent of our Global Positioning System (GPS).

China has constructed hundreds of miles of high-speed rail lines, opened dozens of new airports, built superhighways and dams, and created the largest wind and solar energy industries in the world. We are beginning to see innovation emerge from China, too. Its high-voltage DC power lines, transporting green energy hundreds of miles, will be the most advanced in the world. Innovation is blossoming even in the oil and coal industries, where massive investments are spurring the development of new techniques and equipment. Faced with a decline in US market support of clean energy technologies, one of the US companies I am associated with recently sold over twenty years of Department of Energy–supported commercial and engineering research in advanced clean coal and fuels technology to a private Chinese company for less than a tenth of the original investments. While the US clean-tech sector struggles for support from Wall Street, state-supported Chinese demand for these technologies will bring them to market.

A strong, party-directed effort will spread industrialization into China's heartland and to its western region. Some 250 million people will be moved into urban housing; another 600 million will be forced to remain in agriculture, albeit with better income security and benefits. Under an innovative program designed to recruit high-level talent, China is welcoming home from abroad its most talented and experienced expatriates in business, offering them high responsibilities and higher pay then they have received in the West. China has greatly expanded its military spending, so that it has the second-largest military budget, second only to the United States, in the world, and it is rapidly creating strong, modern armed forces.

China is continuing to procure overseas mineral assets, and it is actively seeking engineering and construction opportunities abroad to enlarge its businesses and prove its engineering skills, and, in so doing, expand its influence, even in Europe. In November 2013, a large Chinese delegation headed by Premier Li Keqiang visited Romania; the premier signed agreements with the

Romanians promising billions of dollars of investments, including two new nuclear reactors. Around the same time, Albania received a $4 billion Chinese offer to develop a deep-water port for Albania on the Adriatic, in order to provide improved sea access into southeastern Europe. During the May 2013 summit meeting between President Obama and President Xi Jinping, Xi reportedly demanded that the United States treat China as a "global equal." And it is pushing hard against its neighbors, demanding concessions, aggressively asserting its claims in historical territorial disputes, and exploiting legal and geographic ambiguities. So much for keeping "a low profile."

However, unlike in the 1990s, when Western leaders could argue that with "constructive engagement" China would inevitably become more democratic and open as it grew economically, expectations are now moving in the opposite direction—China is likely to become increasingly closed as it uses material prosperity and nationalism to maintain the party's legitimacy among the people rather than relying on the consent of the governed. A Chinese campaign in the summer of 2013, based on the authoritative "Document No. 9," warned the Chinese Communist Party cadre that they must eradicate seven subversive ideas, including Western constitutional democracy and universal human values. There is thus little evidence of the hoped-for benefits of "constructive engagement," or of a convergence of Chinese and Western values, and every reason to foresee an increasing divergence of interests.[30]

What went wrong with the US policy of constructive engagement? If there was a turning point in China's assessment of its opportunities, it could be found in the financial crisis of 2008 and its aftermath. China saw the United States as a failing system, its government unable to manage its politics or its economy, and vulnerable to being replaced as the world's leader. In 2011, I was warned by a well-connected Chinese source that the new leadership in China intended to dominate the South China Sea; that its regional rivals, such as Vietnam, would bow to its ambitions or "be taught a lesson"; and that if the United States interfered, our assets would be targeted. By April 2013, the warnings had become even more ominous: "We can see your stealth aircraft"; "We have our own GPS and can shoot down yours"; "We know your technologies from all your companies and from NASA, because Chinese scientists work these for you"; "You will not have any military relations with the Philippines unless we allow it, because China provides them $3.5 billion per month in remittances through Hong Kong"; "Chinese shipyards are working twenty-four hours a day, seven days a week"; "More than thirty ships were launched between October 2012 and April 2013"; "By 2019 China will have four aircraft carriers deployed . . . and its GDP will be equal to that of the United States." While the warnings seemed bellicose and blunt, my source has generally provided an accurate guide to the intentions of what may be, at least, a powerful faction within China's leadership, and at least some of his assessments have proved accurate.

China's strategy of seeking significant concessions from regional neighbors and greater influence abroad is double-edged: it aims to build legitimacy at home through nationalism and the delivery of prosperity while gaining greater security and control over events abroad. The Chinese press, in pummeling Japan and other neighbors on historical injustices and territorial claims, whips up nationalism, builds legitimacy for the party, and enables the party to implement what US critics would see as repressive measures in order to maintain domestic control and drive the economy forward. Meanwhile, relentless Chinese pressure on these regional neighbors—diplomatically, economically, and militarily—is intended to weaken their governments and provide China with greater influence.

China could also use its increasing economic power to dissuade potential alliances of other states that might challenge its aims. And it could use its proxy, North Korea, to raise tensions in South Korea and the West, or perhaps to engineer US disengagement from Korea. China's long-term strategy with Japan has yet to emerge. We must realize the enduring humiliation and lingering insecurity inflicted by Japan's brutal invasion of China in 1937. America has never experienced such an event in its history. Even today, many senior Chinese see the US military as a check on Japan's militarism.

Further afield, China is using its enormous savings to acquire, through state-owned enterprises, a vast network of mineral and hydrocarbon resources in Africa, South America, and even North America. China exploits commercial business transactions to acquire influence, technology, and market-leading positions in key economic sectors, such as renewable energy, computing and electronics, and large-scale engineering. Meanwhile, China is developing its own technologies, upscaling its manufacturing, and slowly allowing the value of its currency to appreciate, with the potential, ultimately, of displacing the dollar as the world's primary reserve currency, all under the direction of the Communist Party leadership.

The Pentagon's annual unclassified report on China in 2013 assessed China's strategic objectives and summarized them as "perpetuating Chinese Communist Party (CCP) rule, sustaining economic growth and development, defending national sovereignty and territorial integrity, and securing China's status as a great power." The report notes that Chinese leaders have characterized the first two decades of the twenty-first century as a "strategic window of opportunity" to achieve these objectives. The Pentagon report goes on to say that "China balances the imperative to reassure countries that its rise is 'peaceful' with the imperative to strengthen its control over existing sovereignty and territorial claims. . . . Many Chinese officials and the public see the US rebalance to Asia as a reflection of 'Cold War thinking' and as a way to contain China's rise." When the United States exercises its legal obligations to allies in the territorial disputes over obscure islands in the Pacific, and especially those near Japan, it provokes Chinese nationalism, opens old wounds and insecurities, and damages China's image of the United States as a reliable global partner. Some in the United States see in these frictions confirmation that China remains a threat in Cold War terms.[31]

But the deeper strategic challenge for the United States is not simply to avoid open conflict with China, but to deal with the more fundamental challenge to the global architecture of trade, law, and peaceful resolution of disputes that the United States and its allies created after World War II. China's strategic rise to global power—patient, nuanced, and far-sighted—implicitly threatens all of this. As we collaborate with China economically and diplomatically, we must understand that, just as the United States seeks the worldwide adoption of democratic values and American norms for international behavior, China's strategy will be to seek structures and relationships that support its values of Communist Party rule and its declared policy of nonintervention in foreign states. The ascendancy of Chinese self-interest as an organizing principle would mean a fundamental weakening of Western institutions, the rule of law, and other Western values, and perhaps their replacement with a more traditional, Beijing-centric approach. This would be a step backward, toward nineteenth-century ideas of the balance of power and spheres of influence, and away from the global community that most in the West see as an inevitable and desirable future.

China doesn't seek conflict—it can achieve most of its goals by adroitly combining traditional Chinese diplomacy with its vast economic power. But neither will it shirk conflict. It will use its military regionally to intimidate, and if necessary will strike sharply to "teach lessons" to its neighbors. It has in the past used its military "preemptively" rather than defensively. Conflict could come to the region. This is the lesser challenge posed by China's rise—that an ascending power seeking recognition of its power, and its rights, would pressure, threaten, bluff, and, perhaps deliberately or perhaps through miscalculation, spark conflict.

Former secretary of state Henry Kissinger has expressed the challenge in these terms: "The issue before the world is whether, as China gets stronger, we in the West can work with China. And the issue is also whether China can work with us to create an international structure in which, for the first time in history, a rising state has been incorporated into an international system and strengthened peace and progress."[32]

As the renminbi becomes convertible and appreciates, and if China becomes the world's largest economic power, Shanghai will becoming increasingly powerful in global banking. US influence with the United Nations, the International Monetary Fund, and the World Bank may shrink in significance, increasingly reflecting China's priorities and interests, or these institutions may be replaced by emerging institutions which more expressly recognize Chinese self-interests. Western law, which in the nineteenth century was hugely instrumental in dismembering parts of China through claims of "extraterritoriality," has few friends in China. It is viewed as something created by foreigners to serve foreign interests, not China's. And certainly Chinese leaders would view much of the US-inspired international system in precisely this way.

The Chinese leadership resists formalizing difficult relationships in specific agreements, as we did with the Soviet Union in the 1970s and 1980s. For example, the Maritime Code of Conduct adopted at the Western Pacific Naval Symposium, designed to prevent miscommunications from escalating into conflict, while most welcomed, is a non-legally-binding protocol for firing colored flares, and has nothing to do with the underlying territorial disputes. Rather than abiding by legal codes and procedures,

China seems more inclined to use its economic power—investments in raw material production and infrastructure that dwarf anything the United States may be able to offer—to create and retain relationships. China's imports could be secured by long-term, fixed-price contracts—a strategy that would displace market volatility into the West. Manufacturing might be geared increasingly for China's internal markets, just as the United States has been urging China to do for some time, to feed a rising consumer class. Chinese economic power could be used to disrupt trade and economic organizations that are potentially hostile to China's interests, through the commercial influence of the economies represented in those organizations.[33]

China could use the Shanghai Cooperation Council or a similar organization to harness its near neighbors, including even Russia. In a grand strategic sense, China may well seek to co-opt Russia for its energy and military technology. China could also attempt to use Russia to distract and disrupt the United States and its allies in Europe and to detract from America's focus on the Pacific. China's leaders might feel they could tolerate some degree of disorder, struggle, and conflict beyond their borders, so long as that disorder did not disrupt China's smoothly functioning economy or the Party's political control. To support its strategy, China will have a growing military power and reach that could be deployed for deterrence, influence, intimidation, and perhaps, as a last resort, actual combat.

Americans should expect China's leaders to seek to limit and curtail Western efforts to inspire democratic reforms or to promote a human rights agenda. Although the United States views these rights as universal, China's leaders do not. Because of cultural differences and a desire to promote their own interests, they deeply disagree with us on these issues. If the Chinese Communist Party's "Document No. 9" accurately represents President Xi's views—and all his actions thus far appear consistent with this document—China's security concerns will be directed not only at internal threats (from Tibetan nationalists and from its own Muslim Uighur population in Xinjiang Province, for example), but also at the institutions, organizations, and practices that continually threaten to export democracy and human rights into China. These Western principles are in direct opposition to what the Communist Party views as its authority to guide the evolution of its own political development.

China's new strategy was partially unveiled at the Third Party Plenum in November 2013. Much attention was devoted to the announcement of major reforms, especially the reform of land ownership and a greater reliance on market forces in connection with investments, innovation, and finance. Although no exact timelines were announced, the economic reforms reflect a shrewd understanding of the limits of China's current, administratively directed economy. (By early December, one of my Chinese business friends was telling me, "Good news: Chinese companies can now invest up to $1 billion abroad without state approval.") But, as several commentators on the plenum noted, gone were the protestations of humility. China was prepared to emerge in its full stature and aim toward its rightful position in global leadership.[34]

Like the other challenges facing the United States today, the challenge posed by China is not a conventional military challenge and cannot be viewed in military terms alone—though military capabilities are an important component of dealing with China. We are engaged with China on many levels and through many channels—private, commercial, scientific and technical, educational, and diplomatic. China also has a voice in US security issues, including terrorism, cyber-threats, and the global financial system. And finally, it is important to engage China in discussions about what may prove to be the most challenging of all the issues we face today: global climate change. China, claiming it is still a developing country—even with the world's second-largest GDP—is now the world's largest emitter of carbon.

We simply cannot march forward alone in dealing with other long-term challenges when our relationship with China may well hold the key as to whether our own efforts at managing global challenges are successful. Some of our interests are intrinsically intertwined, totally unlike the period of the Cold War, when our greatest challenge was that we faced an adversary whose interests were often entirely distinct and directly in conflict with our own.

CHALLENGE FIVE: CLIMATE CHANGE

The scientific consensus that the earth is warming and that mankind's activities are largely responsible for this climate change is well-established, and is in most developed nations accepted as scientific truth—though roughly half of Americans do not accept this.

The International Panel on Climate Change (IPCC), created in 1988 under the auspices of the World Meteorological Organization and the UN Environment Program, has produced regular reports and marshaled evidence from scores of scientists, sparked the creation of climate forecasting models, underscored the urgency of addressing climate issues at the national and international levels, and provided guidance to policymakers worldwide. The first section of the IPCC's Fifth Assessment Report, entitled *Climate Change 2013: The Physical Science Basis*, was released in late 2013.[35]

The latest report affirms with 95 percent confidence that the planet is warming and that human activities represent a chief cause of that warming. Summarizing the scientific evidence from numerous other studies, it finds that "warming of the climate system is unequivocal," and that many of the changes that have been taken place since the 1950s are "unprecedented over decades to millennia." It also finds that "it is extremely likely that human influence has been the dominant cause of the observed warming since the mid-20th century."

The report also looks to the future, basing its predictions on data that has been collected and fed into refined climate models. These projections are worrisome. Temperatures will continue to rise; the oceans will continue to warm and become more acidic; and the contrast in precipitation between wet and dry regions and wet and dry seasons will continue to increase. Meanwhile, sea ice and glaciers will shrink, and sea levels will rise. These projections are based on various scenarios depending upon the projected quantities of greenhouse gas emissions. In the IPCC's worst-case scenario, in which greenhouse gas emissions continue to grow, the report predicts a mean global temperature rise of 3.6°C by the end of the century—which may not sound that dramatic, but would indeed have dramatic consequences as a worldwide average. Other outcomes under this worst-case model include a 0.63-meter rise in the mean sea level, a loss of Arctic sea ice becoming especially acute by about 2050, and a mean 34 percent weakening of the Gulf Stream by 2100. Of particular concern is the prediction that temperature and precipitation changes will not be distributed evenly, but will instead be concentrated in certain regions. The Arctic, for example, may warm as much as 11°C by the end of this century, with increases in precipitation by as much as 50 percent. The Mediterranean Basin, Central and Southeast Europe, and southern Africa may experience a 10 percent to 20 percent decline in precipitation.

But even under the scenario in which greenhouse gas emissions are reduced, there are significant changes: temperatures rise, especially in the Arctic; sea levels rise; Arctic sea ice is greatly reduced; and the oceans become more acidic. Carbon dioxide and other greenhouse gases already in the atmosphere would continue to affect the climate.

Climate changes are expected to impact everyday life in multiple ways. One of the pivotal studies of global warming was done for the British government in 2007 by economist Nicholas Stern. *The Economics of Climate Change*, known as the Stern Review, details the severe impacts that would result from even relatively moderate temperature gains of 2 or 3 degrees. These impacts include increased flood risks during wet seasons and reduced dry-season water supplies to one-sixth of the world's population, a group that includes the people of India, Southeast Asia, and the Andes region in South America. As carbon dioxide is absorbed by sea water, the study says, ocean acidification is likely to have greater effects on marine life and fisheries. Droughts and excessive heat are likely to impact agriculture, especially in Africa, but also in places like Romania and other countries in southeastern Europe and the Mediterranean littoral.[36]

These are effects severe enough to be ranked as a national security challenge for the United States as well as other countries. The Center for Naval Analyses (CNA) was one of the earliest organizations to cite climate change as a threat to US security. "In already weakened states," according to a CNA study released in 2007, " . . . drought, flooding, sea level rise, retreating glaciers, and the rapid spread of life-threatening diseases will themselves have likely effects: increased migrations, further weakened and failed states, expanded ungoverned spaces, exacerbated underlying conditions that terrorist groups seek to exploit, and increased internal conflicts." The report also concluded that climate change could "act as a threat multiplier for instability" in many parts of the world, especially countries that are "already on edge in terms of their ability to provide basic needs: food, water, shelter and stability." Furthermore, "weakened and failing governments, with an already thin margin for survival, foster the conditions for internal conflict." These lines of thought have been echoed many times in other articles and testimony, and are now regarded as established facts within the senior ranks of the armed forces.[37]

The impacts are already with us. We don't need to rely on models and forecasts to see the leading edge of how climate change impacts national security. In 2010, droughts in Australia and Russia drove up the world price of wheat, impacting a number of countries, including Syria. Meanwhile, Syria was itself experiencing a drought. Poor land-reform policies implemented by the Bashar al-Assad regime resulted in hundreds of thousands of poor farmers losing access to water, and hence, their livelihoods. They were the tinder that fueled the uprising against Assad. Across much of Africa, spreading drought is forcing migrations, encroaching on previous patterns of economic activity, and causing rising tensions and internal conflicts. Populations from Somalia and Sudan in the east to Chad and Niger in the west are on the move. The terrorist threat has found readily exploited vulnerabilities in these regions.

Of course, there are serious US domestic consequences also, judging by the impact on the United States of hurricanes in 2005 (Katrina) and 2012 (Sandy). The damage these hurricanes left behind caused significant displacement issues, especially in New Orleans, and cost billions of dollars. Still, the United States has resources to cope with such disasters to soften the blow. Many countries do not.

Viewed as a factor within ongoing economic development processes, the consequences of foreseen climate change appear manageable at first blush. After all, climate change is caused by human activities associated with economic development, and greater economic growth provides more resources—so couldn't those resources be used to adapt to the effects of climate change, or to take actions to mitigate them? Climate-change author William D. Nordhaus says this approach would be expensive; aggressive policies would have to be put into place, such as taxes on carbon emissions and strong incentives to reduce emissions. Furthermore, many of the earth's systems could cross tipping points beyond which they would become unmanageable. Nevertheless, the world must tackle these problems; if we continue down the current path, disaster lies ahead. Many of the models predicting climate change are based on averages and generalizations, Nordhaus points out; but it is the specific cases—the vulnerable populations, in the areas most susceptible to extreme effects, and when they are in weakened states—that should drive concerns for global warming.[38]

Climate scientists are aware of the limitations of the predictive models, which are incomplete approximations at best. The models cannot fully simulate heat exchanges within the ocean, the reflective effects of clouds, or a number of other factors. As temperatures rise globally, for example, there are "nonlinearities"—discontinuous effects and positive feedback mechanisms whose onset and impacts are only partially included in even the most advanced climate models. There is evidence for nonlinearities in the history of the ancient earth: As Nordhaus points out, for example, some 12,000 years ago the earth experienced a rapid cooling over the course of just a few decades, for reasons not yet understood, and this cooling triggered a partial return of the glaciers characteristic of an ice age.

Should these nonlinear mechanisms kick in as temperatures rise, they could lead to sudden, devastating changes affecting people worldwide. Among these potentially dangerous discontinuities could be a sudden collapse of the Greenland or Antarctic ice sheets, causing up to a twelve-meter rise in sea levels worldwide (which would mean the end of coastal cities). Recent analysis shows that the collapse of at least one of the Antarctic ice sheets is underway, and, because of local geologic conditions, is irreversible. Or imagine a sudden shift in the Gulf Stream caused by increased meltwater from the Greenland ice sheet, which might dramatically alter the climate of northern Europe. Or there might be some critical temperature at which other processes kick in—for example, the release of vast stores of methane from the frozen soils and cold ocean bottoms of the Arctic.[39]

The potential of methane release is particularly troublesome. Methane—the most common ingredient of natural gas—is a colorless, odorless gas that retains heat in the atmosphere even more powerfully than carbon dioxide. Many millions of tons of methane are trapped in the Arctic under permafrost and in the deep seabeds. Some leaks naturally into the atmosphere, but thawing of the permafrost would greatly increase these releases. At some point, as warming continues, these releases may accelerate rapidly. Should a significant portion of the Arctic methane "burp," warming would be sudden and possibly irreversible. Other "feedbacks" would also be accelerated, such as glacial melt. All bets on the manageability of climate change would be off: the damages would be far greater than the models can predict, and civilization itself might be acutely impacted.[40]

The climate is already changing, and the impacts of these changes are sufficient to threaten US and global security. Mankind's future will depend on what we do to restrain the release of greenhouse gases. And there may be much less margin for warming without catastrophic change than current models suggest.

SOME ADDITIONAL COMPLEXITIES

This set of five strategic challenges—terrorism, cybersecurity, the US financial system, the rise of China, and global climate change—collectively constitute a set of challenges that is fundamentally different from the ones we have dealt with in the past. Each is a long-term, persistent challenge, rather than acute or transitory. Not one of them is brand new, however; they have all emerged over many years—and have been controversial topics through several US election cycles. They do not involve an obvious enemy, and there seems to be no single, obvious fix or cure or invention that will make them go away. Living with them on a long-term basis has inured us to them; we often do not even sense their effects. Perhaps we have become like the proverbial frog thrown into a pot of cool water, only to be slowly cooked.

These threats are also interrelated. Terrorists are using the same global communications networks that pose a cyber-threat. China is the world's greatest emitter of greenhouse gases. Climate change creates fertile conditions for terrorist recruiting in countries that feel its affects the most. And each threat is deeply connected to economic growth and development. Climate change has been driven by economic growth and will in turn affect the economic growth (or lack thereof) of the future. Terrorists have exploited the anger and psychological dislocation of global economic development to foment violent resistance. And so on. So although each is described separately in this chapter, our policies must take into account that they are intertwined.

Moreover, these challenges are each fundamentally international in character. They emerge from within the complexities and competing interests of innumerable state actors, nongovernmental organizations, enterprises, and financial institutions. Border fences, visas, quarantines, embargos, and health inspections cannot prevent their contagion—nor can they remedy their impacts.

Finally, none of these challenges can be met by relying on government or the private sector alone. They cannot be met simply by strengthening our military forces, or by increasing our diplomatic efforts. In fact, government actions alone cannot correct the vulnerabilities or meet the challenges. Nor can these challenges be met by relying solely on private-sector initiative, innovation, or self-regulation—they are too long-term, too broad, too complex, and too fundamental to be left to market forces. They impact the common good and community interests, not just private profits or efficiencies in capital allocation.

Although none of these challenges alone is existential—in the sense that any one of them is likely to destroy the United States—collectively they constitute a fundamental, long-term, existential challenge to the international system and America's place within it. They should be at the center of our national conversation; they are exactly the grounds over which a national strategy must be unfurled.

We cannot shoot our way out of this situation; nor can we afford to wait for the shooting to start to find a national purpose and craft a strategy. War could happen, of course. But when I hear my Chinese friends expressing concerns about America's vitriolic politics or consumer-driven economy, I often warn them, half-jokingly, "Please don't give us a 'cause'; there was once another nation in Asia that looked at the United States and thought our time had passed. . . . "

But if we rely on external crises to bring us together, we are relying on an obsolete and dangerous "engine" for consensus. Our global economy is too interconnected, our world is too small and environmentally challenged, and the urgency of strategic challenges—terrorism, cybersecurity, the financial system, the ascent of China, and climate change—will simply brook no delay.

To face these challenges, we need some degree of political consensus—and the public and private resources to bear these new burdens. But these elements, too, are problematic.

CHAPTER 4

American Power at an Inflection Point

Zbigniew Brzezinski, former national security adviser to President Jimmy Carter, is one of America's foremost strategic thinkers. In 2011, he wrote, "Our strength abroad will depend increasingly on our ability to confront problems at home." Brzezinski's view that America is overburdened by its problems is widespread. American power in 2014 was at an "inflection point." An inflection point is a dramatic turning point, a point signaling a significant change of direction, either positive or negative. For the United States, this inflection point signals the change from superpower status to a position in which US power seems to be waning. Meanwhile, as a nation, we are drifting; to stop this decline and retain America's capacity to influence world events, we need a national strategy, significant policy change, and new economic tools.[1]

As the National Intelligence Council's *Global Trends 2030* report put it, "with the rapid rise of multiple other powers, the 'unipolar moment' is over and Pax Americana—the era of unrivalled American ascendancy in international politics that began in 1945—is fast winding down." Hardly a week goes by without another reminder—results on educational achievement, world opinion polls, relative economic growth rates, comparisons of sovereign debt and wealth, growth of per capita income—that, in relation to our global competitors, America is sliding.[2]

Such a trend seems a far cry from the sense of American triumph after the fall of the Berlin Wall, the rollback of communism from Eastern Europe, and the American military triumph in the First Gulf War. Or even from the early years of the twenty-first century, when, boosted by new technologies, a booming stock market, eight years of job creation and economic growth, and unbeatable armed forces, the United States seemed unstoppable. For those of us who worked through these periods, the turnaround in expectations seems sudden, unnecessary, and unwarranted.

However, three factors stand out as distinctly different from earlier periods: the prospect of long-term US budget deficits; the fractious nature of US politics; and the worldwide perception that America is slipping.

THE RISING NATIONAL DEBT

As of May 2014, the US national debt stood at almost $17.5 trillion.[3] Americans have always worried about the national debt. We have fought virtually every war on debt, especially World War II. We carried this debt into the Cold War years. Efforts were made to deal with the national debt and annual budget deficits during the Nixon administration—which led to the creation of the budget committees in Congress—as well as during the administrations of George H. W. Bush and Bill Clinton. Under President Clinton, the United States actually went into budget surplus for fiscal years 1998, 1999, and 2000. When a new president assumed office in 2001, he faced the prospect of perhaps wiping out the national debt entirely.

However, as a result of the combination of tax cuts, two wars, the financial crisis, and government programs to speed our recovery from the crisis, the national debt has risen dramatically. Since fiscal year 2007, debt held by the public has more than doubled, rising from about 35 percent of GDP to more than 70 percent. In the fiscal year ending in September 2013, for the first time since World War II, US total national debt exceeded our GDP. While there are no hard and fast limits on how large our debt can be, this debt must be repaid, and that repayment must come from the US budget—ultimately, from the American public.

In 2012 the net annual interest payment on our debt—payments made to the "public" rather than to other government entities like the Social Security Trust Fund—amounted to $220 billion, or a little over 6 percent of total US federal outlays. Should interest rates return to "normal" levels, those payments will double or triple. In addition, "tax expenditures"—deductions given for home mortgages and other special interests—approach the size of total discretionary federal spending—about one-third of the budget—and most are mandated by law. These "tax expenditures" also contribute to the deficit.

Future interest payments and tax expenditures will come at a time when the percentage of mandatory spending in the US government will continue to rise, driven by so-called entitlement programs like Social Security and Medicare. These programs grow as a function of the number of qualified beneficiaries and legally driven payment rates. There is no "discretion" by the executive branch as it prepares its annual budget submission to Congress in how much of federal receipts can be allocated to cover these demands. As the US population ages, a greater percentage of the population is eligible for these programs; the consequence is to curtail the amount that can be spent on other federal programs, whether in national security, education, research and development, infrastructure, or NASA programs. If spending is not cut, taxes have to rise. According to projections by the US Government Accountability Office, interest-rate payments plus payments for Social Security, Medicaid, and Medicare could consume the entire federal budget by 2030. The debt added due to the financial crisis has increased to the point of urgency: we must address these future obligations. In addition, other financial risks will impact the federal government, including federal support for housing, pensions, flood insurance, and even such institutions as the money-losing United States Postal Service.

Adding further to the pressure, our economic growth rate, based on a declining rate of population growth, is expected to slow in comparison to earlier decades. We are expected to grow more slowly than some other economies in Asia, and especially China. The United States' relative dominance in the world economy has shrunk, going from approximately 50 percent in the period right at the end of World War II to approximately 25 percent today. This change was due at first to the fact that war-damaged economies were rebuilt; then the US share held steady for around four decades. But now, with the rise of China and other economies in Asia, the US proportion of world GDP seems likely to fall further, along with our economic power vis-à-vis China—though, of course, the policies we Americans choose will certainly affect how much, if at all, our relative power declines.[4]

The long-term factors behind the trends associated with relatively slower growth are many and varied, including the rise of the US financial sector, which gave us easier access to credit and three decades of consumer-led growth fueled by rising indebtedness and inflated house prices; long-term reliance on imported oil; the relative improvement in literacy and education in the rest of the world during this period; trade liberalization, which has permitted US manufacturers to outsource to lower-cost areas; inadequate growth of domestic manufacturing and other processes that could provide an offset to our imports; and even such factors as the US legal system and immigration policies. British historian Paul Kennedy created a stir in the late 1980s when he noted

America's declining share of world production and its balance-of-payments problems, high consumption, low personal savings rates, sinking rates of investment in R&D, and excessive defense expenditures. He predicted the rising influence of the Asia Pacific region in global affairs.[5]

Scientist and policy analyst Vaclav Smil, writing more than twenty years later, pointed out, even before the financial crisis, that the United States "had enormous government budget deficits, soaring trade deficits, worsening current account balances, a deteriorating international investment position, excessive private indebtedness, and weakening currency." Although "all these undesirable trends were punctuated by periods of recovery or rebound," he wrote, "long-term directions have been disheartening." Historian Niall Ferguson targeted our over-allocation of resources to entitlement programs benefiting the elderly as a betrayal of future, yet-to-be-born generations. He claimed that over-regulation and overreliance on the legal system and lawyers, as well as the overweening power of the state, had caused the slow-down in economic growth rates in the United States and other Western economies.[6]

Each causal factor in the relative decline of the United States has its proponents, and the proponents are prepared to go into great detail about why. A full examination of all of these factors is beyond the scope of this book. But the trends are worrisome, particularly in the context of a rising China, and detailed studies of causes, implications, and interrelationships continue. The diffusion of manufacturing and research has further depleted America's technological edge. Worldwide, the numbers of patent applications are growing, but America's share in this intellectual property is declining. As the World Intellectual Property Organization (WIPO) indicated in a 2013 report, patent applications in China are growing rapidly. Packaging and selling intellectual property has also become a growing business, and off-shore sales of patents and other restrictive technology agreements—many of which were originally funded by the US Department of Defense—constitutes a further erosion of US economic advantages.[7]

America's educational system has been examined relentlessly. In the early and middle years of the twentieth century, the United States had the world's best-educated workforce. In America, unlike many other countries, a high-school education was compulsory, and with the advent of the GI Bill, colleges and universities were no longer the province of the elite. The 1950s and 1960s saw the rapid growth of statewide systems of public universities. Vocational-technical schools and junior colleges also helped to raise college opportunities for young Americans. Until the early 1970s, the American workforce was adding an average of one year of education per decade—but this trend crested in 1973, and others nations have rapidly advanced the educational levels of their workforces. The diffusion of educational opportunity now seems to be turning against the United States. Today, other countries are catching up. The Internet opens up access to online courses at the high-school and university levels worldwide. Countries as diverse as Saudi Arabia and China are racing to build modern university systems—and in their competitive efforts to attract foreign students, US universities themselves are undercutting what had been a privileged American advantage.[8]

Of course, these trends are trends relative to other powers—not necessarily against some absolute standard. In some ways they help the United States in its participation in a global economy, strengthening US trading partners and developing markets for advanced technology. In other ways they reflect American successes at promoting peaceful development and economic growth abroad. We should be, and are, pleased that other nations are finding their way out of poverty, as this has been a US aim for many decades. These trends also miss the wide span of US "soft-power"—our influence on culture, values, and ideas around the world—which is very high, and the attractiveness of the United States as a place to live, work, and do business. But the trends also show a decline in the elements of US "hard-power" potential relative to other states. This issue would need to be addressed to a large degree by the allocation of resources to research and education, innovation, infrastructure, and procurement—in other words, budget.

If we continue on the current path of slower growth, rising debt, and greater mandatory expenditures, the scarcity of funds will limit the flexibility of the US government to make effective strategic, long-term choices. The constant competition for these relatively shrinking public resources leads to squabbling, complaints, and a public perception that the United States lacks the resources, the will, or in some cases, the skills, to accomplish the kinds of programs that were once commonplace. It was telling in 2013 when the government of Japan offered to loan the United States the money to fund a high-speed rail link between Baltimore and Washington, DC.

It is not easy for the government to raise additional resources. Federal revenues come from personal income, capital gains, and inheritance taxes, excise taxes and duties, corporate taxes, and other measures. Each has been under unrelenting pressure for decades. Personal income tax rates were slashed under President Ronald Reagan in the early 1980s, then raised again when the cuts proved to be excessive. President George H. W. Bush faced heavy opposition within his own party when he raised income taxes in 1990. President Bill Clinton raised taxes only as part of a bipartisan balanced budget effort in 1994, but capital gains and qualified dividends are now taxed at a lower rate than ordinary income. Under the George W. Bush administration, major income tax cuts were implemented. The federal tax on gasoline has not been raised since 1994. The ceiling at which the inheritance tax kicks in has been raised, costing the government billions in lost tax revenues.

In American politics today, there is strong and continuing pressure not to raise but instead to reduce taxes. Prospective candidates for public office in the Republican Party usually pledge that they will not raise taxes and, thus far, these pledges have been remarkably powerful in deterring tax increases. Nor can Democrats make much headway simply by proposing tax hikes. For several years there has been discussion of a grand bargain, which would raise revenues slightly in return for much larger reductions in federal spending, and especially entitlement programs—but Republican Party opposition to any tax hikes has defeated attempts to construct the grand bargain thus far.

The financial constraints on the US government are real, and they are growing. They will need to be addressed—and they will be, through a combination of various revenue and spending proposals, argued out again and again in the public and political dialogue of American democracy. In the meantime, they constitute a very real factor limiting America's ability to respond to the strategic challenges we face.

THE FAILURE OF PUBLIC DIALOGUE

The current limitations on federal resources result in part from the fractious political landscape in the United States in the past few years. The stark partisan divisions undercut the focus on long-term trends that matter to the economy and beyond. And the continuing debate over limited government resources seems to be the bread and butter of political differentiation.

Partisan competition has very deep roots in America. This was recognized during the writing of the US Constitution. It was the Founding Fathers' genius to acknowledge that such competition was inevitable, and to deal with it through the separation of powers between the various branches of government and through a system of checks and balances. James Madison and Alexander

Hamilton addressed the problem of "factions" in Federalist Paper no. 51, writing, "Let interest counteract interest, and ambition counteract ambition." This was the genius of the American Constitution—that it provided the mechanism to bring such competition into the structured machinery of government in a way that allowed issues to be addressed and resolved. And in general, it has worked, except for the question of slavery.

But the current tone of partisan competition seems particularly vehement. In fact, some of the most heated arguments stem from a long-running debate about the public interest versus economic freedom that dates back more than one hundred years—to the beginning of the twentieth century, when the Progressive movement emerged in response to the extreme concentration of corporate wealth that was then taking place and the accumulation and abuse of political power locally and nationally. Then a national outcry curbed the powers of corporations in a series of constitutional amendments, sweeping laws, and structural changes in American society and the economy, providing the basis for America's twentieth-century power.[9]

During the twentieth century, academics added their authority to the debate. In the 1930s and 1940s, the work of British economist John Maynard Keynes provided a foundation for a larger government role in the economy. In his 1936 book, *The General Theory of Employment, Interest and Money*, Keynes formulated the idea of "aggregate demand"—the sum requirement for goods and services within an economy and its impact on national income—to explain why cutting government expenditures in times of economic contractions would be harmful, producing results exactly the opposite of those intended.

Keynes' prescription rested on the idea that the operation of supply and demand in free markets, even with clear-thinking participants and perfect information, might not stabilize an economy at full employment. Even though individuals and families should live within their means, government deficits weren't always bad, he said, and government surpluses, or even balanced budgets, weren't always good. More fundamentally, governments should always be able to intervene and tinker with the operation of an economy with some degree of legitimacy, seeking not only to prevent banking failures and securities fraud, but also to regulate the rate of inflation and to promote full employment. Keynesian economics became economic orthodoxy.[10]

The challenge to the Keynesians came primarily from the "monetarists," led by University of Chicago economist Milton Friedman, and therefore often called the "Chicago school" of economics. In the 1960s, Friedman theorized that the more fundamental force on the economy was the money supply, and that the function of government, through its central bank, should be to aim for price stability, balancing the demand for money with its supply. This approach implied a much more limited role for government. It also reinforced a return to the roots of academic economics, the study of supply and demand, and the theories of the efficient allocation of resources. Together, the idea of free markets perfectly allocating resources—"leave it to the private sector"— and the monetarist critique formed a powerful—and appealing— intellectual bulwark against the further growth of government's role in the economy.

Since then, much additional study has refined and sharpened ideas in economics. Market participants are not always rational; nor do they always have perfect information, or the freedom to act on it. Government spending leaks into foreign economies, and therefore government deficit spending may not offer a full, direct stimulus to the domestic economy, and impacts unevenly over time. Monetary stimulus must be adroitly managed to actually raise demand, not just prices. These and many other refinements have been argued through the halls of academe. All of this has been exquisitely but imperfectly modeled in the field of econometrics.

Still, these two schools of thought are in competition, with the monetarist school emphasizing greater market freedoms, a lesser role for government, and a larger scope for private actions, appealing to the financial services industry and business in general. The monetarist view remains dominant today in the West, though Keynesian thought experienced a resurgence in 2008 among those supporting the idea of a fiscal stimulus to jumpstart the economy, and in particular, in critique to the circumstances contributing to the financial crisis and growing inequality of wealth and income in the United States.

During the past half-century, however, continued efforts by government and elected representatives in Congress to address their constituents' needs have resulted in the proliferation of programs. Overlapping, redundant, and sometimes wasteful programs in social services and health care have drawn the ire of the Republicans, in particular. Such programs are nothing new—as a White House Fellow in the Office of Management and Budget in 1976, I worked at the direction of James T. Lynn, who was then director of the Office of Management and Budget, on identifying a number of these programs in the areas of nutrition and family assistance and presenting these findings to Congress. Not surprisingly, each program had its advocates among the congressional overseers; recommendations for change met with strong resistance, sometimes for sound reasons. Despite years of effort to eliminate them, apparent inefficiencies still abound in government programs. A 2013 study for Congress by the Government Accountability Office, for example, found tens of billions of dollars in federal expenditures that could possibly be saved by reconciling fragmented, overlapping, and redundant programs. The criticisms of "big government" are not without substance.[11]

President Ronald Reagan popularized much of the "big government" critique. In his words, "The nine most terrifying words in the English language are: 'I'm from the government, and I'm here to help.'" He also said, "Government is like a baby. An alimentary canal with a big appetite at one end and no sense of responsibility at the other." Reagan's words captured a powerful strand of American political thought that reverberates to this day.

The clashes in Congress between the Democrats and the Republicans over fiscal policy today are a new chapter in this long-running debate. Democrats have repeatedly cited the Keynesian idea of aggregate demand to argue for fine-tuning the economy through stimulus—that is, with deficit spending and low interest rates. And this means government funding of state, local, and federal programs. The Republicans, in turn, loathe deficit spending and want to cut many of those programs. They cry that government spending is ineffective and inefficient, that the deficit is dangerously high already, and that pumping up the economy will create so much demand that prices will rise and we will return to the kind of double-digit inflation that afflicted the United States in the late 1970s. The two parties have made an identity crusade out of an economic argument.

The heated partisan atmosphere has spilled over into much of the other work that needs to be done in Congress, especially the work of protecting national security. Again, this is nothing new. Like the economic debate, the debate over national security has roots in the past. In the aftermath of the Vietnam War in the 1970s, the Republican Party positioned itself to be the strong party on national defense. By the late 1980s, Republicans were actually seeking favor from the military. I remember Republican Congressman Newt Gingrich, for example, explaining to some of us at that time that his stepfather had served in the military and that he had grown up at Fort Benning. Politics was like war, he said, and he wanted to learn lessons from us. It was flattering and charming. In the 1990s, several Republican senators were totally candid in seeking to co-opt senior officers to the political bickering. One told me, "Surely, you don't want to go to the Balkans and fight Bill Clinton's wars." Another Republican, in the privacy of a helicopter flight while visiting troops in Bosnia, sought to draw me out by commenting, "It must be really tough, considering who you're working for." Huh? "Senator, I don't understand what you're suggesting," I answered. "Well, you know, Clinton," he replied, implying that the president wasn't an effective commander in chief, and apparently, seeking my confirmation of that.

Partisanship is exacerbated by the need for money in political races, which opens the door to lobbying. Recent Supreme Court decisions have further opened the door for money in politics, undercutting years of effort by progressive reformers to limit political and campaign finance spending. The twenty-four-hour news cycle, the chaotic media environment, gerrymandering, and the increased transparency of Congress further impact the ability of Congress to reconcile competing ideas and interests. Well-meaning advocates of good governance have pointed out that the combative atmosphere in Congress, available for public viewing on TV every day, can make lawmakers inflexible and unable to compromise and to engage in the kind of "horse-trading" and "log-rolling" that were the hallmarks of earlier eras.[12]

Today, the two major American political parties have been forced further apart than at any other time since World War II, and perhaps since the American Civil War. There is no longer an overlap on issues between conservative Democrats and moderate Republicans. The filibuster, a technique for blocking the vote on pending legislation in the US Senate, has seen record usage in recent years. Senatorial "holds" on nominations for appointed positions in the administration and federal judgeships have been increasingly frequent. Even discussions of "secession" by certain states have been floated, perhaps half humorously, in rancorous public dialogue not seen in the United States within recent memory.

One of the two major political parties has twice sought to cause the United States to default on its debt payments, simultaneously blocking budget agreements for over two years. Thus it has chosen a default position of sequestering revenues rather than the option of compromising with its political opponents. Yet many saw this as a proper and necessary means of addressing one of the most pressing and fundamental problems facing the United States. The conflict absorbed much of the energy that Congress might otherwise have dedicated to grappling with America's unquestionable challenges. It also lowered public trust in government as well as foreign expectations about our future as a nation. It was the latest chapter in America's declining faith in our capacity to face the future.

AMERICA'S DECLINING INFLUENCE ABROAD

America's weakened financial position and fractious politics have not been lost on the rest of the world. America is perceived abroad as having more limited resources than in the past and a difficult, perhaps broken, political system. There is widespread acknowledgment that the United States' long and frustrating engagements in Iraq and Afghanistan were largely unsuccessful. And these perceptions impact American influence in the world.

These views are in part a spillover from perceptions within America itself. According to Pew Research Center data, growing numbers of Americans believe that US prestige and influence are in decline. Some 53 percent of respondents in a December 2013 poll said that the United States was less important and less powerful now than ten years earlier. Fully 70 percent believed the United States was less respected abroad. Columnist Frank Bruni, in a *New York Times* opinion piece in early May 2014 citing a collection of data—opinion polls, World Bank data, expert political opinion, educational attainments, crumbling infrastructure, and a diminished middle class—pointed to what he called "a faded tapestry of American possibility." He asked, "Isn't pessimism a self-fulfilling prophecy?" And public opinion abroad seemed to agree.[13]

A BBC poll in May 2013 found that only about 45 percent of respondents abroad had a mainly positive view of America. A Pew Research Center Global Attitudes Project poll released two months later found that the United States is viewed favorably in Europe and Northeast Asia, but unfavorably in the Islamic world, and increasingly, unfavorably in China. America's "soft power" and culture are admired in Africa and Latin America; however, a growing number of people around the world, especially the Europeans, now view China as the world's leading economic power. The Pew survey summary noted that "throughout much of Europe, the prevailing view is that China will ultimately eclipse the US as the leading superpower. And this is the majority or plurality view in five of the seven Latin American nations polled." The October 2013 shutdown of the US government provided China with an opportunity to attempt to further buttress its standing in world opinion. For example, Xinhua, the official Chinese news agency, stated that "it is perhaps time for the befuddled world to start considering building a de-Americanized world."[14]

In addition to the perception of weakness stemming from the US military withdrawals, proposed cutbacks in defense spending, and coarse and fractious politics, there is a widespread belief that the US economic model simply doesn't work very well anymore. High rates of joblessness, long-term and chronic unemployment, high youth unemployment, rising income inequality, lack of significant investment in many sectors of the economy, undistributed and unused piles of corporate cash, declining levels of new business formation, and uncharacteristically low rates of economic growth, along with high annual budget deficits, all combine to give the impression abroad that something is systemically wrong in the US economy.

Former Australian prime minister Kevin Rudd, a longtime China expert, puts it in stark terms. In a personal conversation in

December 2013, he told me, "If you Americans don't grow your economy, clean up your politics and fix your educational system, you will lose Western civilization." Losing Western civilization would be the mother of all inflection points.

THE INFLECTION POINT IN PERSPECTIVE

Inflection points—moments of dramatic change—can be managed or even reversed. This is true even for the most dramatic of these turning points. The United States has done it before, and we could do it again. In the 1930s, too, during the depths of the Great Depression, capitalism looked like a failure, and the United States looked like a power in decline. In late 1937, eight years after the onset of the Great Depression, and after a strong recovery in employment and manufacturing in 1934–1935, the US economy once again slumped. Manufacturing employment, payrolls, and production declined month after month. Unemployment rose to 19 percent. All the remedies that the United States attempted to put into place seemed to fail.

What brought the US economy out of the Depression was US rearmament in preparation for World War II—and then wartime production itself. With so much slack in the US economy, the industrial mobilization was stunning. Real US GDP grew by 8 percent in 1939, 8.8 percent in 1940, 17.7 percent in 1941, 18.9 percent in 1942, and 17 percent in 1943. The US gross national product (GNP) in 1939 stood at $91.3 billion, measured in 1939 dollars; by 1945, the GNP, in 1939 dollars, climbed to $166.6 billion. Production of war material surged. Summarizing the achievements, a 1992 book noted that, "practically the entire American durable goods industry" was converted "to war production and the application of mass production techniques to manufacture of instruments of warfare." In 1942, American war production equaled the outputs of Germany, Italy and Japan combined. Millions of new workers entered the workforce, and unemployment dropped below 2 percent in 1943. US workforce training was implemented, minorities and women were increasingly integrated into the US economy, and both corporate profits and wages increased. Nevertheless, it was a difficult and somewhat chaotic period, and marked by some degree of labor strife.[15]

The upturn was largely financed by an explosion of government debt. Civilian demand was suppressed during the war, in part by rationing, in part by sales of savings bonds, and in part by the absence of certain consumer goods. But the activities of war succeeded in banishing the Great Depression. US production constituted 54 percent of the world GDP at the end of World War II. Partly this high percentage was due to the fact that the industrial capacity of Germany and Japan had been destroyed, along with the Soviet economy; and Great Britain was also struggling because of the war. Unfortunately, it had taken a war to persuade Americans to work together.

Today, although government and personal debt is high, the US economy still has substantial resources available to it, including capital, labor, and industrial capacity. Capital consists of corporate retained earnings—monies held within corporations, plus excess capital within banks and financial institutions, including private equity funds and hedge funds. American nonfinancial corporations retained some $2.2 trillion in 2013. Private equity funds in 2012 held almost $1 trillion of investible capital. And according to a 2013 database, hedge funds held another $2 trillion in 2013, some of which would have been investible. Altogether, growth in the US economy is not capital-constrained.[16]

US unemployment in November 2013 stood at 7 percent (10.9 million people); in addition, there were another 7.7 million people working part-time "for economic reasons" (that is, they would rather be working full-time). Another 2.1 million people were labeled as "marginally attached," meaning that they wanted to work, but had given up looking. To this could be added another 19.3 million "noneconomic" part-time workers, some of whom, presumably, would move into the labor force full-time under the right circumstances. In other words, slack labor in the US economy is very nearly on par with the situation before World War II. It is certainly well above the 4 percent level that nominally constitutes full employment. Meanwhile, US industrial capacity utilization at the end of 2013 stood at 79 percent, with manufacturing below 77 percent.[17]

These are all resources that could be used but are not. If the capital were invested in the United States, in job-producing activities, the economy would quickly rebound, and growth would accelerate. How much? Costs for job creation range from perhaps $50,000 per job in small retail businesses to more than $300,000 per job in industrial and highly capital-intensive businesses. But, to be conservative, assume that every $1 million of investment creates four jobs. This means that $100 billion in investments creates 400,000 jobs, and $1 trillion in investments would create 4 million jobs. There are several trillions of dollars on the sidelines of the American economy, and many more trillions beyond our borders that could be invested here.

What would it take to unlock this money? In general, businesses invest with a variety of motives—for the expectation of near-term profit, for example, or to capture market share or develop new technologies or processes. Business investments are deterred by market uncertainties, uncertainties about taxes, regulations, permitting, technology risks, and many other factors. A *Financial Times* analysis from July 2013 looked at a variety of excuses, including general economic conditions, regulation, corporate cultures, executive pay, and "monopolistic rents," acknowledging each, but finally concluding that matters of corporate governance and compensation should be viewed as important macroeconomic policy matters. In other words, look to the incentives.[18]

Investing is a function of the emotions—it is not purely rational. Keynes attributed the propensity to take investment risks to "animal spirits." In boards of directors meetings around America, shareholders' representatives weigh risks and benefits as they consider the best use of corporate funds. And today, American businesses are, in general, disinclined to take risks and make investments. This may be a function of relatively slow growth in consumer demand, or demand for their particular products. But it has an irrationality to it, as though, in many sectors, the "animal spirits" are lacking. Partly this is a function of individual and collective experiences with the financial crisis and its aftermath; many of us watched helplessly as otherwise sound smaller companies in various sectors were dragged into bankruptcy by customer uncertainty, declining markets, lack of timely credit, and contagion. It is a sobering emotional experience, and collectively, many boards of directors are exercising much greater caution going forward. Institutional investors behind today's market are also restraining companies' investments. This restraint is due to the same psychology at work in many investment fund managers. It is sometimes expressed in the way managers allocate investments, how they approach due diligence requirements, or how they manage investment approval processes.[19]

Interest rates are near their all-time lows, and credit markets are working, especially for large corporations. But banks themselves are still cautious in lending to small businesses. The total value of small business loans in the fourth quarter of 2012 was 78 percent less than in the second quarter of 2007. Small businesses claim that banks are no longer willing to step up, while banks complain about the lack of demand and the lack of creditworthiness of prospective borrowers.[20]

Other effects from the Great Recession have accentuated existing trends. Without remediation, they will further undercut US economic strength. In most sectors, corporate profits were driven up by efficiency enhancements that didn't translate into increased hiring. This reflected a deepening of long-term trends: in each successive recession for the past thirty years, businesses have reduced employment sooner in order to protect profits, and have delayed hiring full-time employees, instead using temporary and part-time workers for as long as possible. Income growth for the "bottom 99 percent" has virtually stalled, and for the bottom 90 percent, real incomes actually declined. Government investments in R&D, though crucially important for basic research, have fallen, and productivity improvements have slowed. Larger firms were able to capture market share at the expense of smaller firms—but it is the smaller firms that create jobs.[21]

During the most damaging period of the financial crisis in early 2009, an experienced investment banker called me aside from a board meeting of a major international company. "Wes," he said, "I don't know what you're going to do in the next few years—perhaps you will go back into government. But if you stay in the private sector, do not invest your own money in building businesses; this financial crisis will hold down the world economy and especially hit small, start-up businesses for at least five years." He wasn't wrong. He and I had watched together as some of the most promising businesses in private equity portfolios failed, even with the backing of Goldman Sachs—and he sensed the psychological impact on the investment community as well as the deep economic challenges confronting the United States.

The financial crisis seems to have hastened America toward the "inflection point," the point at which the nation could turn a corner and enter a period of decline, in fact as well as in perceptions at home and abroad. The triple crush of government debt, vicious partisanship, and crippling public opinion, added to the financial crisis, weakens American influence in the world. Without a strategy that infects public opinion, and that provides a rationale for new policies and attitudes, the US economy could simply "dawdle" its way through a vicious cycle of caution and disappointment. Already, we seem to be entering a period in which, some believe, American power and influence may not be quite adequate to manage the foreign policy risks of multiple crises and challenges. Many in the world, seeing challenges in the Middle East, Asia, Africa, and with Russia, are asking, "Where is American leadership?" and "What will happen to the rule of law, progress in building international institutions, and the mechanisms for peaceful resolution of disputes, if America isn't able to retain its global leadership role?"

But perhaps this inflection point is also a gift to American leadership—in the same way that the march into World War II in Europe provided the impetus for pulling the United States out of the Great Depression. The last time we had such slack in the US economy was just prior to World War II. Would it be possible to use the urgency and imminence of the strategic challenges sketched out in Chapter 3 to confront the inflection point itself, and to pull America back together? Can we muster the will and the resources needed to put America back on track? Can we convince the American people and their elected officials that "we have to *do* something"?

We have the means. After all, we are still the world's largest economy, and we do have real economic strength—abundant natural resources, including water, minerals, and biomass; robust agriculture; low-cost energy; the world's best university system; leading technology in energy, communications, computing, aerospace, and automotive industries; marketing skills and customer services; and our cultural assets and edge in entertainment. America offers one of the world's safest and lowest-risk business environments and is the world's leading storehouse of "intellectual property."

Moreover, we possess key advantages in dealing with each of the challenges that we are facing. We are isolated geographically from the nexus of Islamist terrorism, and our culture has been inherently assimilationist in absorbing immigrants and their children, regardless of religious background, nationality, or ethnicity. We created the Internet, and the largest of the Internet companies, as well as much of the Internet's backbone, is located within the United States; we should be able to use our accessibility to deal effectively with cyber-threats. Although it was American mortgage-backed securities that served as the agents of infection in spreading the financial crisis, the scale of the US economy, and the dynamic responsiveness of the US Federal Reserve, give us powerful economic leverage in international circles. Unlike the Soviet Union during the Cold War, which tried to build a separate economy with its allies, China has increasingly integrated its economy with the world economy. China is in fact heavily dependent on US markets, and, as our largest overseas creditor, on the value of the US currency. Consequently, we have a great deal of influence over China. And as the largest and still the most innovative economy in the world, the United States has the power to take the lead in dealing with climate change.

Additionally, we have tremendous potential support from our allies abroad. Most of Europe is hungry for American leadership, especially Eastern Europe and the Baltics. The austerity policies of the eurozone, the limitations of the European Central Bank, and the frictions and tensions created by unemployment and immigration have, unfortunately, tarnished the allure of European unity. Although the United States needs a strong Europe as its partner, today's European weaknesses provide an opportunity for even closer collaboration with Europe economically, diplomatically, and militarily. Despite the best efforts of the European Union—and the forbearance of the United States in this process—the European Union lacks a unified foreign policy and the defense organization to back it up. Europe lacks a common perception of threats and challenges, as well as the public support it would need for increased defense expenditures. European forces face severe shortfalls in heavy lift, strategic communications and logistics, reconnaissance and surveillance, deployable forces, and precision airpower. The North Atlantic Treaty Organization, of which the United States is the leading member, remains the foundation of European security. And in the Middle East and Asia, friends and allies are seeking our support.

Finally, we have our values—what America stands for. We Americans still believe—and others in the world believe with us—that the United States is the land of opportunity. Immigrants come here to seek financial prosperity, security, and freedom for themselves and their families. They seek dignity and self-respect, a new life, and new opportunities. I have heard the stories again and again from those who have come to our country. They risk the security of the familiar, taking hold of their courage and determination, and they find the future they were seeking, whether they come from Asia, Central or South America, Eastern Europe, Africa, or the Middle East. They have found here in America the same opportunities that earlier centuries of immigrants found—the Italians, the Germans, the Jews of Eastern Europe, and the Irish, the Scots, English, and Dutch. There is real power in these values and in their expression in our political system—power to transform ourselves and help change the world.

The inflection point may yet be reversible. But to consolidate and apply these assets, we need something that helps us set priorities, maintain our focus, and build our strengths, even as we adapt to the exigencies of the moment. We need transcendent ideas. We need a strategy.

CHAPTER 5

Reversing the Inflection Point

The five top long-term challenges facing the United States—
terrorism, cybersecurity, the financial system, China, and climate change—are clearly not subject to simplistic solutions. Each
is integrally connected to one or more other challenges; none can
be addressed solely within US borders. Viewed together, these five
strategic challenges could provide just enough of a challenge to
America to provide a bipartisan rationale for pulling the country
closer together—without having to find an enemy. But we cannot
expect to easily address these challenges unless we reverse the relative decline of American power. We have to pull back from the
inflection point, reverse course—and restart America's economic
engine.

ENERGY INDEPENDENCE PLUS

One starting point exists that could supercharge the US economy,
change the impression that the United States is a declining power,
and give us the additional means we need to address the long-
term challenges we face. And it could be implemented without
any significant costs to the taxpayers. This starting point is energy
independence. Energy independence would allow us to capture the

$200 billion to $300 billion we spend each year importing petroleum. And it is such a powerful idea that it could be a key component in our overall national strategy by itself.[1]

Our dependence on imported oil currently functions like a "tax" on America. It takes away this $200 billion to $300 billion from our economy each and every year, an amount equivalent to 1.2 to 1.8 percent of GDP. This is money withdrawn from consumers through the gas pumps at filling stations across the nation, from airlines paying for imported jet fuel, and from trucking and shipping firms. It is money that cannot be otherwise spent on consumer goods, invested in new technology, or used to support the economy in other ways. It is simply a wealth transfer to nations that sell us the petroleum.

If we had the means domestically to produce this fuel, we could retain these billions within the economy. Imagine: Taxes alone on these revenues might total $50 billion to $90 billion per year, and other monies, cycling through a multiplier of paychecks, consumer spending, and investment, could provide an additional 1.5 to 2 percent growth in real terms to the US economy. This benefit alone is sufficient to obviate the most pressing quarrels about spending priorities and entitlement programs, about whether and how to improve our infrastructure, and about how much to invest in American education. Greater revenues would help drive down the national debt, increase employment, and provide a means for easing the hostile partisan fight over the budget. Reducing that deep divide, and all the fractiousness that goes with it, would also strengthen America's hand in the world. And we now have the potential to achieve energy independence, and even to go well beyond energy independence to become the leading fuel and energy exporter in the world. These changes would not only transform our economy but also restore power and influence to America. Energy independence could become the centerpiece of a new American strategy, built not on military might but on economic strength.

Energy independence is not a new idea. Every president, beginning with Richard Nixon, has advocated energy independence. It was the pursuit of energy independence that led to the formation of the Department of Energy in 1977. Since then, many billions of dollars have been spent on research and projects designed to move the United States toward energy independence, including efforts in solar, wind, biofuels, clean coal, and nuclear power. Many of us have been advocating an even more aggressive pursuit of energy independence in speeches, articles, and discussions with administration officials. President Obama campaigned for the 2012 election on a strategy of using all available forms of energy to move us toward energy independence (the so-called "all-of-the-above" strategy).[2]

What's changed over the past forty years, however, is that the price of oil has become high enough to make "unconventional oil" and other sources of fuel profitable—and we know that high prices worldwide are likely to be sustained. In 2005, an effort was made by some of the Gulf states to undercut Iran by driving down the price of oil; they attempted to flood the market, and the price did decline, but only briefly. Today the global demand for oil is more than 90 million barrels per day—and rising—as a function of global growth, and particularly growth in former Third World countries. Conventional oil exploration and production cannot grow to meet this demand. Discoveries of conventional oil that is recoverable have continued to decline over the years. Hence the rise in production of unconventional oil from shale, from oil sands, and from very deep in the oceans. Even with oil provided by these alternatives, the price of oil, currently around $100 per barrel, is unlikely to decline much, if at all, in the near future, and is likely to rise in the 2020s.[3]

The United States and our Canadian partners are the leaders in the technologies that enable access to unconventional and deep offshore oil, such as horizontal drilling, 3D seismic techniques, and "fracking," as well as the means for extracting oil from Canadian oil sands, and we have enormous resources of unconventional oil here in the United States. Now, at last, we can achieve energy independence, and even go beyond, to become a leading exporter in world energy markets. This is "Energy Independence Plus."

Incidentally, by energy independence, we are really speaking about not depending on importing oil for transportation purposes. For all practical purposes we are already independent in electric power production. So discussions about energy independence are really discussions about petroleum—not coal-fired power plants, solar energy, or wind, or hydropower, or nuclear. These sources of electricity will only replace petroleum when there has been a significant investment in electric automobiles—and thus far that has not happened. Ninety-nine percent of the oil we consume is used in transportation or in petrochemicals, so "energy independence" is really about increasing our production of petroleum and its substitutes and simultaneously reducing domestic demand for oil.

Estimating future oil production is difficult, but it appears that we will not meet the goal of full energy independence if we simply extrapolate current trends. In October 2013, for the first time since 1995, US oil production exceeded oil imports. But this still left us importing over 35 percent of the oil we need. In December 2013, the Energy Information Administration (EIA) released a preview of its *Annual Energy Outlook*. This report predicted that US oil production would rise to some 9.5 million barrels per day in 2016, but that this amount would slowly decline in later years. And while oil imports are predicted to decline as US fuel economy measures take hold, we will still be importing 25 percent of our oil. At the projected 2016 low point of oil imports, the United States will still be importing almost 5 million barrels per day. This amount will slowly rise to 6 million barrels per day by 2040 as demand increases and production falls. With oil prices estimated to rise to $141 per barrel by 2040, in the Department of Energy's "reference case," this will keep the cost of imported petroleum near or above the $200 billion mark indefinitely. The Department of Energy also assumes that biofuels will not meet the United States' mandated target of 36 billion gallons per year, and that natural gas will provide only about 3 percent of the liquid fuels requirement for transportation. In other words, if current trends continue along the lines of Department of Energy estimates, we will likely spend between $5 trillion and $7 trillion on imported oil over the next 25 years.[4]

Moreover, unless we achieve energy independence and even more—enough for exports—we leave OPEC countries (and speculators) in charge of oil prices. So the goal needs to be more far-reaching than just energy independence: the goal needs to be full US energy independence, plus substantial exports. Also, there is urgency: each additional year of delay costs another $200 billion or more that is lost to the American economy. We should aim to attain "Energy Independence Plus" as rapidly as possible.

How do we achieve it?

Full energy independence means domestic production of at least an additional 5 million to 6 million barrels per day of liquid fuel above and beyond the anticipated growth in US production. It will take action by both the private sector and government to bring us to full energy independence and beyond.

Energy markets, and especially liquid fuels, are highly competitive. I walked into an energy conference at the congenial Aspen Institute a few years ago. Unlike most Aspen Institute conferences, in which heated intellectual argumentation is mollified by the delightful surroundings, this was an inward-facing dust-up of the first order. The big oil companies were against each other, oil was against gas, oil and gas were together against electric-powered cars, and everyone was against biofuels (except for me; I believe they constitute a genuine American home-grown technology with vast potential). The total liquid fuels market is on the order of $600 billion annually, so it is a major piece of the economy. Thousands of businesses depend on the energy industry, and millions of people are employed in it—everyone from the land agents who secure mineral rights for oil companies to the individual corn farmers who deliver their grain to ethanol plants. Every fuel has its advocates, and each of the advocates wants a greater share of the market. And each will promise you a much brighter future, if everything is done his or her way. Quarrels and disputes—personal, public, political, and legal—are endemic. To move to energy independence and beyond, the US fuels industry has to stop fighting itself for the US market and move to address the worldwide market, where there are plenty of opportunities for all. This shift requires a change of attitudes and effort in the private sector, as well as appropriate support from the government for fuel exports.

Government can do a great deal to bring about this transformation. Despite the competition, energy markets are not "free markets." It is not possible to "leave it to the private sector." Production of oil is regulated by various federal and state agencies, depending on where the property is and who owns it. As one friend of mine from Oklahoma explained to me, "In some counties here, you can get a permit to drill and frack in a day." New York State, in contrast, has a moratorium on fracking in place as the state awaits environmental and health studies, and this moratorium has lasted for years. In most states, inspectors monitor the drilling, along with the Occupational Safety and Health Administration (OSHA) and the Environmental Protection Agency (EPA).

Drilling on federal lands goes through an arduous permitting process, and production from these lands has declined in recent years. Getting the oil from the well to the refinery is usually by truck initially, and then by pipeline or rail, and that process, too, is heavily regulated. It is difficult to get permits to construct new pipelines, and any failures in transport, such as pipeline leakages, are reported, investigated, and subject to financial penalties. Actual composition of the liquid fuels is regulated by the Environmental Protection Agency under the provisions of the 1990 Clean Air Act. So it is a highly developed and regulated market, with major players spending millions of dollars on lobbying and advertising to keep their share and keep others out.

Lots of money is donated to foundations and universities for studies, too—and you can usually find someone to study just about anything, in return for grants. In some cases, individual advocates become major personalities, like my friend T. Boone Pickens, who has become the apostle of natural gas. The studies and the speeches and the lobbying are all part of the "influence game" in Washington, DC, and in state capitals, with legislators championing their constituents' causes. Sometimes there is a more subtle overtone to all of this, too, because neither the regulators nor the legislators are in lifetime sinecures—many will eventually transition to the private sector. Still, a government strategy to more strongly encourage increased production of fuels, and to promote sales abroad, would go a long way to reducing the wasteful and destructive competition between types of fuels and facilitate more efficient use of all our resources.

We expect strong downward pressure on US demand for liquid fuels, even as the economy grows. The automobile fleet mileage standards put into place by the Obama administration in August 2012 call for a fleetwide average fuel economy of 54.5 miles per gallon, double the existing standard. In principle, this requirement should reduce oil consumption by 2.2 million barrels per day by 2025, and subsequently by up to 4 million barrels per day. These savings are already in the Energy Information Administration forecast of imports, and they are insufficient to take us to energy independence. To the extent that they are not realized—and there is some expectation that the savings may fall short, based on past experience and some loopholes in the standards—then even more oil must be produced beyond the anticipated 5 million to 6 million barrels per day increase projected by the EIA.[5]

So to become energy independent, we need to produce more fuel. And here's how: by extending oil production in federal lands, continuing investments in new oil-related technologies, and accelerating permitting. We should retain the 2007 Renewable Fuel Standard (described below) for biofuels, as well as adopting an "open fuel standard"; make the greatest possible use of natural gas in compressed or liquid form, or by converting it to liquid fuels such as diesel and jet fuel; and use enhanced coal-to-liquids technology with carbon capture. Energy Independence Plus is achievable, if we take account of the following points.

Oil Production. The US oil industry is without doubt the strongest, most flexible, and most innovative industry grouping in the world. Crushed periodically by price collapses, new discoveries, and OPEC's skillful manipulation of supply, and buoyed by (sometimes) incredible profit margins, new technologies, and very determined leadership, American companies large and small have somehow survived and prospered enormously. Today, the oil industry will be quick to tell anyone that the greatest opportunities are here at home. The combination of private ownership of mineral rights in the United States, well-organized and responsive capital markets, skilled technicians, continual scientific research, and entrepreneurial spirit makes America's domestic oil industry unique.

There are potentially billions of barrels of additional oil to be recovered from existing wells using new techniques and yet-to-be-developed technologies. Every month brings increased discovery and experimentation in the quest to go after old reservoirs containing hundreds of millions of barrels as well as tight oil to be released by fracking. (Fracking usually releases a combination of oil, natural gas liquids, and natural gas; the greater the proportion of oil, the more valuable the well.) Between April 2013 and December 2014, the Department of Energy's estimates for "tight oil" production (requiring fracking) in the United States for 2016 rose by 2 million barrels per day.

Although oil companies guard their figures carefully, industry publications suggest that the Permian Basin in Texas and New Mexico, for example, which is today producing some 1.3 million barrels per day, could produce much more when various shales in the area are exploited. The Eagle Ford Shale in South Texas may contain more than 25 billion barrels of oil and natural gas liquids; production in the Eagle Ford quadrupled between 2011 and 2012, and doubled again in 2013, to yield over 1 million barrels per day. Some oil industry analysts expect production to reach 1.8 million barrels per day by 2022. The Energy Information Administration projections for the growth of future production have been continuously revised upward in recent years. We should expect to see another (unanticipated) 1 million barrels per day or more from tight oil production by 2016 if existing trends continue. In addition, companies are anxiously searching data for old wells and looking for opportunities to produce more oil from previously declining reservoirs.[6]

Although oil production on private land has been booming, production on federal lands, which were responsible for about a quarter of US oil production in 2012, has risen only modestly since 2008. There are 113 million acres of federal land available for exploration and production. About another 166 million acres are off-limits or inaccessible. Firms must pay for rights for leases to explore these lands, and also pay royalties on production. According to a Congressional Research Services study, gaining approval to drill from the US Bureau of Land Management (BLM) has become increasingly arduous for companies in recent years, despite more rapid processing of applications within the BLM. According to the study's author, "A more efficient permitting process may be an added incentive in developing Federal resources, which may allow for some oil and gas to come on stream sooner."[7]

A 2011 study by the energy consulting firm Wood Mackenzie found that opening up additional federal lands, onshore and off, could add 2.8 million barrels per day of additional production by 2025. By 2025 this decision would also create 530,000 new jobs. The revenue due to royalties and taxes "is estimated to rise by a cumulative of $20 billion by 2020 and $150 billion by 2025." A Congressional Budget Office (CBO) study noted estimates of about 175 billion barrels of oil equivalent (BOE) in undiscovered reserves on federal lands, including deep waters in the Gulf of Mexico and outer continental shelf (most of this was *not* in the Alaska National Wildlife Refuge). The CBO study estimates $2 billion in additional leases and royalties through 2022 from further opening of federal lands outside the Alaska National Wildlife Refuge. A Louisiana State University study of the potential benefits of the CBO analysis went further, citing full economic benefits of $127 billion per year to the US GDP over the next seven years from fully opening federal lands, along with 500,000 new jobs. If we could open and incentivize access to these areas, we might reap, conservatively, another 2 million barrels per day.[8]

Of course, there are challenges involved in the expansion of production, including use of water, and its reuse, in fracking; the risks of spills and contamination; inadvertent methane leakage from wellheads; and rapid expansion of infrastructure. But these are risks known by the industry and targeted by investments in new technologies and new servicing companies. Although dealing with these risks will be a major concern for the nation, pursuing increased production will stimulate new technologies, and it could be a significant investment opportunity and source of profits for many firms in this sector.

Oil from Oil Shale. A heavy oil known as *kerogen* is trapped in shale rock formations in parts of Wyoming, Colorado, and Utah. The amount of kerogen that is locked into oil shales in these states is estimated at some 2 trillion barrels, with almost 1 trillion barrels estimated as recoverable. Production was attempted in the 1970s, during the first oil crisis, but as prices of oil returned to lower levels, these efforts were abandoned. The high price of oil is now stimulating renewed efforts.

Although Shell recently abandoned an effort in this area, new technologies using horizontal drilling and high heat could yield highly economic in situ recovery with little environmental degradation or atmospheric release of carbon. So long as prices for oil remain at or near $100 per barrel, this oil will be brought to market eventually. With the right technology and investment, this resource could yield perhaps 500,000 barrels per day or more indefinitely. Government approvals and incentives will be essential to hasten its effective development.[9]

Biofuels. Ramped-up production of liquid fuels should include a significant biofuels component. Under current laws, highly detailed annual targets are mandated for the biofuels component of gasoline and diesel fuels. Biofuels already provide approximately 10 percent of US liquid fuel. Each year the biofuels component is scheduled to rise until, by 2022, the United States will be blending 36 billion gallons of biofuels annually. This will constitute some 30 percent of the US gasoline supply. The Renewable Fuel Standard (RFS), which was created by the 2005 Energy Policy Act and expanded in the 2007 Energy Independence and Security Act, has become the focal point of a fierce fuels-industry fight, which broke into the open in the autumn of 2013 with several congressional proposals to kill or modify the law. And for the first time, acting in accordance with its mandate, the Environmental Protection Agency proposed scaling back the total volume of renewable fuels to be placed into the nation's fuel supply.

At stake in this fight is the potential to substitute up to an additional 2 million barrels per day of biofuels for imported oil. (Also at stake are vast oil-refinery profits from domestic fuel sales, the development of advanced biofuels, and a whole range of impacts—intensely debated—on farm income, grain prices, air quality, and America's home-grown biofuels industry.) With the passage of the 2005 and 2007 energy legislation, capital flowed into the ethanol industry. Virtually overnight, production shot from about around 100,000 barrels per day to over 900,000 barrels per day of grain-based (mostly corn-based) ethanol. Investments in advanced biofuels were choked off by the financial crisis of 2008, and many promising technologies foundered. These interruptions opened the RFS to continuing criticism for overpromising advanced fuels, such as cellulosic ethanol.

Still, despite the difficulties associated with funding, the industry has moved forward with many different formulas and pathways into advanced fuels, chiefly ethanol, but also new fuels like biobutanol and methanol. In 2014 we should see the first commercial-scale, second-generation biofuel production, with three large plants coming online using corn residue as feedstock. Other commercially viable systems using other feedstocks and/or producing different products are also in the works. The Department of the Navy has done pioneering work in providing purchases for some of these advanced biofuels, but new fuels will soon be commercially viable, at scale, without any subsidies.

Meanwhile, blocking biofuels growth has, unfortunately, become an important objective of the oil industry, and has been pursued by legal challenge, politics, and advertising. Canned research reports have been generated, and a great deal of behind-the-scenes lobbying has been underway for some time. A vast publicity campaign in 2008, paid for by the Grocery Manufacturers Association, raised the issue of "food versus fuel," and the slogan gained traction quickly. Droughts and speculation in grain markets since 2008 have actually been responsible for most of the rise in grain prices; and as of this writing, corn prices in the United States are around $5 per bushel, slightly higher than the average cost of production, having declined by over 40 percent from the high levels associated with the drought of 2012. Still, congressional hearings have been held and modifications of the Renewable Fuel Standard have been discussed to favor the oil companies. It is symptomatic of America's fuels market—industries fighting with each other for the US domestic market, when the world at large is hungry for American liquid fuels and natural gas. Reaching energy independence in the shortest possible amount of time means opening up opportunities for biofuels, not closing them off, as part of what President Obama termed his "all-of-the-above strategy."

In practice, higher volumes of renewable fuels mean that in the near term, it will be possible to change the mix in some newer automobiles from 90 percent gasoline and 10 percent ethanol to offer blends of 85 percent gasoline and 15 percent ethanol, as well as the now-conventional E85 blend for flex fuel vehicles. By 2022, when the law is fully implemented, it should be possible to have designed automobiles able to run efficiently on blends of 70 percent gasoline and 30 percent ethanol. All of this is technically feasible, and it will produce higher mileage efficiencies, reduce US demand for crude oil, and retain tens of billions of dollars inside the US economy.

The United States just has to be willing to stick with the existing law. If we stick with this law, we will reduce the need for imported oil by almost another 2 million barrels per day. Excess fuels can be exported. The area of biofuels is a new technology sector, and the United States is in the lead. The technologies themselves can be licensed and exported. In later decades, fully renewable, advanced, carbon-neutral biofuels will be able to provide liquid fuel sufficient to further reduce dependence on petroleum.

Natural Gas. The opportunities for powering automobiles and trucks with natural gas, compressed or liquefied, are just being understood. The United States currently uses approximately 26 trillion cubic feet of natural gas per year—but we have natural resources of more than 3,000 trillion cubic feet or more. T. Boone Pickens says that industry sources are privately acknowledging that these natural gas reserves are at least 4,000 trillion cubic feet, and probably higher. No one really knows how much is there, because, like oil reserves, natural gas reserves are computed as a function of both geology and technology; estimates tend to be conservative. And as technology improves and production rises, the amount of the resource that can be recovered also increases and so reserves increase.

Theoretically, a unit of natural gas (1,000 cubic feet) has approximately one-sixth the energy of a unit of oil (1 barrel, or 42 gallons), but it stands today at less than one-twentieth the price. So, using natural gas for vehicle propulsion, even counting the costs of compressing or liquefying, offers potentially huge financial advantages—on the order of perhaps one-third the cost of using gasoline or diesel.

The challenges here are financial and technical. Conversion of existing vehicles is expensive—some $2,500 for an automobile, and perhaps $75,000 for a large tractor-trailer rig. Mileage per volume is somewhat reduced, especially with compressed natural gas, and the infrastructure to "fill-er-up" along the way doesn't exist. Thus far, use of compressed natural gas (CNG) and liquefied natural gas (LNG) has been limited to fleet vehicles in urban environments, where they can return to their origin for fuel, or some long-haul truck fleets on designated routes. According to the American Gas Association, there are about 140,000 natural-gas-propelled vehicles on the roads today. However, railroads and trucking firms are seriously evaluating using liquefied natural gas in place of diesel. Work is underway to build LNG fueling stations along the interstate highway system. The Energy Information Administration expects LNG to replace perhaps 700,000 barrels per day of diesel by 2040.[10] We could do more.

Gas-to-Liquids. Natural gas can also be converted directly into liquid fuel, such as low-sulfur diesel, by using a petrochemical process. In most countries this process doesn't make economic sense, because the price of gas is relatively high compared to the price of oil. But unlike the case for oil, there is no world price for natural gas. So in the United States—where long-term gas prices are predicted to remain at $5 and below, and oil is predicted to remain at around $100 per barrel (conservative financial estimates often use $80 per barrel as the "safe' price)—conversion plants could be very profitable, even though they require investments in the billions of dollars. Roughly speaking, every $1 billion of investment in gas-to-liquids will produce some 10,000 barrels per day of fuel.

Planning for the first such plants is already underway. In terms of scale of effort, organizing 100,000 barrels per day of additional fuel from gas-to-liquids processes shouldn't tax either US engineering and steel or financing. Efforts like this, which typically take five years from planning to production, could bring another 500,000 to 1 million barrels per day of fuel to US markets without impacting gas pricing.

Coal-to-Liquids. Techniques of extracting liquid fuels from coal were originally developed by the Germans in the years prior to World War II. The United States bombed twenty-six of the so-called "syn-fuels" plants in Germany as part of the World War II bombing campaign, and urban legend has it that after the war, the South Africans somehow acquired the technology. A huge company, Sasol, emerged to claim the proprietary rights to one of the key technologies involved. The United States also tried its hand in this technique, known as the Fischer-Tropsch process, in 1949 and again in 1980. Both efforts were halted after the price of crude oil undercut plant economics.

Originally the technology was environmentally dirty, but several modifications have made coal-to-liquid conversion increasingly efficient and capable of carbon capture. At the low end of expectations, coal-to-liquid technology can convert a ton of inexpensive coal—say at $10 to $20 per ton—into more than a barrel of a refined product such as jet fuel or diesel at a total cost of between $30 and $50 dollars per barrel.

China is investing tens of billions of dollars in coal gasification. The United States has huge coal reserves, including the relatively wet, poor-quality lignite coal preferred for the principal coal-to-liquids technologies. Here, as in the gas-to-liquids case, every $1 billion of investment should result in more than 10,000 barrels of premium fuel. The United States could meet its entire liquid fuel needs by tapping these vast resources. Given the right incentives, coal-to-liquids technologies could begin producing 1 million to 2 million barrels of fuel per day within the next decade. Moreover, investments in coal-to-liquids facilities could provide a durable source of low-cost fuels for years after fracked wells are depleted; if there are to be any hydrocarbon-based fuels or petrochemicals in America in the long term, coal-to-liquids production will probably prove the most economical means of providing them.

In total, the hydrocarbon resources available could easily take the United States *beyond* energy independence: the components named above include at least an additional 1 million barrels per day from unanticipated new fracking or extending the life of old wells; 2 million barrels a day from new federal lands efforts; 2 million barrels per day from biofuels; 1.2 million barrels per day from natural gas and gas-to-liquids technologies; and another 1 million to 2 million barrels per day from kerogen oil and coal-to-liquids technologies. This adds up to 7.2 million to 8.2 million barrels per day of additional production. Liquid fuels in excess of US domestic needs can be exported. Even if, as some studies suggest, tight oil production will decline somewhat after 2020, there is more than ample potential in oil shale, advanced biofuels, gas-to-liquids, and coal-to-liquids to sustain and even increase US liquid fuels production for decades to come.

Export markets for fuel are growing annually; domestic US producers and refiners just have to reach them. Combined, each of these lines of effort should make the United States more than liquid-fuels-independent in less than a decade—and we should be in a position to earn valuable foreign exchange and to command additional weight in world economic affairs from a dominant fuels position.

In addition, by pursuing Energy Independence Plus we will be increasing employment at home—a matter of critical importance—as well as boosting GDP. In the oil industry, which is typically capital-intensive, job creation currently runs at the rate of $300,000 of investment per new permanent job created. The billions and billions of dollars of investment and production will create millions of new jobs in exploration and production, the construction of pipelines and facilities, and ancillary employment—accounting, food services, transportation, and many other fields, in the industry itself and the broader economy.

Based solely on America's shale resources—and not factoring in biofuels, kerogen, gas-to-liquids, or coal-to-liquids—a McKinsey Global Institute study in 2013 estimated a boost to the US GDP of $115 billion to $225 billion annually in the energy sector by 2020; an associated boost in energy-intensive manufacturing industries of $55 billion to $85 billion; and a wider ripple effect into professional services, construction, transport, and trade, driving an additional $210 billion to $380 billion incremental increase in annual GDP. This would be a total of almost $700 billion added to our annual GDP from shale alone by 2020. This McKinsey document goes on to estimate that building out the infrastructure for this production would draw almost exclusively on private capital, creating up to 1.6 million construction jobs in the near term. Factoring in the additional energy efforts, America could easily double or perhaps even triple its GDP growth rate in the near term, create several million jobs, and restore the "magic" to America's economy.[11]

Further reinforcing the impact of pursuing energy independence, a 2013 study by IHS estimated that by 2020, the full value chain, from upstream production through energy-related chemicals, of unconventional oil and gas would be creating 3.3 million jobs, and adding over $468 billion to annual GDP. The study further estimated that tax receipts to federal and state treasuries would rise to more than $125 million annually by 2020. In addition, it found that second-order effects would increase US manufacturing by some $258 billion annually by 2020. And these estimates pertain only to shale—not to biofuels, oil shale, gas-to-liquids, use of compressed or liquefied natural gas, or coal-gasification-to-liquids. Just imagine the potential economic growth awaiting us if all these elements of energy independence were included in economic forecasting.[12]

Exporting LNG. A bonus play in energy independence is to facilitate the export of natural gas, in liquefied form. The international market for LNG is large and growing, and there is a significant price disparity between natural gas prices in the United States and prices in Europe—with the latter more than twice the US price—and Asia—where the prices are almost five times the US price.

Our free-market system and virtually unlimited capital can make us a leader in this international market without driving up the price of natural gas at home. Investments could be made in pipelines to bring the gas to the shoreline, liquefaction plants, and shipping—all opportunities for additional American job creation. And, as with increased oil production, with LNG production there would be an immediate favorable impact on the nation's balance of payments.

Less expensive electric power. A second bonus effect of increased gas production, mentioned in the McKinsey study, will be to lower the cost of electric power generation in the United States and to reduce overall carbon emissions. The impact has already been felt as utilities have begun shifting to lower-cost natural-gas-powered electricity generation. This trend will continue as coal-fired power plants are gradually shut down or refitted to burn natural gas. And this benefit, in turn, as noted by the McKinsey and IHS studies, incentivizes energy-intensive manufacturing industries. But also, it encourages the relocation here of industries from overseas. Already there are reports of European heavy industry relocating to the United States to take advantage of the cheaper energy and natural gas here.[13]

In sum, aiming for Energy Independence Plus offers America an incredible bounty of accelerated economic growth and job creation, and a sure path to reversing the "inflection point" discussed in Chapter 4, all without reliance on war as an engine of change and prosperity.

IMPLEMENTING ENERGY INDEPENDENCE PLUS

Implementing Energy Independence Plus is essentially a matter of federal leadership: announce the goal, and then establish the incentive programs to achieve increased production and exports.

Exploitation of petroleum and natural gas on federal lands should be expedited. Export permission should be granted for the export of US-produced crude oil; we will soon be producing above the point of our own needs. Increased exports of natural gas should be approved, and the approval process should be streamlined. Natural gas liquefaction plants should receive expedited environment permitting. The Renewable Fuel Standard should be retained. An "open fuels" standard should be adopted to break the grip of the big oil companies on the service stations and allow free competition among fuels at the pump, including methanol, ethanol, and compressed and liquefied natural gas.

In fact, almost all the agencies and bureaus needed to implement this strategy are in place, from the Departments of State, Interior, Agriculture, and Energy down to the Environmental Protection Agency. Some additional staff and administrative support will be required to facilitate faster permitting for projects. Small government grants and large federal loan guarantees could be made to encourage startup of commercially mature but currently difficult-to-initiate projects like gas-to-liquids and coal-to-liquids conversion plants. Greater interagency cooperation on promoting energy production—for example, among various agencies in the Departments of Commerce, Interior, and Agriculture—will also be required. Much emphasis is already on the table for improving America's manufacturing sector for export; using these agencies to increase America's energy output—also for export—could provide a substantial boost for business development, infrastructure, and employment.

But the challenge is less administrative and financial than it is a matter of sound policy choices, and the politics of making them. Climate change is a very real problem—probably the most fundamental of the challenges we face. The transportation sector is the nation's second largest contributor to greenhouse gas emissions. Energy Independence Plus explicitly acknowledges that we will continue to rely on fossilized carbon in transportation for many years to come. Indeed, that is precisely the prediction of the Energy Information Administration in extrapolating current policies. To deal with climate change, we need to move away from fossilized carbon as a fuel as rapidly as possible. But there are some 250 million cars and light trucks on the road today, as well as heavy vehicles and aircraft using petroleum-based fuels. Replacing this inventory will take many years, even under the most optimistic scenarios. This poses a significant problem, but at the same time provides the crux of a solution. We should make the most of our hydrocarbon resources now while concurrently establishing stronger incentives to move more rapidly and completely away from fossilized carbon and into renewable fuels and electric power in the future.[14]

Helping us craft this balance between the demands for economic growth and energy and the need to deal with climate change will be the environmental movement, one of the largest and most influential of the many movements and nongovernmental forces in the nation. Without the support of the environmentalists, there will be no Energy Independence Plus. With their support we can have both Energy Independence Plus *and* global environmental and climate leadership.

Environmentalism in the United States began as early as the 1800s, with the aim of conserving natural resources and our American heritage, including fisheries, forestry, water, soil, and wildlife. But the modern environmental movement began in the 1960s with concern over air and water pollution. The first Earth Day in 1970 captured the attention of tens of millions of citizens. Rachel Carson's book *Silent Spring*, first published in 1962, became the touchstone and rallying point for environmental awareness and activism. Major new organizations, such as the Natural Resources Defense Council, Friends of the Earth, and the Environmental Defense Fund, took their place alongside older organizations, like the Sierra Club and the National Audubon Society. The movement was effective in forcing attention on and urging resolution of egregious environmental problems, including acid rain, and the pollution of the infamous Love Canal. Partly due to its own success, the passions of the environmental movement have cooled. It takes an issue like the Keystone XL Pipeline, a project designed to bring carbon-intensive tar-sands oil from Canada into the United States—and epitomizing the deep conflict between efforts to secure greater energy security and efforts to deal with climate change—to provide the focal point for reenergizing the environmental public.

Winning support for Energy Independence Plus requires a grand political compromise between, arguably, two of the most powerful interest groups in America, the oil lobby and the environmentalists. It is a contest that, unfortunately, also aligns along the partisan divide between Republicans and Democrats. It could be seen as a fight between those who want to increase the production of liquid fuels and those who want to protect the environment, or between those who deny climate change and those who recognize its great dangers. Without political leadership, it could provoke the kind of gridlock that has characterized the approval process for the Keystone XL Pipeline.

But in fact, this is the very crux of developing a new strategy for America. It is both possible and necessary to push for Energy Independence Plus now, in the near term, and at the same time take the global lead in phasing out carbon fuels and reducing greenhouse gas emissions. Uniting these two seemingly divergent aims, and the forces behind them, could provide an incredibly powerful boost to American leadership and influence worldwide, for it will provide not only the increased hard power of a reinvigorated economy, but also the soft power gained by a demonstration of the effectiveness of the American political system and global leadership on the climate issue.

Crafting this strategy requires a grand political compromise. This compromise needs to address three issues. First, as explained above, it needs to address how to expedite the increased production and exportation of liquid fuels and natural gas. The oil and gas industry, and the energy sector in general, along with much of the investment community, will be strongly in favor of this plan. The environmental community will be strongly opposed. So the second issue that needs to be addressed is how to minimize potential environmental damages as energy production is expanded. This second issue is important not only because of the need to win the support of environmentalists, but because it is the right thing to do for our common good. The third issue will be how to provide the economic incentives that will phase out reliance on carbon-heavy fuels in order to reduce the greenhouse gas emissions driving climate change.

Minimizing the potential environmental impact of increased hydrocarbon production can be achieved through a variety of policy, budgetary, and regulatory actions. Additional environmental clean-up funds could be allocated, and environmental oversight at the state and national levels could be expanded. The oil and gas industries could be required, through legislation, to adopt a self-regulating framework, as the securities industry was in the 1930s.

The simplest and most effective means of phasing out fuels with a heavy carbon footprint would be through a straightforward carbon tax, complete with scheduled biannual or triannual increases. As taxes increase, consumers, and hence vehicle manufacturers and the entire fuels industry, will have progressively greater incentive to shift to more environmentally friendly fuel. The tax could be collected at either the retail or wholesale level. As a benchmark, a tax of $25 per ton of carbon would be expected to add about 21 cents to the cost of a gallon of gasoline, well within the range of price fluctuations on gasoline; at this level, it would provide approximately $25 billion of additional revenue annually. One advantage of the tax, as compared to the proposed cap-and-trade legislation defeated in 2009, is that it would generate additional revenues.[15]

The question facing the United States is whether within our political system we can come to grips with the policy challenges entailed by these proposals, and resolve them. The conventional wisdom says, "No, this is too tough. The groups engaged are too powerful. The political conflict will be too great." But this view can be proved wrong: both sides in this debate have something to gain. The oil industry and its affiliates, including biofuels, would receive much greater government support in production and marketing. The environmental community would get adoption of carbon pricing and real action in dealing with climate change.

It will require adroit political leadership to broker the compromise. But there are many variables available to the mediators: the federal lands to be opened; the manner of expediting approvals for exploration, construction, and export; new and more stringent environmental mediation measures; the initial value of the carbon tax and its stepped rate of increase in the years ahead; how its revenues will be used—and more. And managing opposing perspectives of different groups in such a way as to best achieve the public interest and highest common good is precisely the virtue of our democratic system.

It isn't simply about compromises between rival interest groups; it is really about the future of America—economic growth, a long-term perspective on the challenges ahead, and America's security and future strength. The American oil and gas industry, as well as the biofuels industry, can readily accept that increased production of fuels would restart the American economy and boost America's strategic power. This connection is harder for environmentalists to accept. But they must recognize the imperative of America's economic revitalization. The aims they seek for the environment cannot be attained with a weakened, divided

America that must turn inward to cope with continuing political disarray. Instead, both sides must agree on a long-term strategy, a strategy that incorporates compromises on the immediate goals of both sides, but for the purpose of reaching a higher good for all.

Adopting Energy Independence Plus with a carbon tax could give us full US energy independence in seven to ten years, as well as a reinvigorated America economically and a powerful position in global climate leadership. This is the right way to reverse the inflection point and head in a positive direction once again. Already some of my "centrist" friends, like former White House chief of staff Mack McLarty, are arguing for some kind of compromise; he calls for launching a broad-based discussion about America's energy priorities and policies.[16]

There are alternatives to this approach to economic growth and a recovery from the inflection point, of course. For one, placing a real focus on the nation's housing problems, by enabling homeowners to refinance underwater mortgages to current market values, would be a major step in a positive direction. Such measures have been blocked so far by those fearing they would adversely impact the financial institutions holding current housing debt. This problem could be worked through, of course, but attempting to do so would involve a politically charged minefield of blame and gains. Another approach would be infrastructure funding. But achieving a significant infrastructure fund has also been impossible in the current partisan atmosphere.

Other alternatives include putting greater emphasis on privatizing science and commerce in space, or renewing our focus on improving US export competitiveness by strengthening US manufacturing technology, and simply waiting for the psychological trauma of the financial crisis to fade. And, in the longer term, there is much to be gained from new policies and emphasis on education, to restore to the United States the advantages in the workforce that it once held. These ideas are not new, and some efforts along these lines are underway now, with positive but limited results. None of these alternatives, however, is as promising for the country in the near term, strategically or economically, as adopting Energy Independence Plus, and coupling it with a carbon tax to give us a reinvigorated economy plus global climate leadership. And with the resources gained through economic growth under this strategy, each of these other alternatives can be more intensively pursued.

CHAPTER 6

New Tools for a New Era

The United States has a wide array of tools necessary for strong diplomacy and global leadership: great diplomats, a strong military, and effective representation abroad; a legal and ethical framework for foreign policy; and relatively well-funded economic assistance and development programs. Many of these tools are carryovers from the Cold War, a time when we needed a strong military force structure and a nuclear "triad" of manned bombers, intercontinental ballistic missiles, and ballistic-missile-firing submarines. Some of the tools, such as Special Forces and economic sanctions, were sharpened considerably in the post–Cold War period. The bottom line, though, is that we need some new tools for a new era.

The post–Cold War environment has continued to evolve since the early 1990s. Some small countries are growing rapidly in population and political power. Trade everywhere is growing—even with former Cold War adversaries. International capital flows, concerns for food security, and China's fierce quest for overseas sources of energy and minerals have driven development in Africa and South America. The old Cold War paradigm of "at least he is our dictator, not their dictator," is over; people in most developing nations expect economic development and more open, democratic, and honest government. Countries formerly behind the Iron Curtain, even though relatively developed, have the same needs for honest government and economic growth and development.

In the aftermath of World War II, the United States struggled with how to use its newly created nuclear weapons to assure its security when it no longer possessed a nuclear weapons monopoly. Eventually, America's strategists recognized that although nuclear weapons provided the power to deter, to threaten, and possibly to stabilize, they could not replace the role of conventional armed forces in demonstrating "presence" and commitment. Nor could they be used very well to fight terrorists, provide peacekeeping and peace-enforcement, occupy territory, seize terrain, or overthrow a country's government.

Similarly, the growth of economic interdependence within the global economy calls for a rethinking of the basket of tools we use in advancing American interests. Economic interdependence impairs the effectiveness of both nuclear threats and conventional military action against major opponents; economic sanctions are also less useful when we are confronted by major powers that are well-integrated into the global economy. As we are discovering in the Ukraine crisis, in an era of global economic interconnections, the imposition of sanctions can be self-deterred, because such sanctions often bounce back on those who impose them. Though targeted sanctions against individuals or individual institutions may avoid some of the drawbacks of the broader sanctions, we need a more powerful form of economic leverage—leverage that is positive rather than negative.

In working with companies in Africa, Asia, the Middle East, and Eastern Europe, I have often recalled the advice of Lebanon's prime minister, Rafic Hariri: work the economy—or, as he put it, "You have to start with economic rights." In other words, create meaningful employment opportunities. Ever since World War II, the United States has tried to do this for people and nations around the world. The State Department has placed increased emphasis on development in general, and in particular on "economic diplomacy," helping US companies gain contracts and sales abroad. In some cases this strategy has also reinforced US exports of our manufactured goods.

But experience over the past twenty years in global economic growth, as well as our own need to promote peaceful development abroad, shows not only that these tools are complex, and often not well-coordinated, but also that they need updating to keep up with new opportunities and realities. Some twenty-four different federal agencies are involved in the development assistance effort. Their programs often have conflicting objectives. Much could be done to make the US assistance programs more efficient and effective. The Quadrennial Reviews of Diplomacy and Development, initiated in 2009 under Secretary of State Hillary Rodham Clinton and US Agency for International Development (USAID) Administrator Rajiv Shah, have aimed to bring greater focus to US government assistance and development efforts, as well as strengthening US diplomacy.[1]

USAID has some excellent programs to provide vital assistance to certain countries in infrastructure, health, agriculture, and other sectors. Much of the assistance is in the form of humanitarian relief. Other assistance is technical in nature, contracted for delivery by nongovernmental and private voluntary organizations. In some cases infrastructure work is funded. Spending on foreign assistance can be controversial at home.

In 2013, I visited USAID efforts in two African countries, where some remarkable Americans were busy helping to provide electricity, health, and nutrition to citizens. One of these programs ran into the hundreds of millions of dollars annually; it was for electric power and road construction and paving. Proud of their efforts, and eager to justify their programs, one of the young administrators asked me, "How can we get more publicity at home for what we're doing here?" I had to explain to her that, actually, getting publicity isn't always a good idea. "Our folks in Arkansas," I said, "would like some of that road construction money right there at home, as well as help with the electricity grid." The generosity of the American government and the selflessness of our public servants abroad in helping other governments and peoples are always heartwarming. But in many cases, there may be other ways to help.

As one student of US development assistance noted in 2013 Senate hearings, "at a time when most low-income countries are growing quickly and receiving windfall gains from resource discoveries, demand for traditional grant aid will be diminishing. . . . What countries want, and where the United States is really best placed to help, is with other types of development finance: debt, equity, venture, and other kinds of patient capital that can leverage private capital and be deployed for long-term development."[2]

In 2003, the United States created the Millennium Challenge Corporation, which provides grants and loans to specific projects in developing nations, and to lower middle-income countries, in order to reduce poverty, providing they can establish government programs to improve the transparency, honesty, and effectiveness of their governments. This program was originally intended to push many billions of dollars of development into infrastructure in these countries, based on their commitment to free markets and democratic governance, without regard to their priority in US foreign policy. Twenty-six countries have been helped to date, and a number of others have received "threshold funding" to help them design qualifying programs. Although the programs typically run for five years, positive impact was quickly noted, as countries such as Yemen and Niger worked to improve governance simply to qualify. Thousands of farmers, many kilometers of roads, and hundreds of educational facilities and sanitation systems have been built.

In practice, however, Millennium Challenge has proved more difficult than anticipated. First, the level of funding has been lower than expected, due to the government-wide effort to reduce US budget expenditures; instead of the anticipated $5 billion per year, annual program appropriations in recent years have averaged a little less than $1 billion. Only a quarter of the funds are available to the lower-middle-income countries, making it much more difficult for such countries to win programs (or, as they are called, compacts). Programs to improve governance take longer to design and implement than expected, and there is also backsliding and failure. Measurements of success and long-term impact have been difficult and somewhat controversial. Though the program has not yet met its lofty aims, it remains an important tool of American diplomacy.[3]

Many countries, especially US allies in Eastern Europe and other middle-income states, are left out of many of these programs. These countries fall into the gap between the most needy countries chosen for economic assistance and ordinary trading partners and allies. Yet these nations are sometimes at the very nexus of the destabilizing competition redolent of the Cold War. At the time of writing, Ukraine is the most obvious case in point. Its economic dependencies on Russia have created vulnerabilities that have been exploited in repeated crises since 2000. Bulgaria and Romania have also found themselves at risk, despite being members of the European Union.

Desperate for economic development and jobs, these countries often succumb to aid and investments with obvious strings attached. Major investments by large corporations are helpful, but only under the right conditions and with the right payoff for the host nation. Too often, these investments are somewhat exploitative in nature, demanding concessions on taxes and other matters in arrangements that actually take advantage of the host government's weaknesses. Loan guarantees can sometimes be helpful, but more than half a century of loan-guarantee experience with development finds them also inappropriate in the cases of greatest need. The State Department's Global Partnership has been a good step, but experience has shown that other alternatives are needed.

We need a more powerful means of bringing resources abroad to back entrepreneurial talent. We have recognized this need for years, and in response, the concept of microfinance and various other methods of extending credit financing, loan guarantees, and insurance for exports have come about. The Export-Import Bank of the United States and the Overseas Private Investment Corporation provide loans and loan guarantees to back US businesses abroad. These agencies are actually profitable, and they return their earnings to the US Treasury. But they usually back the more established firms.

CREATING A SOVEREIGN WEALTH FUND

The next logical step for the United States would be to create what is known in the investment world as a "sovereign wealth fund." This type of fund would provide equity investments into US companies, joint ventures, and host-nation entities. These investments would go to create businesses and profitable infrastructure, without requiring payback, and would come with management or management assistance and oversight. This funding would be "risk capital." The fund could retain and reinvest its earnings, or could return earnings to the general US Treasury. The concept behind the fund would be to use its equity to secure debt financing through large banks and international institutions, such as the World Bank; securing the debt financing for major projects typically requires a substantial equity investment—as much as 30 to 50 percent, depending on the risks associated with the project.

A US sovereign wealth fund would be able to undertake significant equity investments that the private sector alone might find too challenging. If the United States had such a fund, it could invest abroad in development projects, earning returns that would ultimately accrue directly to the US taxpayer in financial terms, as well as indirectly, through improved regional stability. The fund would operate on a for-profit basis, using resources raised by the US government, pursuing investment objectives approved by the US government, and operating not in competition with the US private sector, but to lead, shape, and reinforce private-sector efforts.

Sovereign wealth funds are not a new idea. Countries as diverse as Norway and Kazakhstan have used earnings from the sale of oil in this way, placing the funds not into their treasuries along with general revenues, but into state-managed investment funds. The earnings are then invested for profit at home and abroad. The United States could do the same thing with the some of the additional revenues generated by our pursuit of Energy Independence Plus.

A US sovereign wealth fund is not without questions, issues, and controversies. Among them would be how the fund would be resourced and governed, how its investment objectives would be determined, how much risk it should take on, whether it would compete with and drive out private funding, how its profits would be disbursed, whether it would drive out small or large firms, whether it would inhibit or enhance host-nation development, and whether it would subject the United States to criticism abroad.

In this case, the sovereign wealth fund would be resourced by some of the additional tax revenues yielded by greatly expanded US oil and gas production. It should have primarily a strategic purpose, and only secondarily a financial purpose. That is, its investments should be directed toward countries whose economic development offers high-priority payoff to the United States, such as improved regional stability, conflict avoidance, and reductions in terrorist recruiting, as well as more general humanitarian and economic benefits to the population there.

Here is the most compelling logic: rather than, say, sending hundreds of millions of dollars of military assistance training into a developing country in order to promote stability, why not bring in US capital and management to spearhead development and infrastructure projects? In 1996, instability was rife in West Africa, particularly in Liberia; later, the same was the case in Sierra Leone. In an effort to assist African countries, the United States created the African Crisis Response Initiative—training battalions of soldiers in a number of African countries so that they could serve in peacekeeping missions in neighboring states. The cost ran into the hundreds of millions of dollars, and, while necessary at the time, resulted in more "militarization" rather than in more economic development. If we have the resources available to invest proactively, to create employment and an economic future, we may be able to dispense with some of the military programs that we have relied upon. Of course, the sovereign wealth fund's aim would be to invest profitably, but by using US government resources up front, to lead private investment and debt into strategic countries. USAID is working towards this.

Simply put, after the controversies are taken into account, there remains the need for the United States to engage more constructively abroad in today's more risk-averse capital environment. There is no reason that US engineering firms, for example, cannot be resourced to compete for projects in Africa or Asia, when firms from Asia can come into even the United States to compete for projects here with financing from their own governments.

In fact, the United States works with a small venture fund today, called In-Q-Tel, which is technically independent but operates under a contract with the Central Intelligence Agency. In-Q-Tel supplies start-up funds for intelligence-related technology companies, helping them commercialize to provide products back to US government agencies. As we ramp up energy production across the United States, couldn't we ask our oil producers who are working on federal lands to pay a few dollars extra into a US sovereign wealth fund that could be used to promote for-profit development abroad? Such a project would extend US influence around the world and promote broader US goals of human dignity, employment, and responsive government.

Such a fund could even help at home to break through Wall Street's current allergy to bolder investments, if it was properly directed. One problem the wealth fund would address is the broader commercialization of US-government-sponsored technologies, particularly those technologies which can reduce greenhouse gas emissions and help us adapt to climate change. Even though our national labs and agencies have a mission to commercialize the technologies they develop, this is a tough problem, and fraught with hazards. Small teams often try to take such technologies out of the labs only to founder in the so-called "valley of death," the gap between first investments and development and subsequent major investments leading to large-scale marketing and sales. If a US sovereign wealth fund was available, it could help fill in this gap. This same problem even afflicts larger companies. One company I'm associated with received hundreds of millions of dollars of government support over a period of several years for its research and development efforts in energy, then had to sell its technology, which was fully functioning, to a private overseas company for less than ten cents on the dollar—to be placed into service in China. This technology could have been retained in the United States if a sovereign investment fund had existed to support it.

Incidentally, many American states, including my home state of Arkansas, have recognized the need for something like a wealth fund to provide grant money to assist major business development and investment. In some cases this might be an appropriated fund drawn from general revenues; it other cases it is money raised by special bond issues. Governors and their staffs often have extraordinary development resources at their disposal. We need to provide our national government with a comparable tool, especially for use abroad.

BETTER USE OF THE PROFIT MOTIVE

A sovereign wealth fund could not only drive strategic investment in infrastructure and necessary industrial projects, but could also accelerate the emergence of stronger, more entrepreneurial economies. On one of my business ventures, I went to Africa to study a for-profit agricultural development investment handled by an Israeli firm for the Angolan government. The Israelis had examined commercial fruit, vegetable, and agricultural product sales in Luanda, Angola's capital and largest city. Because of Angola's oil-dominated economy—it exports almost 2 million barrels per day—Luanda is also one of the world's most expensive cities, and most of its food was imported from Portugal or elsewhere in Europe.

After assessing demand, the logistics of delivery, the costs and methods of processing, and the soil and climate, the Israelis created agricultural villages. Individual farmers were responsible for their own production; processing and movement to market was handled by a community-owned effort. This type of village followed an Israeli model called a *moshav* (as opposed to a *kibbutz*, where everything is collectively owned and managed). The farmers in these villages, who were demobilized former soldiers, were learning farming, sending their children to school, going to school themselves at night, and hiring others to help them manage their efforts. The individual farmers were earning approximately $400 per month, and the villages were spreading prosperity in rural Africa.

The model provided rural development and job creation—for profit. And as the Israelis explained to me, the profit motive was essential in keeping all the parts of the system working and improving. Free enterprise works. Why couldn't the US government do that? I thought. Rather than just underwriting US firms exporting manufactured goods, like the US Export-Import Bank, or loaning money to US companies that work abroad, like the Overseas Private Investment Corporation, or paying local contractors to build infrastructure, or teach farming techniques, as USAID sometimes does, why not co-invest with governments or local organizations for profit, and then keep our share of the profits in-country, reinvesting it to keep the benefits there? Countries in Africa are resource-wealthy and are blessed with energetic, ambitious businessmen—but they are short of the specific financial and technical skills necessary to interface with international capital markets and large corporations. These skills were precisely what the Israeli program was building—not through a business school, but through hands-on labor and the profit motive.

The United States certainly has the entrepreneurial talent to make such programs work. Across America in every city are struggling entrepreneurs seeking their fortunes and their families' futures in alternative energy, finance, farming, housing, construction, real estate, and retail. Sometimes they are young people looking for their first traction in the job market, but they are often well-educated, capable people in the midst of their careers. Sometimes they are experienced, competent, and ambitious people who have simply been made redundant at home because large US corporations have flattened their organizations, or because they have suffered from the continuing slow growth of employment here. This is talent that is needed at home, of course. But opportunities for small businesses in many sectors and most communities have been difficult to develop since the financial crisis.

This is precisely the kind of entrepreneurial talent needed in developing nations. For years we have too often tied US assistance to the procurement of US products; now it is time to link US assistance to our most important asset—our people—and fund them to go abroad, to teach, learn, and help promote economic development there. Using a sovereign wealth fund for resourcing, the United States could promote joint venture, for-profit economic development programs—businesses—that could reach out to our entrepreneurs and draw them into business and project development abroad with benefits, both there and for the United States. In the process we would accelerate the rapid development of free-market practices and entrepreneurship in Africa and promote more rapid and stabilizing economic and political development.

BROADENING OUR ECONOMIC FOCUS

We now have a much better understanding of how to use these new tools to create strategic impact, as well as for profit. A World Bank–sponsored study of how nations grow, led by Nobel Prize–winning economist Michael Spence, offered key pointers in this regard. The study showed that nations in poverty can achieve economic growth by paying attention to market dynamics, but they have to have strong, pragmatic support from government. It is the government that sets the right policies and invests in the right infrastructure, including transportation and education. As Spence noted in his book *The Next Convergence*, "effective governments and markets are both essential. . . . They are not in competition with each other but rather complementary parts of the process."[4]

Spence's work on economic development strategy provides a powerful argument for a more strategic approach by governments. Simply providing the right legal framework, with minimal actions or interference by governments, is inadequate. The role of governments is critical, not only to provide the right legal framework, but also, pragmatically, to identify and incentivize development in the sectors of greatest strategic advantage for each country. This is not central planning; the price signals from markets are essential. Nor can the economy be rigidly controlled.

Rather, it is an emphasis on seeking and strengthening precisely what economists since David Ricardo, the early-nineteenth-century economist, have cited—comparative advantage. It emphasizes a pragmatic, market-based approach that concentrates on enhancing sectors that offer potential advantage and can draw in foreign and domestic capital. International consulting firms, such as McKinsey Global Institute, are being hired by governments to provide advice on economic growth strategy—and tie it to specific investment objectives, firms, and timelines.

While US missions abroad often cooperate with host-nation governments in their economic forecasting and development efforts, we need the sharper, more pragmatic focus of Spence's approach in our work with foreign governments abroad. Working to counter corruption, and introduce more market-oriented legal structures and new techniques is inadequate.

In countries throughout Eastern Europe, US guidance has been all-important in setting government directions and priorities, yet in the immediate aftermath of the Cold War, the Chicago school of economics seemed to influence all advice, and governments found themselves cutting taxes, privatizing formerly state-owned industries, and then facing charges of corruption and economic crimes. The "leave-it-up-to-the-market" approach of the 1990s undercut the legitimate and even essential role of governments in these countries, that of protecting the common interests of their citizens. In Eastern Europe, hasty privatization of state-owned assets created "oligarchs," not economic progress, and today most of these countries are struggling with economic stagnation. They are also suffering crises of government legitimacy as a consequence.

Although the United States' role in emphasizing the rule of law and private enterprise has been crucial, we should have the skills and tools to help governments identify strategic sectors and formulate pragmatic approaches to strengthening these sectors. It's always possible to hire a McKinsey to help the country formulate and implement an economic development strategy—but we should also develop and use our own insights and experiences, so that we can most constructively engage and assist national governments.

Incidentally, Spence's general approach can be applied to advanced developing economies like that of the United States. This is, after all, what virtually every US state tries to do in its own economic development efforts. Spence's analysis aligns with many others in concluding that the US financial sector has been overdeveloped, that the information revolution enabled the easy outsourcing of jobs, and that infrastructure—including R&D and transportation—has suffered from systemic underinvestment. Most importantly, Spence concluded that macroeconomic policies—working toward price stability and a balanced budget—are simply inadequate. He stated that, in addition, public-sector investment and adaptive policy reform are important elements in facilitating structural change and in sustaining growth and employment.

Spence is just one of many economists who advocate for something more than fiscal repair to achieve the kind of long-term, sustained growth necessary for the economy. That group includes other Nobel Prize winners, such as Joseph Stiglitz, Paul Krugman, and Alan Blinder. This approach to economic development, of course, is precisely what the United States will be undertaking by aiming for Energy Independence Plus and global climate leadership.

The three new tools I am suggesting—a US sovereign wealth fund, public-private partnerships for profit abroad, and US-led strategic planning for national economies—could provide tools for the US foreign-policy toolkit that have long been missing. However, like all new tools, we will have to learn when and how to use them. They are meant to be "market-extenders." That is, the tools can enable the United States to lead abroad in economic development in ways that have not heretofore been possible, particularly in cases where the private economy and US investors are unwilling or unable to participate. The effort to create "earnings," "cash flow," and "profits" will not only produce results in specific projects, but will accelerate the accretion of business skills and job creation and growth in these economies.

If the United States uses these three tools, it can stake out an economic role in the world that gives it more influence in the era ahead. This role is different from what can be achieved through most current forms of assistance, or through NGOs—however well-meaning those forms of aid may be. These new tools, linked to for-profit investment strategy, will be more rewarding (and more salable to US voters) than our current programs and more constructive than militaristic approaches to foreign policy.

The tools do involve "encroachment" by government into private economies, but these encroachments fill in the missing elements required to promote proper economic development, just as Ike's creation of the military-industrial complex took us through the Cold War and brought vast benefits to the civilian economy. Where private capital will not venture because the risks are too high or the benefits not easily demonstrated, a sovereign wealth fund can take the lead; where skills and business development are weak, US for-profit partnerships with locals can impart these skills; and where economies are struggling with competing and conflicting demands, growth strategies can help prioritize efforts, strengthen pragmatic policy developments, and reinforce government legitimacy.

CHAPTER 7

Answering the Strategic Challenges

With the reinvigorated US economy surging on more rapid exploitation of energy resources, a carbon tax, and new economic tools added to the already impressive array of US diplomatic, economic, and military resources, the United States will be able to address the long-term challenges it faces. But addressing long-term challenges successfully requires substantial public support, not just smart policies. Strategies must be simple, consistent, and easy to understand. Truly effective strategies are simply "absorbed" into the public and private conversations. They become fundamental, like the strategy that guided the United States during the Cold War: deter nuclear war; contain Soviet expansionism. Although there was lots of discussion about the ways and means, and strong criticism as the war in Vietnam failed, the strategy itself was so clear that it enabled the country to meet its challenges and emerge as the sole superpower.

Today—as we are bringing the troops home—can we now find another motivation, rather than imminent conflict, or a hateful enemy, to help all Americans work together for our long-term well-being? Can we craft a simple idea, so clear and compelling, that it can frame the problems we face, put into perspective the acute crises that inevitably arise, and guide us in dealing with the serious long-term challenges we face?

Today, "Energy Independence Plus," and a carbon tax for global climate leadership, can serve as the basis for a new national strategy. Frame it as an "Energy-Enabled Strategy for Growth, Responsible Development, and Security." "Energy-Enabled," certainly, because the innovative production of more liquid fuels from petroleum, biofuels, natural gas, and coal resources is at the heart of this opportunity. "Strategy" because we must think long-term; we recognize that if we can deal with deep, long-term challenges to our values and national well-being at home and our national interests abroad, we will also have the strength to deal with the acute crises that inevitably arise. Economic "Growth," derived from greater energy production, provides the job opportunities Americans seek, as well as both resources and leverage to address the major challenges we face. "Responsible Development" based on a progressively escalating carbon tax will help us transition away from hydrocarbons. We must use these hydrocarbon resources intensively now, to get the American economy back on a high-growth path, but we must move beyond these hydrocarbons as rapidly as renewable electric-power and electric-vehicle technologies can be scaled. And we need to assist other nations in the same transition. "Security" is what we are aiming for—security from terrorists, cyberwar, financial calamity, an adverse realignment or collapse of the international system, and the profound dangers of global climate change. Let's call it "Energy-Enabled Strategy," or "E2S," for short.

E2S is a long-term strategy aimed at securing our future; it labels no enemies or adversaries, and is directed against no other power. Instead it aims to promote a better future for all Americans, and in so doing, to enable America to continue its historical leadership role in helping others. It is a very simple theme, easily understood. It is based on genuine partnership between America's strong private sector and the US federal government, using private enterprise where market-based incentives can deliver private and public good, and using government to provide the strategic direction, services, and regulatory functions that the private sector itself cannot deliver.

E2S: ADDRESSING THE FIVE KEY CHALLENGES

Using American strength gained through Energy Independence Plus and global climate leadership to face the long-term challenges described in this book reverses the inflection point. It requires little other than the concert of policies, some new tools and perspectives, and adroit leadership; the other resources are readily available. No sons or daughters need be sacrificed; there need be no cramping of civilian consumption, or vast national sacrifices. The political trades needed to achieve energy independence and carbon pricing, and to enhance investments in national infrastructure, are readily available. Stopping the bleeding in residential real estate is more difficult, but in a recovering economy may be possible. Renewed robust economic growth will do much to reduce the passions of partisanship, as well as to raise American prestige and influence abroad. Taking the lead in dealing with climate change through a carbon tax will drive American technology forward and also provide America enormous influence extending well beyond this issue. This bipartisan solution will buttress worldwide appreciation of our political strength. Enhanced economic tools will put us back on a fair footing with our competitors abroad, further enhance our own economic performance, and even promote more effective measures to deal with climate change.

Having reversed the inflection point, we can work on the long-term challenges, so long as we continue to place short-term crisis response in the proper perspective and stretch the public dialogue toward the longer term—and so long as we use our government, instead of treating it as our enemy. Here's how energy independence, global climate leadership, and the new economic tools outlined in Chapters 5 and 6 can help to address the five key challenges described in Chapter 3.

Terrorism. The current US counterterrorism strategy, published in 2011, is well-balanced across the immediate and longer term. It prescribes adhering to US core values, including respect for human rights; encouraging responsive governance; maintaining respect for privacy and civil rights; and balancing security with transparency—though Edward Snowden's disclosures have certainly tarnished the US reputation in some of these areas. The strategy also is strongly supportive of working with our allies, including building various security arrangements and leveraging multilateral institutions. It prescribes using every element of our government, and getting the balance right between immediate action and long-term progress.[1]

But what we can improve is how we undercut the conditions that provide fertile ground for terrorist recruiting and organization. In this regard, three sets of policies need to be followed: first, we need to deny terrorist organizations a free "home base" where they can train, organize, and equip themselves with newer technologies and techniques; second, we have to undercut the sectarian motivations and rationale for terrorism; and third, we must promote fair, sustainable development in the ungoverned or poorly governed areas.

Conventional US diplomacy, partnerships with the host nations, and law-enforcement and military antiterrorist efforts are well-advanced. However, a significant challenge remains in ungovernable areas. It is precisely here that the new US tools and the resources derived from energy-enabled growth can prove extremely valuable. These economic tools, coupled with technologies in distributed energy, communications, and education, will enable the United States to work with host-nation governments to extend the reach of development into the hinterlands and to bring economic opportunities to millions of isolated and potentially disaffected individuals who might otherwise be vulnerable to terrorist recruitment. Under this plan, they would be more able to participate in their own economic and social advancement, and their vulnerability for recruitment by terrorist groups would be reduced.

In a host-nation development plan, profit-motive-based developments would bring in US entrepreneurial talent to partner with host-nation businessmen, and sovereign wealth fund monies would seed major efforts and attract the follow-on private and international funds necessary for project completion. US leadership in global oil and gas markets, and our excess production capacity, would provide us with additional non-defense resources needed to address the terrorist threat. Perhaps equally important, US production capacity could reduce the power of some exporters to arbitrarily hike prices; oil and gas price volatility should decline significantly as increased US production came on stream.

Still, the United States must understand that part of the solution is intrinsic to the Muslim world. Until Muslims understand that terrorism is both the murder of innocents and suicide, both of which are deeply condemned in Islam, terrorists will still find recruits. The United States must not be hesitant or afraid to talk about "Islam" with Muslim countries—terrorism is an ideology, and we and our partners must share efforts to defeat it as an ideology, just as we defeated communism.

Cybersecurity. Although there is an increased awareness and emphasis on cyber-threats today, and the Cybersecurity Command is operational and protecting the US government, our economy is still acutely vulnerable. The private sector and free markets will not provide us with cybersecurity. Individual businesses are reluctant to admit and report data breaches; the bad publicity associated with the reports may be more damaging to their business than the cyber-losses themselves. Some cyber-losses are covered by insurance, and any businessperson is going to weigh the cost of the fix versus the cost of the insurance to cover potential losses. But, ultimately, the social costs of cyber-theft and cyber-attack are felt throughout the systems that make up our economy, and these collective costs and vulnerabilities far outweigh the potential for individual harm. Accordingly, the US government will have to take a larger role.

The least of the problems is to know what to do. Dealing effectively with the threats will require at least three sets of measures: the first set is technical, the second is related to the domestic end of the problem, and the third is an international matter. On the technical side, the vulnerabilities of the Internet itself need some correction. First-generation efforts are capable of enabling large Internet service providers to scan incoming and outgoing streams of digits for "malware." These efforts have not reached maturity. Some cyber-crime, cyber-espionage, and cyber-strikes can still get through these gateways. And no matter how vigilant, any software-enabled security effort can, theoretically, be defeated by other software, whether implanted from within or passed through in disguise. So these efforts will need to be ongoing.

The nature of the Internet protocol could also be changed to require positive identification and authentication of senders for each message. The current Internet protocol was created for constrained data capacity, but today's Internet has more than sufficient bandwidth to accommodate full return addresses and to require multiple "hand-shakes" between the senders and intermediate routers. These changes should be sufficient to further stymie efforts to disguise the origin of messages. Technical solutions would do a great deal to reduce crime and espionage on the Internet.

Within the United States, however, efforts to promote the identification of users are highly controversial and strongly resisted. Regrettably, major privacy forces are mobilized by any suggestion that Internet users should be identified. The needs of privacy are likely to be further compromised moving forward. Business councils and trade associations, and the firms they represent, will need to accede to a greater degree of federal involvement in cybersecurity. Federal standards for security must be established, monitored and revised where necessary, and enforced. And businesses must invest appropriately and invite federal scrutiny.

Each addressee in a business transaction represents a point of access for intrusion and disruption, so entire chains of suppliers, producers, customers, and clients must be properly protected. We need to think of the Internet as being less like a playground and more like a rail network. It has become essential to trillions of dollars of business; it's not unreasonable to secure it. You and I don't get to run our own trains on the railways; nor should people be able to interfere with the smooth and safe operation of the Internet. Only the federal government is adequately resourced and informed to provide this foundation of security, though private firms will continue to screen for security and implement private efforts.

This teamwork between the public and private sector will need to be legislated, because it involves sensitive commercial considerations, such as intellectual property protection, as well as personal privacy considerations. In addition, it will be costly; businesses will have to pay for their own protection and, in fairness, also pay for the federal protection and oversight required. Business investments in cybersecurity are, of course, expensed and tax-deductible. However, partial financial compensation could be provided through "tax-expenditures," such as accelerated depreciation or tax credits for enhanced cybersecurity investments.

In the area of critical infrastructure, such as the power and petrochemical industries, the United States must team with operators in order to sanitize and safeguard our systems. The first order of business is eliminating the "cyber-bombs" that may have already been implanted in industry hardware or software.

In addition, the US government needs to impose certain controls and obligations on the public Internet and its service providers. Among these are the obligations to note, investigate, and take action on reported cyber-crimes, including identity theft, with an obligatory linkage to federal cyber-crime task forces. There should also be a "quick disconnect," such as a national security override that could be selectively or fully implemented to isolate the US network from overseas networks, or to isolate certain regions to prevent contagion of an attack. These are simply the normal measures that should be available to a sovereign state. We have something analogous in the Emergency Broadcast System (now called the Emergency Alert System), which was put into place for TV during the Cold War and is still in use for civil emergencies.

On the international level, the United States needs to work assiduously for the right kind of international protections, including the rights of governments to search and challenge the sources of suspected cyber-crimes. The United States has been understandably reluctant to do this because it has used the Internet in its own offensive national security efforts. Indeed, some believe that many of the vulnerabilities of popular software programs are the result of collusion to allow openings for National Security Agency intrusion and offensive action. However, we ourselves are the most vulnerable of nations. And in attempting to preserve our options for offensive use of cyber-espionage—where we have arguably the most effective and sophisticated capabilities—we have left ourselves exposed defensively. Given the vulnerabilities of the United States, and the difficulties in detecting and tracing attacks, the defense is more important than the offense. We should be using our leadership to create stability in international networking, because we will benefit from this stability more than any other nation—and Americans will need to have more trust in their government to do so.

The more difficult problem is political. We need greater public trust in government, willingness to invest in security, and international partners. Moving forward with E2S will address some of these obstacles. An improving economy should reduce political division, provide business and government with increased resources for investments in cybersecurity, and enhance respect for the US government abroad. More fundamentally, we cannot succeed in E2S unless we strengthen cybersecurity.

Finance. The essence of the financial challenge is the protection of the US economy from an additional collapse, and to assure this protection at a time when the country has less capacity for additional debt than in 2007. The Financial Crisis Inquiry Commission did not complete its report until after the Dodd-Frank reform legislation that was directed at fixing the crisis had already been passed. An important next step is to review the full expression of Dodd-Frank, after it has emerged from its regulatory interpretations, in order to measure its effectiveness against the factors that caused and spread the crisis, and to test it against other possible challenges to the financial system. Does it actually provide sufficient protection against excessive debt and regulatory failures to prevent the next financial crisis?

We should also establish a series of financial-preparedness exercises, involving Treasury Department, Federal Reserve, and banking officials, to bolster their ability to work through challenging scenarios that could take place in the future. After all, challenges to the banking system, whether caused by some vast, unanticipated cyber-failure or a systemic failure in some other country, should be anticipated, war-gamed, and prepared for, just like the challenging scenarios that the Departments of Homeland Security and Defense prepare for as a normal part of training. The

Financial Stability Oversight Council, as well as the Consumer Financial Protection Bureau, should issue their own periodic systemic reports and assessments, as well as addressing whatever specific issues arise.

In this assessment, certain regulatory loopholes engineered into Dodd-Frank should be reexamined. Principal among these is the naked credit default swap. Allowing private markets in these major transactions precludes transparency and efficiency. It also increases the exposure of the both individual institutions and the system to risks that are not well-understood. Another issue that has not been resolved has to do with the standards applied by credit ratings agencies; asking "Who grades the graders?" is critical in assessing systemic risks in debt markets. A third issue is compensation: "clawback" provisions should be incorporated into all short-term compensation that flows from initiating long-term debt, in order to align the incentives structure with the performance of the underlying debt product. A fourth issue is the scale and nature of financial firms' participation in agricultural and mineral commodities markets. Although these markets appreciate the participation of outsiders, as it provides a certain degree of liquidity, market supply is, in the near term, fixed, and additional demand quickly inflates prices. This effect was particularly noticeable in the summer of 2008, when crude oil prices spiked to the $150 per barrel range. Working these issues in the highly politicized and heavily lobbied Washington regulatory environment will be exceedingly difficult, but it must be done.

These difficulties raise the larger issue of whether the regulatory approach itself is viable. When it was conceived in the 1930s, financial and security-industry regulation was in essence a trade-off. These sectors were rescued during the Depression by government action; in return for restricted competition and continuing government protection, they accepted restrictions on their activities. That consensus disappeared decades ago; today it is completely gone.

Sitting with a major bank a few months ago, I listened as smart young bankers discussed current banking regulations and restraints and plotted new financial "innovations" to work around them—I wondered whether this was the beginning of Financial Crisis II. Rather than shrinking big banks under Dodd-Frank reform, we have enshrined them as "systemically important financial institutions"—in popular lingo, the ones that are "too big to fail"—and then tried to prescribe a path for dismantling them in a crisis to keep them from causing serious systemic problems. Given the scale and incentives of the financial system, it is natural to expect its participants to continue to find ways around regulatory restrictions. They will generally seek combinations of greater leverage, less transparency, and faster payouts—all the tendencies that regulation is attempting to corral. When these tendencies are combined with the complexities of large modern banks, and the propensity for large financial institutions to "capture" their regulators, legitimate doubts can arise about whether regulatory reform, in and of itself, is sufficient to provide the financial system and our economy with the stability we need.

If regulation itself is inherently inadequate, then perhaps the implications of the increasing financialization of the US economy should be more deeply considered. The financial sector has assumed an ever larger role in the nation's GDP, and the nation relies on ever-increasing amounts of debt. Should these trends be reversed? Some believe these trends lead to instabilities in the financial system as well as to disproportionate increases in income and wealth at the top of society. Gerald Epstein, codirector of the Political Economy Research Institute at the University of Massachusetts, for example, said in an interview that "at the macro level, because of instabilities and distorted incentives, financialization can undermine the overall growth and development of the economy so that in the end, the real opportunities for investors and workers—except perhaps for the very wealthiest members of society—are diminished."[2]

While some economists continue to argue strongly that minimally regulated access to credit is essential to economic growth, and that financial innovation is critical in moving the economy forward, the weight of recent experience suggests that concerns about excessive financialization have some merit. Policies to address these concerns could include taxes on financial transactions; reductions or termination of favorable tax treatments for certain classes of dividends and capital gains (why should "unearned income" be taxed less than income earned by work?); requirements for greater reserves to back up debt; efforts to have originators of debt retain some liability, even as it is securitized and sold; measures to increase market transparency; and measures to reduce or delay executive compensation. In general, these measures would seek to redirect banking efforts away from trading and toward their original functions: providing credit for operations, production, expansion, and innovation in business enterprises.

The tendency toward financialization is a global phenomenon, so solutions must be sought not in the United States alone but globally. As global capital flows, especially from Europe, contracted during the financial crisis, the growth of global financialization eased, but renewed growth will once against accelerate it. Much discussion is directed toward the International Monetary Fund (IMF), whose policies promoting the liberalization of financial markets to encourage freer capital flows are believed to have promoted financialization. The United States has extraordinary influence within the IMF, but of course its influence also reflects the policies and pressures within the US political system, and so will be reflective of overall financial system reform efforts at home. As US efforts to stabilize the US financial system are implemented, parallel measures will also be needed internationally.[3]

Dealing with the global financial system probably requires reconsideration of some of the basic precepts that have driven modern economies. Free capital flows from the United States to emerging markets can be simply overwhelming; they can inflate and then depress such markets. Efficient market theory assumes that markets are transparent, that market participants are rational, and that each participant has all available information. It assumes that markets will find equilibrium at full employment, and seeks to minimize government's role. There was even an assumption that adopting these policies would promote income equality—while in fact the opposite seems to be the case. These tenets of the so-called neoliberal school are the foundations of globalism—yet these theories are seriously questioned in economics today.

US economic growth derived from energy independence and global climate leadership can provide a substantial margin of safety for the economy. Additional investment in oil, gas, and biofuels—and later investments incentivized by the carbon tax—will drive investments in infrastructure, ancillary services, and new technologies; soak up much of the liquidity parked today with the Federal Reserve; and raise overall demand in the economy without incurring additional federal deficits. More robust economic growth will help break the current cycle of business stock buybacks, reduced investments in new product development, and white-collar downsizing—all of which have helped to promote financialization as a reliable source of profits.

China. Our aim should be to bring a growing China smoothly and peacefully into the international system, and to have it shoulder responsibilities commensurate with its wealth and power and congruent with the values and aspirations of other nations. In approaching this effort, the United States must look beyond historical parallels in dealing with China.

In scale, China's economic growth, and the challenge it presents, is far different than that of Japan in the 1980s. The population of Japan was only one-third that of the United States; China's population is more than four times greater than the US population. The rise of Germany in the early twentieth century is sometimes cited as a parallel. But this comparison is also inadequate. Germany was an ascending power willing to wage war to gain a more powerful international position. It never had the population or industrial capacity of the United States; nor did it have the strong leadership backbone of a single political party, above the rule of law, as China does. China is not the new Soviet Union, economically isolated from the larger world, either. China is larger than 1980s Japan; potentially more powerful than pre–World War II Germany; and more economically integrated with the United States than the Soviet Union ever was during the Cold War. The United States cannot rely on historical precedents in approaching China.

For over two decades, the US strategy toward China has balanced on a knife-edge between a policy of "engagement" and a policy of "containment," a version of the policy the United States followed toward the Soviet Union during the Cold war. Since the dispersal of the democracy protesters at Tiananmen Square and other actions across the country in 1989, US military-to-military engagement was suspended, and the US-China relationship cooled. In 1996, the United States sent two aircraft carriers toward China during a period of rising tensions associated with Chinese missile "tests" directed toward Taiwan. China has been denied the right to import various high-technology defense-related goods, despite growing Chinese trade, and US weapons were sold to Taiwan. When I visited China Aerospace Science and Technology Corporation, the Chinese combination of the US Air Force Space Command and NASA, its chairman complained that the United States would not sell communications satellite technology to China. True. The technology was among numerous restricted items controlled under US International Traffic in Arms Regulations. China interprets all of these measures as evidence of US containment policies.

The Obama's administration's pivot to Asia, announced in late 2011, was perceived by China as being directed against China. The military component of the US policy of "rebalancing," for example, has been greeted with skepticism in China. The United States has not only shifted forces but also updated defense treaties as part of this pivot. The United States has also initiated the Trans-Pacific Partnership, an effort to create a large free-trade zone encompassing nine countries, but excluding China, and has endeavored to participate far more actively in various regional summits and dialogues. Still, the United States also created a US-China Strategic and Economic Dialogue, high-level meetings designed to discuss and resolve key issues and to promote stronger relations between the two countries.[4]

However, as China has pressed its territorial claims on the South China Sea and East China Sea more forcefully, including suggesting an old claim for Okinawa, the United States has been drawn more directly into controversial regional issues. The South China Sea is an important international waterway; to the north, the United States has a long-standing defense treaty with Japan, which has been the anchor point of US security policy in the Pacific since the end of World War II. In the past four years the United States has found itself courted by China's neighbors, who are anxious for reassurance and support against what they see as China's excessive claims—but also wary of provoking China. The United States, in turn, has provided regional allies much of the requested support, while it also has pressed for international dialogue on these territorial issues. Nevertheless, China perceives the United States as the ultimate source of resistance to its expanding claims, particularly as China's military declarations raise issues of access to what we believe are international waters.[5]

China, in turn, has attempted to engage the United States directly and more exclusively, calling for a special bilateral relationship in which the two nations would "remove obstacles" and "accommodate each other's interests." Although China may have more benign motives, many see such proposals as a continuation of a long-term Chinese policy to pave the way for its geographic expansion of presence and influence. As the United States becomes engaged more directly and places greater emphasis on its relationship with China, we may subject ourselves to greater pressures in regard to China's expansive territorial claims. It will be in China's interest to force us progressively to choose, on issue after issue, between China's favor and the interests of our allies and China's neighbors in the region. "China is larger and is far more important; why would the United States not side with China?" is a familiar question in China.[6]

The United States, of course, will aim to deflect these direct choices into multilateral forums in which we can reinforce established law, procedures for dispute resolution, and the larger international structure as it has emerged since World War II. We see value in structure and procedures, in fulfilling commitments to allies, and other obligations. China, in contrast, believes that this structure and those obligations are heavily tilted against it.

In the end, the degree to which we can manage a balanced relationship with China, directly and bilaterally, depends on the relative strengths of the United States and China. Restoring vigorous US economic growth, fixing our unemployment problems, refurbishing our infrastructure, improving US public education, and demonstrating that the US political system works are all key elements of establishing the proper foundation for US-China relations. In addition, US allies in Europe are also critically important. If we can establish firmer collaboration with Europe on vital macroeconomic, technology transfer, and investment policies, we will be in better shape worldwide, and particularly with respect to the weight we can bring to our relationship with China.

E2S—the vigorous pursuit of US Energy Independence Plus and global climate leadership—provides the foundation for all of this, for if we become the world's leading energy exporter, as we strengthen our economy we will create a more balanced US-China economic relationship. We will also then be able to reduce Europe's susceptibility to Russian energy-based intimidation. Already, Chinese firms are combing the United States, seeking opportunities for long-term purchases of exported US natural gas—and these are contracts we should welcome. Using a US sovereign wealth fund, or something similar, to fund infrastructure and energy developments in Eastern Europe and Africa would also restore balance to what has been a largely unchallenged Chinese economic penetration of resource-rich African countries and a prospective move into Europe. And if we can combine our increasing exports of petroleum products and natural gas with environmental leadership in a grand political compromise toward climate change, we will have further enhanced the United States' credibility and its power to deal with other vital issues.

The military dimension will also be important in shaping the outcome of the US-China relationship. By 2019, Chinese military strength—including aircraft carriers, land-based aviation, submarines, and ballistic missile technologies, all of which could be directed against US aircraft carriers in the East and South China Seas—will prove a formidable technological challenge for the US armed forces. Even without any military confrontation, the balance of power in the western Pacific will shape the Chinese predisposition to push, threaten, or compromise. The Chinese must understand that their expanding military capabilities have consequences both regionally and for the United States. For example, the United States must not rule out the need to strengthen its ballistic missile defense as China rattles its intercontinental ballistic missile capabilities. And we should be very candid in explaining this to the Chinese.

We should also anticipate further Chinese efforts to enlist Russian military cooperation, not only in offsetting US power in the

Pacific, but also in seeking diversionary efforts toward Europe. We must help China understand that a closer, more assertive alignment with Russia will provoke the United States and our allies into a response. The military component of US rebalancing must continue to be resourced, but not so narrowly focused on the Pacific as to invite trouble in Europe or elsewhere. E2S will provide the robust US economic growth needed to support continued investments in US defense capabilities and will augment US moral authority through powerful action to address climate change, which is plaguing China's image and air as well.

Through our own economic growth, continued military strength, and unflagging diplomacy, we must work to transform what China perceives as its interests—such as expanding its territorial reach—into broader interests as a global leader that will secure China's future in the global community. China should take pride that these territories—Taiwan, for example—have built strong economic bonds with China. Taiwan's current course of development certainly poses no threat to China. China must be helped to understand that its neighbors' actions on security are largely reactions to China itself. We should promote the opposite: helping China to bask in the economic achievements of its neighbors, and to be proud of its own soft power as its neighbors freely seek the advantages of closer ties.

Americans, in turn, must accept that China has a right to its own system of government and its own standards. China's governance is for the people of China themselves to determine. However, on the matter of human rights, the United States should insist that China, like every other member of the United Nations, abide by its commitment to the United Nations Universal Declaration of Human Rights. In this respect, the United States must both be insistent in each meeting and consistent over time. We must help China see a distinction between its principle of "noninterference in internal matters of other states" and respect for basic human rights and dignity. (For our part, we must also demonstrate our own acceptance of the responsibilities of global leadership. For example, the United States should move forward on matters such as the International Criminal Court and the United Nations Convention on the Law of the Sea.)

The United States need not acquiesce in China's current view that China will inevitably replace the United States as the world's leading power. The United States and China have disparate systems. But US natural resources, the rule of law in the United States, the United States' entrepreneurial culture, and its vast head start in higher education and science are strong factors in our favor. People from all over the world want to live and work in the United States, including wealthy Chinese. They seek the protection of our laws and the individual freedoms they find here. China does not provide these same attractions. E2S can provide us the confidence that opens the door to long-term, peaceful, and constructive work with a stronger China. We should welcome and encourage Chinese leadership on "soft-power" issues like humanitarian assistance, or cooperation to prevent piracy in the Indian Ocean. At the same time, we must work early and in private to head off confrontations such as future territorial disputes. We should routinely anticipate China's future territorial moves—China's demands are consistent—and we should seek to engage China in constructive exchange about these security issues before confrontational decisions are made on both sides.

US and Western leaders must also resist the tendency to overestimate the power of their personal diplomacy and relationships. China will gratefully accept any concessions offered in the name of building personal relationships, but it is unlikely to reciprocate. China operates on its long-term interests—not on personal friendships with foreigners. This might seem obvious, but the pattern of Western diplomacy indicates again and again that our elected leaders are vulnerable to foreign suasion. I saw it repeatedly in the

Balkans and elsewhere: emissaries of popularly elected governments generally played for the headlines from a visit; no one wanted to be seen as failing, and so there was a tendency to "give away" too much and seek too little. China's leaders understand and exploit this tendency.

In our dealings with China we need an assertive, patient diplomacy backed by a strong and growing US economy; supportive allies; and a US military capable of standing toe-to-toe with China in a crisis. With these pieces in place, we can succeed in helping China assume its rightful place as a global leader, and perhaps an equal of the United States, in a manner that promotes global prosperity and stability. But it is clear that diplomacy and military capabilities alone will be insufficient to manage the relationship with China; we must continuously demonstrate our power and competence in technology, job creation, and economic growth, and the strength provided by hydrocarbon exports and strong policies to reduce carbon emissions does exactly this.

Climate change. US adoption of a carbon tax, albeit in conjunction with the push toward Energy Independence Plus, will establish the United States as the global leader in tackling climate change. It will constitute a powerful symbol, set a strong example, and serve to reduce the continued growth of demand for petroleum. Nevertheless, due to rapid economic development elsewhere, global demand for oil will rise in the years ahead—from a total demand of approximately 90 million barrels per day to perhaps 120 million barrels per day over the next fifteen years. Increased US production will delay expanded production of "dirtier" oil elsewhere, while the carbon tax will spur other nations to take similar measures to reduce their demand for carbon-heavy fuels. The theme would be "Hydrocarbons now, as we transition beyond hydrocarbons."

US exports of liquefied natural gas to China will be especially valuable in the near term, as it will offset the use of coal for electricity generation, resulting in large net reductions of carbon emissions. Think of it as the Chinese buying "clean air" from us, rather than exporting their pollutants to us. Crafting the move toward full energy independence, and at the same time initiating carbon pricing, would provide a platform for global US leadership. We can scale the price as necessary to move us along the path to much greener energy at a rate that is technologically, economically, and politically feasible, and use the US carbon price to drive international action.

In terms of public diplomacy, America's elected leaders should treat actions to deal with climate change at home and abroad as opportunities for job creation, economic growth, and profit—not as costs to be avoided. In the calculation of short-term profits, any investment is an expense affecting the bottom line, stock values, and even executive compensation. But investments in measures to alleviate climate change are investments in the future. In this sense they are similar to investments by earlier generations in canals and highways, and perhaps even more powerful, since they are usually derived from new technologies and processes.

Increased investments in alternative forms of energy will also be essential. This starts with the administration's current efforts to penalize carbon dioxide emissions from electric power generation. Natural-gas-fired generation provides a substantial improvement over coal, but still emits greenhouse gases. Wind and solar power are increasingly price-competitive with current coal and natural-gas-fired generation. But these, of course, are no replacement for liquid fuels for transportation in the near term.

Solar power is an excellent case study in how to view policy changes on such issues. The United States was an early leader in this technology as a result of President Jimmy Carter's initiatives to reduce our dependence on imported oil. But inconsistent public policies and the high prices of small-scale solar technologies scuttled the early solar efforts in the United States. Germany's strong leadership in renewable electricity pricing, reflected in the European Union's renewable energy goals over the past decade, brought solar power leadership to Europe for a time.

But now China, hungry for new sources of power, has made investments to scale in solar technologies and—especially in the wake of the financial crisis—has captured worldwide production. Western investors are wary of competing with Chinese production today—they sense that the money and expertise that would need to be committed would be overwhelming. As a result, the future of photovoltaic technology may well lie with China, and with it, the promise of reliable, increasingly economical, clean electricity. Solar developers and installers in the West are taking advantage of the low-cost solar panels that China is making, and solar power is at "grid parity" or below in some locations, especially during peak pricing periods. ("Grid parity," in simplified terms, means that the cost of the power generated by an alternative energy source is equal to or below the cost of power generated by more traditional sources.) With the manufacturing comes the innovation, and that innovation is likely to be vested in China. It is an opportunity perhaps lost to the United States.

Still, there is a large number of related technologies in which the United States has every opportunity to compete. This includes everything from improved insulation to utility-scale battery storage, more efficient cooling and heating systems, so-called balance-of-systems elements in solar installations, photocell plating, and perhaps more revolutionary solar-electric materials on the nanoscale. These and other more revolutionary technologies need the right market conditions to draw in the investors and customers necessary to scale. Bringing these technologies to market will create hundreds of thousands of new jobs and billions of dollars of profit.

For now, the United States is very much alive in this field. The squabbling over tax incentives for solar, amounting to a few bil-

lion dollars per year, seems silly from the perspective of the potential gains from leading in these new technologies, as well as from
the perspective of the ultimate improvements in energy production that could be made. If Americans can agree politically on
E2S—a "Hydrocarbons now, as we transition beyond hydrocarbons" compromise, we will avoid many of these self-defeating political disputes.

The case for dealing with the threat of climate change has to be
made in many ways. We can start by citing the following: the future damages that can be avoided; the reduced insurance and remediation needs in business and agriculture; the new technologies
and new industries that could emerge; the increased employment
in new professions and skills that pursuing these new technologies
will create; and, ultimately, the fact that we will be working to
bring about a better and more peaceful world. The Obama administration's 2014 National Climate Assessment is a very good start
at seizing and retaining public focus on climate issues, but needs to
be followed up by the full panoply of studies, hearings, public an-
nouncements, visits, and a more or less continuous campaign to
keep climate change "front and center" in the media.

In a busy twenty-four-hour media environment, climate change
is often submerged by news stories with more immediacy: crises
abroad, domestic economic news, sports, and celebrity gossip.
Climate change is a continuing, creeping process, and one with
very little money behind it at present—no sports wagering, movie
contracts, or stock market leaps. All of this tends to make it slip
away from public consciousness. Nevertheless, the case for dealing with climate change can be made with clarity, and we should
expect our leaders to make that case clearly and often enough to
penetrate even the cluttered media environment.

Pursuing progress in dealing with climate change is not at all
inconsistent with pursuing energy independence. In fact, the robust economic growth associated with energy independence, and

the explicit political trade-off it entails with the oil and gas industries, provides us with a long-term, phased approach to moving away from a fossil fuels environment and bringing forward new programs and new technologies to continually reincentivize investment and economic growth. And it is this path, in particular, that will assure critical American leadership in dealing with climate change.

APPLYING AMERICA'S STRENGTH—E2S

A rejuvenated America will have important work to do in the world. It is a world in which America's newfound currency of energy exports, global climate leadership, and new economic tools will be particularly useful.

Europe. Europe remains the part of the world most closely linked to the United States in history, culture, and values. After the Cold War ended, the United States, as part of NATO, led efforts to restore peace and stability in the Balkans and to promote NATO's enlargement to encompass East European nations that were formerly dominated by the Soviet Union. The European Union, with its twenty-eight members, has a population some 50 percent larger than that of the United States, and a gross national product larger than our own. We are bound to Europe not only through NATO but also through many other international institutions, as well as through business investments and deep personal relationships.

Today, Europe is facing multiple challenges, ranging from substantial difficulties recovering from the financial crisis to the inevitable economic and cultural pressures accompanying the assimilation of immigrants from the south and east. The cohesion of the eurozone has been severely tested by repeated crises involving sovereign debt and banks in Europe's southern tier, especially in Greece and Cyprus. Germany has emerged since its reunification in 1990 to become increasingly powerful economically, and its voice has dominated reactions to the financial crisis. Its export-driven economy has profited from the common currency, and even from the weaknesses of some eurozone countries. European defense expenditures have been insufficient to provide Europe with significant expeditionary military capabilities, and its economic security is heavily dependent on Russian natural gas supplies. In the Ukraine crisis, breaking as this book goes to press, Germany has, thus far, played an ambivalent role, torn between its economic relationships with Russia and its commitments to international law and obligations.

The United States needs to strengthen its economic and political ties to Europe. Under E2S the United States could supply Europe with a significant portion of its future natural gas needs, which would be liquefied in the United States and shipped to regasification facilities already being built in some European countries. These exports could be particularly helpful to the Baltics and Germany.

The United States should also use its new economic tools to promote economic development in Eastern Europe. These countries, including Bulgaria, Romania, Slovakia, and the smaller countries of Kosovo, Macedonia, Albania, and Bosnia, have been particularly impacted by the European Union's austerity effort and overall economic climate. Job creation in these countries has been weak, and their economies are struggling under the privatization of old, state-owned assets, new EU regulations and requirements, and the practical difficulties of making young democracies function effectively. These relatively weak coalition governments have well-educated populations, but they need real economic development strategies, robust foreign direct investment in their agriculture, raw materials and infrastructure, and partnerships with US entrepreneurs. In Eastern Europe, a US sovereign wealth fund;

"for-profit," US-led public-private partnerships; and greater commitment to strategic economic development could be extremely useful.

Russia. Under President Vladimir Putin, Russia has become increasingly focused on its use of energy, energy technology, raw materials, and arms exports to extend its reach. Ukraine is the latest victim of Russian pressure, but all around its periphery Russia is continuing to seek customs unions, border-defense and air-defense cooperation, and electric power grid relationships that extend Russian leverage over its near neighbors. Its use of natural-gas cut-offs to threaten Ukraine has been particularly aggressive—and effective in the near term.

Russia is also aggressively pursuing nuclear energy and securing uranium supplies in an effort to position itself as the next-generation energy leader. Its support of Iran's Bushehr Nuclear Power Plant, a project that has drawn much ire in the West, is simply part of a larger Russian play. On one of my trips to Mongolia in 2010, the capital city's business set was abuzz with reports that Putin had threatened Mongolia with doubling the price of the jet fuel and diesel Mongolia purchased from Russia if Mongolia failed to turn over an old uranium mine. The development of the mine had begun in Soviet times, but the incident showed the importance of energy issues to Russia's current goals.

Russia recognizes the possibility that at some point it may have to deal with greatly reduced Western and Chinese demand for its petroleum and petroleum products. Ending reliance on carbon-based fuels will be a painful transition for Russia—and this is real leverage that the United States, in becoming the global climate leader, will hold over Russia. Sanctioning Putin for transgressions in Eastern Europe may be a near-term necessity, along with other measures to restore stability in Ukraine, but we will achieve far more by strengthening the economies of the former Iron Curtain countries using our new economic tools. Simply put, the new element of deterrence for Eastern Europe is not so much military force, but economic progress. Nations that are thriving economically, as a result of strong investment and progressive policies, would be far more capable of resisting the intimidation, threats, and blandishments of Russia, and helping Russia to reform itself, than they would be if they were struggling and vulnerable. Our NATO allies would be well-advised not only to reinvigorate their own military capabilities, but also, and perhaps even more importantly, to invest constructively in the teetering economies of Eastern Europe.

Stronger US leadership in world energy markets will prevent Russia from raising prices for natural gas to Europe and for oil globally. Meanwhile, the United States should work to block and deter Russian interference with its neighbors, through the use of sanctions and whatever other means should become necessary. As the United States pursues stability in the nations beyond NATO's borders, we must try to offset Russia's normal paranoia and help it to understand that this provides the best basis for peace, security, and prosperity for all—it is in no way an encirclement of Russia. These actions must be seen as a temporary exception to a more fundamental effort to pursue dialogue and cooperation with Russia, seeking areas of agreement, working to deepen ties, and continuing to pursue ways to engage Russia's citizenry as directly as possible.

Western Hemisphere. Through the North American Free Trade Agreement (NAFTA), Canada, Mexico, and the United States form a free trade area of 470 million people and $19 trillion. This area is larger in population and much richer than the European Union. Together, Canada and Mexico are the United States' largest export markets. Cross-border supply chains, investments, and travel have all boomed.

Still, Mexico has grown at a slower rate than some other Latin American countries. Its energy sector, in particular, has been choked by government ownership and lack of investment. Mexico's president, Enrique Peña Nieto, has begun to reform the energy sector in Mexico, opening the door for private-sector initiatives and investment. His plan should result in a new surge in Mexican oil and gas production, especially as new US technologies are brought to bear on Mexico's rich hydrocarbon resources. Together with Canada, the United States and Mexico have the potential to dominate global hydrocarbon markets during the coming decade, and perhaps for several decades to come, an incredible turnaround that will bring increased prosperity to all three nations.

Security challenges remain in the region. These challenges include continuing problems with drug trafficking up from the Andean Ridge countries of Colombia, Peru, and Bolivia, the infiltration of terrorist groups into Mexico, and the continuing hostility of Venezuela. Russian arms sales to Venezuela resumed in 2010. A constant factor in the region is the Chinese presence, in the form of growing investment and interest. But the new US economic tools should enable US entrepreneurial talent and larger private firms to engage in joint ventures in more strategic investments in the area.

Africa. Africa's size (some 4,600 miles from north to south and about the same distance from east to west at its widest point), along with its rapidly growing population (more than 1 billion people), make it the world's next growth engine in the decades to come. Its diversity of resources and markets, its rich minerals endowment, and its rapidly developing governments make Africa a prime investment and development opportunity. Petroleum is everywhere, offshore and onshore.

Mali, South Sudan, Niger, Kenya, Uganda, and Mozambique, hardly thought of as oil giants, are being combed by explorations and oil-field developments. Tanzania is counting on rich deposits of offshore conventional natural gas as well as of minerals. Ethiopia and South Sudan are sitting on billions of barrels of oil and are capable of becoming energy-producing giants like Nigeria and Angola. Other African countries, including Zimbabwe, are mineral-rich. Despite continuing political and economic development challenges and multiple conflicts, economic growth in Africa, driven principally by the commodities boom, averaged 5.6 percent per year from 2002 to 2008. This growth slowed during the financial crisis, but it picked back up in 2012, reaching 5 percent. This growth potential makes Africa a more suitable target for many investments, and an increasing number of infrastructure and African investment funds have been formed, especially in Europe, to take advantage of opportunities there.[7]

Over the past decade, China has taken the lead in pushing the development of petroleum and other resources within Africa. Chinese state-owned enterprises, and even Chinese army engineering units, have pursued pipeline and highway development, exploration for oil and gas, and favorable concessionary relationships with local governments in Africa, with little regard to the impact of these efforts on the welfare and governance of local populations. Chinese companies have a notorious reputation in Africa for being quick on the investment arrangements but unwilling to hire locals and to incorporate local capabilities in their projects. Still, Chinese investments have been welcomed in many African countries as the most rapid means of generating economic growth and export earnings. According to Chinese sources, China may put up to $1 trillion into projects in Africa through 2025.[8]

The United States has run increasingly sophisticated development programs in Africa through USAID. In addition, with the formation of the US Africa Command, US military capacities are increasingly deployed to train local African forces, and occasionally to conduct direct action against terrorist groups deemed capable of threatening the United States. New economic tools, such as a US sovereign wealth fund, US-led public-private partnerships, and broader economic strategies for each country, could further speed economic development, guard against further terrorist encroachments, and enable the United States to assist more effectively in the emergence of these developing and mostly democratic states as responsible members of the global community. US global climate leadership could encourage more rapid development of renewable and sustainable energy and more responsible economic growth.

It could be especially valuable to use these new tools to expand the production and use of biofuels within sub-Saharan Africa. These new economic tools and technologies would help to place the United States on par with China in competing for economic access and influence on the continent. And by so competing, greater US-China cooperation might come about within the region.

Central, South, and Southwest Asia. US energy leadership and new US economic tools will also prove extremely valuable in dealing with Central, South, and Southwest Asia. Using our own sovereign wealth fund and for-profit public-private partnerships will accelerate US economic penetration and leadership throughout this area.

India and Pakistan both have vast coal resources that could be turned cleanly into fuel and power with available US commercial technologies. Afghanistan's rich mineral resources are already being exploited by Chinese firms; new US economic tools could enable American firms to compete on an equal basis, a factor of increasing importance as US troop strength is drawn down. These increased economic linkages will give the United States greater power to balance, conciliate, calm, and draw these countries together.

Elsewhere in the region, Sri Lanka, an island nation of 20 million, is pressing forward with development. Bangladesh has established its reputation as an extremely low-cost manufacturing center, but also as a probable terrorist haven. Myanmar, the latest nation in the region to become partially democratic, has benefited from Chinese attentions to its key location: the new Myanmar-to-China natural gas pipeline is now fully operational, and a new port has been built in Myanmar to support Chinese needs there. But the generals still in power in Myanmar have wisely opened the country up to Western trade, tourism, and investment, too. They seek a counterweight to Chinese influence, which new US economic tools under E2S could enable us to supply.

In Central Asia, countries such as Kazakhstan, Turkmenistan, Tajikistan, Uzbekistan, and Azerbaijan are wrestling with modernization, exploiting natural resources, and coping with various spillovers that threaten their security. From the south, there is the danger of fundamentalist terrorists spreading from unfinished business in Afghanistan. From the west and north, there is the steadily strengthening embrace of Moscow, seeking to achieve through customs, power, and military relationships an ever greater degree of control over the external and internal affairs of these countries. To the east is China. The Central Asian countries seek a lifeline to the West.

One of Kazakhstan's leaders said to me in late 2013, "You are going to be increasingly independent in energy. That means you will be less interested in us; we must look elsewhere for help." Our aim through E2S must be to create precisely the opposite interpretation: our greater independence in energy, and the revitalization of US economic growth that comes with it, should increase our capacity to engage and assist other nations, even in Central Asia. New economic tools will enable us to do this more effectively than current methods. A US sovereign wealth fund, and the ability to participate for profit in public-private partnerships and bring in plentiful US entrepreneurial talent, can work to our advantage.

Energy is the common currency of the region. Natural gas and oil, shale, pipeline, and refining capacity are required to meet the fuel needs of a growing population. Renewable electricity is being installed, but at a far slower pace than market needs warrant. Small and medium-sized US companies, struggling for resources and financing at home, could make heavy inroads in these markets, maintaining influence, assisting in peaceful development, and showing US engagement, if appropriate incentives existed.

East Asia. East Asia is currently the fastest-growing region in the world economically. The arms trade is booming in the region, as all of these nations are arming and upgrading in response to what they see as an enormous Chinese military buildup. North Korea is armed and provocative; it has nuclear weapons and long-range missiles as well as a large army, special forces, and the ability to strike and devastate much of South Korea's capital city, Seoul, with virtually no warning. The Japanese are well aware of the North Korean missile threat, but, like other countries in the region, Japan is preoccupied with Chinese actions, capabilities, and intentions. Japan has heard the tough talk about territories and sees the inexorable encroachment on the seas and airspace through which China is staking its claim to global-power status.

The United States has strong allies in the region. But as one of my Chinese friends told me, sneering, "Singapore . . . you have an alliance with Singapore?" They do not sneer at Japan and Korea. But most of the East Asian states are likely to resist polarization in a US-China rivalry. Instead we must seek cooperative relationships through constructive purposes, such as by implementing stronger policies to reduce greenhouse gas emissions.

In East and Southeast Asia, exports of refined products, and especially of liquefied natural gas, will become additional means of knitting the Asia Pacific region together with the United States. Also, the United States remains a critical market for manufactured goods from these countries. But these countries also are connected economically and geographically to China, and China's military rearmament further reduces their space. Using our new economic tools under E2S, we need to give them the economic incentives to work our global agenda, through our institutions, while we work to bring China into the global community in a more harmonious way. These new economic tools can be deployed to strengthen the economic staying power of countries like Indonesia, Vietnam, and the Philippines during China's ascent, even as we enhance US trade with China through our LNG exports.

The Middle East and North Africa. These areas will see continuing strife and struggle. The great Shia-Sunni rivalry that was revived by the overthrow of the shah and the ascension of Ayatollah Khomeini in Iran has reached a culminating point in Iran's quest for nuclear weapons. Iran is likely to end up in much the same situation as Japan—able to produce a nuclear weapon on short notice, but choosing not to do so. For Iran, this outcome provides an optimal trade-off; it allows the country to achieve maximum strategic power in the region while simultaneously slipping free of sanctions, to promote its own internal economic development, and to turn its highly talented, Western-oriented business community loose to bring in much-needed technology and capital.

Two of the states formed by the breakup of the Ottoman Empire almost a century ago—Syria and Iraq—will remain troubled for some time. Syria is the prize, caught between the two great confessions of Islam. Iraq is likely to increasingly move toward Iran and away from the United States despite the almost nine years of strong American presence. Both are likely to struggle to achieve federalist structures of some kind to ease the tragic conflicts of recent years while seeking to further exploit their hydrocarbon resources. This effort is likely to be broken down into stages, however, and this will invite meddling from outside powers and attract jihadists who are seeking to exploit violence and sectarian fears for their own purposes. Meanwhile, other nations on the periphery of Saudi Arabia will make their own accommodations to the stresses of modernization and sectarian conflict. Bahrain, Oman, Yemen, and even Lebanon will likely be adjusting government policies and powers in efforts to maintain security in their difficult neighborhood. Saudi Arabia itself will eventually transition to a new generation of leadership.

The increased US role in global energy markets will stabilize oil and gas prices. For some countries, this will be beneficial, because it will allow them to make plans for the future with greater certainty. At the same time, it will reduce OPEC's power to ratchet up prices to compensate for economic weakness at home. As the manager of one national oil company explained to me in 2013, "Our national budget is built on the expectation of $100 per barrel; we can't live with less than this." Fair enough: US energy leadership also needs prices in the $90 to $100 range to support tight oil and deep-water developments, as well as gas-to-liquids and coal-to-liquids. But we will also have sufficient market clout to dampen OPEC's ability to manipulate prices.

Even Israel, with its huge natural gas finds in the Mediterranean, seems destined to become a net exporter of energy. Israel's security barrier and continuing leaps in antimissile capabilities have done much to reassure its population of its security, as described in Chapter 2, paving the way for a possible peace agreement with the Palestinians. This may happen in the near term, or it may take another decade of maturity and stability in the region. Jordan and Lebanon will need continuing assistance from the United States, including military assistance, in order to weather the storm of sectarian strife in the region.

Across North Africa, the ripples and riptides of the Arab Spring that began with the Tunisian street vendor in late 2010 may eventually lead to stability, but it may take a decade or more, and until then the United States must stay closely engaged. Here, too, oil resources and energy will play a crucial role. Egypt's oil industry, crippled today from losses to the convertibility of the Egyptian pound, will prove a powerful magnet for stability and foreign investment. So long as the price of oil stays high enough, Libya, Algeria, Morocco, and even Tunisia will all benefit from the revenues provided by privately owned, heavily taxed oil properties.

Perhaps more than other regions, the Middle East will be affected by the drive to move away from fossil fuels, which will gain momentum in the decades to come. Already, plans are underway to lay several high-voltage undersea cables to connect vast solar arrays in the deserts of North Africa to Italy, and perhaps elsewhere, and then to the European energy grid. The specific locations and the feasibility of this project ultimately will be driven not only by economics but also by policy choices. Augmented by commercial-scale batteries capable of distributed storage of many gigawatts of power, solar energy could someday provide the majority of all power in the Middle East and Europe. Saudi Arabia and the United Arab Emirates are already invested in solar. Masdar City, a solar-powered, sustainable city, has already been established. These countries are diversifying beyond oil and oil revenues at a brisk pace.

In April 2014, a year after my first meeting with the Syrian opposition, US engagement remained ambiguous. The United States had provided some training and lethal weaponry, attempting to beef up moderate elements in the Syrian opposition. But the aid had been relatively slow in coming, and it had failed to turn the tide on the battlefield in favor of the rebels. In fact, the rebels themselves had fought pitched battles, with the hardline extremists associated with the Al-Nusra Front and the Islamic State of Iraq and the Levant (ISIL) often gaining ground and inflicting significant losses in these fights.

By this time, the Assad regime had used chemical weapons, breaching US President Barack Obama's announced "red line," but the much-anticipated US air strikes failed to arrive. First US action was sidelined by a presidential decision to seek congressional authorization, and then by a bold Russian diplomatic ploy announcing that Assad's regime would give up its chemical weapons entirely. After months of effort, the US-engineered, UN-sponsored peace talks began to take place in Geneva, with no results.

But the United States was nevertheless deeply committed to the region. US troops assured the stability of Jordan, which bore a heavy load of refugees from Syria. US troops and intelligence agencies were also training the Syrian opposition. US diplomacy was engaged throughout the region. Large numbers of troops remained in Kuwait and elsewhere in the Gulf, and the United States was providing on-station ballistic-missile defense for Israel from seaborne assets. No ground troops had gone into Syria, no Syrian targets had been taken out by US airpower, and Assad remained in power. As this book went to press, time was running out to strengthen the Syrian opposition—and doing so would seem to require providing much greater support, including effective air defenses to enable the opposition to force Assad into serious negotiations and block further Russian meddling in the region.

The United States must not disengage from the Middle East. Nor should it be perceived as doing so even as it pivots toward Asia. We should seek, however, to use diplomacy, economic power, our newfound strength in energy, our new economic tools, and military assistance, rather than the deployment of forces, in the region. Where there are terrorists, either in training or active, capable of threatening the United States, we should use direct action by small teams of Americans to strike precisely, aiming to detain, arrest, or, if necessary, eliminate them. And we cannot rule out further deployments of other US forces. The Middle East will remain a volatile region for another decade or more. Nasty surprises are possible, including assassinations, sudden regime change, the emergence of terrorist sanctuaries and training grounds, and continuing threats of nuclear proliferation. But the United States, as it reclaims energy independence and more vigorous economic growth, will be well-positioned to handle tactically whatever challenges emerge.

THE VIEW AHEAD

The well-being of the United States depends on staying engaged globally, continuing to play our role in imparting global stability, facilitating economic growth and development, and encouraging the rule of law and regimes responsive to the needs and interests of their people. There is neither safety nor security in retreat. But we must promote our interests with a different mix of instruments than in the past.

In an increasingly interconnected and interdependent world, force is a decreasingly effective means of advancing American interests. Where force has to be used, it must be used with precision; with meaningful, attainable military objectives; and directed by overriding political and diplomatic aims. The threat of force is more useful—as the Cold War proved—than its deployment. If the US sword is to be returned to the scabbard, it must nevertheless be sharp and ready, and the US shield must be strengthened and extended. There should be no giving away the US superpower influence.

But more useful still is our economic potential. We must revitalize our power in the economic sphere, winning new respect and gaining increased influence by taking advantage of our energy resources at home. A much stronger US economy, increasing leadership in global energy markets and in addressing climate change, and new, positive economic tools to export US entrepreneurial talent abroad will best serve our interests in the decades ahead.

We must take the right lessons from history—especially from our own past. As Americans, we have to use our government—it is our own creation, not our enemy. We must have a long-term vision and face up to long-term challenges. Other nations do; if we do not, we are subject to their designs, whatever our potential power. We have to lead ourselves, not wait for acute crises and times of conflict before we will work together.

Using our new economic strength and leadership in hydrocarbons, we must reinvigorate our partnership with Europe, seeking its continuing growth and its convergence with our policy aims in the important work ahead. Working alongside us, Europe can provide the reinforcing economic and diplomatic power to help manage China's peaceful rise, for example. We must work carefully to assist in the evolution of China's interests and needs so that it can assume a responsible place in the international community without war. Within North America, the Middle East, Africa, and the Pacific, the United States must strengthen economic, political, and cultural ties, helping these rising economies adapt within a global economic system. Meanwhile, we must continuously work on the environmental challenges, especially our carbon footprint, and attempt to reduce the human stresses on the planet. All of this is encompassed in the strategy of E2S.

Can it work? Can we help keep the peace, address serious issues in our grand strategy, and strengthen the global institutions and the emerging rule of law that we believe has served humankind so well? The answer is yes, but only if we strengthen our economy at home by using the natural resources available to us; tend to the long-term challenges we face, working patiently, month after month, year after year; and then use our power to adapt tactically to the needs of the moment. And all of this must be based on a return to greater trust in American government and greater harmony within our political institutions and public discourse. E2S will work if we can begin with a historic political compromise that accepts "Hydrocarbons now, as we transition beyond hydrocarbons." It is a compromise that could reconcile the ongoing conflict between the need to exploit our hydrocarbon resources and the need to face the realities of climate change. It will take skilled leadership to broker the compromise. This leadership will need to shape a greater common appreciation for America's purposes and power at home. It will also need to show why we must move beyond petroleum, natural gas, and other hydrocarbons into a fully renewable economy powered by biofuels, solar, wind, geothermal, hydro, and perhaps nuclear energy.

Will this be difficult? Yes. But dealing with tough issues is precisely the inherent advantage we claim for our own system of government—the unique ability, through informed public dialogue and representative political institutions, to compromise competing interests and find the best way forward. Dealing with energy and the environment today, we have a unique opportunity to restore confidence and trust in government as well as to create an unprecedented US economic renaissance.

If we can come together as a nation around the strategy of E2S and restart our engine of economic growth, the principles of US foreign policy will continue to serve us well. We should stand by our allies and honor our commitments; use force only as a last resort, multilaterally when possible, unilaterally when necessary; support democratic regimes and those with such aspirations; and insist that all nations, whatever their chosen form of government, respect human rights and dignity. We must also be modest in recognizing that however proud we are of our own Constitution, the precise structures and processes of democracy elsewhere will vary to reflect those nations' histories, cultures, and environments. We should use our technology and talents to promote development, fight disease, and ease hunger, bringing others in to share the burdens through alliances, partnerships, and multinational institutions. We must continue to pursue innovations with the specific tools of our foreign policy, especially in the economic development sphere, and insist on measured effectiveness of the resources thus committed.

The United States is an exceptionally fortunate nation, blessed even at a time when its relative power seems to some to be declining. We have incredible natural resources and an innovative and entrepreneurial business spirit. Over four centuries, Americans have shaped modern civilization. Today, we have the power to renew our influence in the world and reunify America at home. We need no war, or adversary. Men and women all over the world know what we stand for—freedom, dignity, opportunity—and they want us to succeed. America is needed, perhaps more than ever, to help shape the global civilization that is emerging. Our work is not yet done.

ACKNOWLEDGMENTS

This book provides a way of looking at the world, and America's role in it. In writing I drew fundamentally on the strategic outlook from my military education and experiences, and I am grateful to all those I served with, and especially the many mentors who helped me see the big picture along the way; men like retired generals Colin Powell, Alexander Haig, John Shalikashvili, Dale Vesser, Maxwell Thurman, and Rick Brown, and friends like Barry McCaffrey, Bob Scales, and especially Colonel (ret.) Roger Nye, longtime West Point professor of history.

But this book has taken me well beyond my military experiences, into business, economics, diplomacy, technology, history, and politics. I'm very appreciative to the friends, business colleagues, and family members who provided me the insights and experiences that led to this book. From the time I retired from the US Army I was treated warmly by the business community and given many opportunities to learn and participate in business.

To Stephens Group, Inc., including Jack Stephens and Vernon Weaver, as well as Warren Stephens, Curt Bradbury, Jon Jacoby, Doug Martin, and Jackson Farrow, I owe my deepest gratitude for giving me a start in investment banking. Thanks also to Don Gogel, Jim Rice, and Jim Rogers at Clayton, Dubilier and Rice, and to Goldman Sachs—Barry Volpert, Peter Weinberg, John Thain, John Thornton, Hank Paulson, John Rogers, Rich Friedman, Karen Seitz, Sanjeev Mehra, Hugues Lepic, François Valentin, Henry

Cornell, Ken Pontarelli, and many others—for letting me learn private equity (and Wall Street) from some of its founders and best practitioners, as well as providing openings into business in Europe, China, Latin America, and the Gulf.

John Borer, Ed Rubin, and Michael Vasinkevich from Rodman and Renshaw gave me the inside view of small banks and "small-cap" companies in the United States, Europe, and China. Later, David Dunn and I founded our own small bank to work early-stage companies and projects, and with Chinese friends Ying Wang and daughter Julie Xu, and partners like John Cavalier, Tom Baruch, and Joe Endoso, are working in consulting, technology, and project development, internationally as well as in the United States, chiefly in energy, but also in technology and general business development.

In the minerals field, Heinz Schimmelbusch of Advanced Metallurgical Group, Valerio Battista of Prysmian, and Stefan Messer of Messer-Griesheim helped me understand minerals, metals, manufacturing, and business from the European perspective, as well as multinational business strategies in general. Steve Feldman showed me how to take precious minerals into the financial community.

In oil, gas, and coal, I learned about upstream and downstream from Ford Nicholson, Bob Cross, Frank Giustra, Wolf Regener, Abby Badwi, Jeff Brookman, Glen McNamara, and Jack Lipinski. In biofuels and agriculture, I had great teachers in Jeff Broin, Tom Buis, Jeff Laut, Greg Breukelman, and others.

I worked on the fringes of transatlantic military and security work with John Caldwell, Christian Gravengaard, Patricia Driscoll, Marcel Boogaard, Mark Hatten, and Mark Nichols.

In technology, information, security, cybersecurity, and disaster relief, Charles Morgan, Jerry Jones, Bill Connor, Mike Steed, James Lee Witt, Harvey Schiller, Bob Marbut, Ron Chaimovski, Chip Smith, Bob Boback, Joe Grano, Terry Matthews, Craig Betts, Tom Yunck, Michel de Rosen, Ron Samuel, David Bair, and Bernie Rice all helped me move beyond my military experiences and see business leadership and entrepreneurship in action. Richard Clarke, an old friend from the Clinton Administration, has been especially helpful over the years in helping me understand terrorists, 9/11, and the intricacies of cyber warfare.

I've worked on renewable energy with Dan Juhl, Frank Epps, John Mitola, John Cavalier, Pedro Barriuso, Sean Klimczak, Jerry van der Sluys, John Callaway, Mike Garland, Bill Lese, Bruce Kelly, Hunt Ramsbottom, John and Jeff Wooley, and my son, Wes Jr.

Eytan Stibbe and David van Adelsburg brought me into Africa, impact investing, and entrepreneurship on a multinational scale. Thierry Deau has shown me how to scale in infrastructure and invest for impact. Petar Stoyanov, Stamen Stantchev, Boyko Noev, Mitko Abadiev, Cristian Burci, Mike Pochna, and many others brought me into business in Bulgaria, Romania, and Kazakhstan. Ron Meer has brought me into real estate.

In all these endeavors, my good friends Steve Bova and Jerry Jones and business partner James Lee Witt were there in Arkansas to share reflections on our respective endeavors. Tom Schueck's lessons in business were also valuable. I have learned from successes, hard times, good and bad decisions, and some outcomes less fortunate than others across more than seventy businesses with which I was associated in one way or another. I've tried to listen and learn from others' experiences as well.

I was fortunate to have a strong academic connection to the University of California at Los Angeles, thanks to Ron Burkle, Frankie Quintero, Kal Raustiala, and Alexandra Lieben, allowing me to wrestle with issues and keep up with elements of the academic community; I also received support from Susan Lemke at National Defense University.

Friends in the International Crisis Group, including George Soros, Steve Solarz, Mort Abramowitz, Louise Arbour, Gareth Evans, Tom Pickering, Chris Patten, Mark Malloch Brown, Javier

Solana, Sandy Berger, Ken Adelman, and Carole Corcoran, as well as Bob Harrison, David Sandalow, and Chelsea Clinton at the Clinton Global Initiative, John Hamre at the Center for Strategic and International Studies, and so many others, provided a sounding board for my ideas as they have evolved.

I also drew on the lessons learned from more than a decade of fairly active participation in elective politics, including a Presidential run, and from my many discussions of the issues with friends, such as former president Bill Clinton; former senator and secretary of state Hillary Rodham Clinton; Arkansas governor Mike Beebe; senators David and Mark Pryor and Blanche Lincoln; congressmen Marion Berry, Vic Snyder, and Mike Ross; Arkansas legislator John Edwards; Little Rock mayor Mark Stodola; the man who headed my own campaign, a close friend who is dearly missed, Eli Segal; and my brother-in-law, Gene Caulfield, who has been a friend and adviser for over forty years. I also would like to thank former White House chiefs of staff Mack McLarty and John Podesta; former secretary of transportation Rodney Slater; and longtime advisers Josh Gottheimer, Tom Baer, Mark Nichols, and Erick Mullen; Don Epstein—who is much more than my speaking agent; Richard Holbrooke, a man whose counsel so many of us have missed; as well as the many state leaders, elected officials, and staff members, assistants, and supporters who befriended and taught me along the way.

In working with the media I learned the twenty-four-hour news cycle with CNN, FOX, and MSNBC, all under various contracts, and also learned from Tom Johnson, Walter Isaacson, Aaron Brown, Wolf Blitzer, Roger Ailes, Davidson Goldin, Dan Abrams, and Gail Chalef, as well as through doing shows with Larry Kudlow, Erin Burnett, Trish Regan, and many others.

Obviously, whatever I took from these experiences is my responsibility alone, but I am tremendously grateful for the opportunities to learn which they provided.

In writing this book, I was fortunate to have the inspiration of friends Steven Nagourney, Hiam Nawas, David Dunn, Anne Marie Slaughter, and Alice Germond, who read drafts, provided insights and sources, challenged ideas, and helped me sharpen my themes, as well as Daniel Yergin and others who helped me marshal the evidence and strengthen my arguments.

Publisher Peter Osnos, publisher and editor Clive Priddle, project editor Collin Tracy, and copy editor Kathy Streckfus have been generous with their time and guidance and scrupulously careful in trying to help me avoid obvious mistakes in a book that tries to sweep across two centuries and cover war, peace, diplomacy, economics, business, commerce, politics, sociology, journalism and media, leadership, and strategy. Any mistakes are mine alone.

My office in Little Rock has been of great help in doing research, proofing the manuscript, and offering common sense as I've gone through multiple drafts and a hectic travel schedule; for this support, I thank Catherine Grunden, Samuel McSpadden, Sarah Stringer, Juli Wood, and Pache Gray as well as good friend and longtime travel agent Bettiane Balzano, who over many years was always able to get me from place to place on time and ready, despite a demanding calendar.

And to my family: wife, Gert, and son, Wes Jr., my deep gratitude for reading and commenting on the drafts, and especially for their support, patience, and sacrifice as I worked, rethought, and revised, and, in general, took time away from them and my wonderful grandsons, Wes and Dash.

NOTES

INTRODUCTION

1. Leslie H. Gelb, "Time to Get Tough with China?" Daily Beast, December 8, 2013, www.thedailybeast.com/articles/2013/12/08/time-to-get-tough-with-china.html.

CHAPTER 1

1. All cited by David W. Drezner in *Foreign Affairs*, "Does Obama Have a Grand Strategy? July/August 2011, www.foreignaffairs.com/articles/67919/daniel-w-drezner/does-obama-have-a-grand-strategy.

2. Ibid.

3. See the following for the reports cited in this paragraph: National Security Strategy Archive, http://nssarchive.us/; Quadrennial Defense Review, www.defense.gov/home/features/2014/0314_sdr/qdr.aspx; Quadrennial Diplomacy and Development Review, www.state.gov/s/dmr/qddr/; Economic Report of the President, www.gpo.gov/fdsys/browse/collection.action?collectionCode=ERP, www.whitehouse.gov/administration/eop/cea/economic-report-of-the-President; Quadrennial Technology Review, http://energy.gov/quadrennial-technology-review; Government Accountability Office, *Serving the Congress and the Nation: Strategic Plan, 2014–2019*, GAO-14-1SP, http://gao.gov/assets/670/661281.pdf.

4. A. Scott Berg, *Wilson* (New York: Putnam, 2013), 446.

5. Ibid., 477; Hugh Rockoff, "U.S. Economy in World War I," n.d., EH.net, www.eh.net/encyclopedia/u-s-economy-in-world-war-I/.

6. Robert H. Frank and Ben S. Bernanke. *Principles of Macroeconomics*, 2nd ed. (Boston: McGraw-Hill/Irwin, 2007), 97; Board of Governors of the Federal Reserve System, "Industrial Production Index," http://research.stlouisfed.org/fred2/data/INDPRO.txt; B. R. Staubee, "The Farm Real Estate Situation, 1932–33," US Department of Agriculture, J Circular No. 309, 1933, https://archive.org/stream/farmrealestatesi309stau/farmrealestatesi309stau_djvu.txt.

7. W. W. Rostow, *The United States in the World Arena* (New York: Harper and Row, 1960), 10.

8. "X" [George F. Kennan], "The Sources of Soviet Conduct," *Foreign Affairs*, July 1947.

9. Francis Fukuyama, "The End of History?" *The National Interest*, Summer 1989. See also George H. W. Bush, "Address Before a Joint Session of Congress," September 11, 1990.

10. White House, *A National Security Strategy of Engagement and Enlargement*, February 1995, available at www.au.af.mil/au/awc/awcgate/nss/nss-95 .pdf.

11. Anne Applebaum, "The Worst Mistake America Made After 9/11," Slate, September 4, 2011, www.slate.com/articles/news_and_politics/foreigners/2011 /09/the_worst_mistake_america_made_after_911.html.

12. Danya Greenfield and Amy Hawthorne, *US and EU: Lack of Strategic Vision, Frustrated Efforts Toward the Arab Transitions*, September 25, 2013, Atlantic Council, available at www.atlanticcouncil.org/publications/reports/us -and-eu-lack-of-strategic-vision-frustrated-efforts-toward-the-arab-transitions; House Armed Services Committee, Subcommittee on Seapower and Projection Forces, December 4, 2013.

CHAPTER 2

1. National Intelligence Council, *Global Trends 2030: Alternative Worlds*, December 2012, 5, available at www.dni.gov/index.php/about/organization /national-intelligence-council-global-trends.

2. Richard Perle, James Colbert, Charles Fairbanks Jr., Douglas Feith, Robert J. Loewenberg, Jonathan Torop, David Wurmser, and Meyrav Wurmser, for the Institute for Advanced Strategic and Political Studies, Study Group on a New Israeli Strategy Toward 2000, *A Clean Break: A New Strategy for Securing the Realm*, 1996.

3. See, for example, Ron Suskind, *The Price of Loyalty: George W. Bush, the White House, and the Education of Paul O'Neill* (New York: Simon and Schuster, 2004).

4. "Deputy Secretary Wolfowitz Interview with Sam Tannenhaus," *Vanity Fair*, May 9, 2003, transcript at US Department of Defense, News Transcript, Press Operations, www.defense.gov/transcripts/transcript.aspx?transcriptid =2594; Robert M. Gates, *Duty: Memoirs of a Secretary at War* (New York: Knopf, 2014), 28.

CHAPTER 3

1. "Ex-NSA Chief Contradicts White House on Terror Danger," Investors .com, May 19, 2014, http://news.investors.com/ibd-editorials/051914-701408 -decentralized-al-qaida-a-growing-danger-ex-nsa-chief.htm.

2. Dana Priest and William Arkin, "Top Secret America: A Hidden World, Growing Beyond Control," *Washington Post*, July 19, 2010, http://projects

.washingtonpost.com/top-secret-america/articles/a-hidden-world-growing
-beyond-control/1/.

3. The Review Group on Intelligence and Communications Technology report is available online at "NSA Review Panel Findings: Liberty and Security in a Changing World," *The Guardian*, December 18, 2013, www.theguardian.com/world/interactive/2013/dec/18/nsa-review-panel-report-document.

4. Domain names are registered and managed by the Internet Corporation for Assigned Names and Numbers (ICANN), but ICANN does not regulate or control the Internet. ICANN is a private, nongovernmental organization, and its mission is to support the principle of an open Internet and free access. See www.icann.org/.

5. Siobahn Gorman, August Cole, and Yochi Dreazen, "Computer Spies Breach Fighter-Jet Project," *Wall Street Journal*, April 21, 2009, http://online.wsj.com/news/articles/SB124027491029837401.

6. Siobahn Gorman, "Electricity Grid in US Penetrated by Spies," *Wall Street Journal*, April 8, 2009.

7. Richard McGregor, "US to Charge Chinese Military Officers with Cyber Syping," *Financial Times*, May 19, 2014, www.ft.com/intl/cms/s/0/2108a726-df58-11e3-a4cf-00144feabdc0.html?siteedition=intl#axzz32QB7zEJe.

8. Mandiant, *APT1: Exposing One of China's Cyber Espionage Units*, 2013, http://intelreport.mandiant.com/Mandiant_APT1_Report.pdf.

9. Joint Security Commission, "Redefining Security: A Report to the Secretary of Defense and the Director of Central Intelligence," February 28, 1994, www.fas.org/sgp/library/jsc/; President's Commission on Critical Infrastructure Protection, *Critical Foundations: Protecting America's Infrastructures*, October 1997, https://www.fas.org/sgp/library/pccip.pdf; White House, *Defending America's Cyberspace: National Plan for Information System Protection. Version 1.0, An Invitation to a Dialogue*, 2000, https://www.fas.org/irp/offdocs/pdd/CIP-plan.pdf.

10. Center for Strategic and International Studies (CSIS), "Securing Cyberspace for the 44th Presidency: A Report of the CSIS Commission on Cybersecurity for the 44th Presidency," December 2008, http://csis.org/files/media/csis/pubs/081208_securingcyberspace_44.pdf; William A. Owens, Kenneth W. Dam, and Herbert S. Lin, eds., *Technology, Policy, Law, and Ethics Regarding U.S. Acquisition and Use of Cyberattack Capabilities*, National Research Council, National Academies Press, 2009, www.steptoe.com/assets/attachments/3785.pdf.

11. "Dow Hits Record High," Daily Beast, March 5, 2013; www.thedailybeast.com/cheats/2013/03/05/dow-hits-record-high.html; Makoto Nakajima, "The Diverse Impacts of the Great Recession," 2013, Philadelphia Fed, http://philadelphiafed.org/research-and-data/publications/business-review/2013/q2/brq213_the-diverse-impacts-of-the-great-recession.pdf; Tyler Atkinson, David Luttrell, and Harvey Rosenblum, "How Bad Was It? The Costs and Consequences of the 2007–09 Financial Crisis," Staff Papers, Dallas Fed, July 2013, www.dallasfed.org/assets/documents/research/staff/staff1301.pdf.

12. Brad Plumer, "How the Recession Turned Middle Class Jobs into Low Wage Jobs," *Washington Post*, February 28, 2013, www.washingtonpost.com /blogs/wonkblog/wp/2013/02/28/how-the-recession-turned-middle-class-jobs -into-low-wage-jobs/.

13. Jim Puzzanghera, "Fed's Low-Interest-Rate Policies Cost Savers $758 Billion, Study Says," *Los Angeles Times*, April 22, 2014.

14. Steven E. Woodsworth, *Manifest Destinies: America's Westward Expansion and the Road to the Civil War* (New York: Knopf, 2010), 9, quoting H. W. Brands, *T. R.: The Last Romantic* (New York: Basic Books, 1997), 601.

15. *The Financial Crisis Inquiry Report: Final Report of the National Commission on the Causes of the Financial and Economic Crisis in the United States* (Washington, DC: Government Printing Office, 2011), xvi, available at www .gpo.gov/fdsys/pkg/GPO-FCIC/content-detail.html (FCIC Report hereafter).

16. Binyamin Appelbaum, "Fed Misread Crisis in 2008, Records Show," *New York Times*, February 21, 2014.

17. Ibid. For a full accounting of the evolution of financial regulations since the Great Depression, see Martin H. Wolfson, "An Institutional Theory of Financial Crises," in Martin H. Wolfson and Gerald A. Epstein, eds., *The Political Economy of Financial Crises* (Oxford: Oxford University Press, 2013), Chapter 9; FCIC Report, xviii.

18. FCIC Report, xvii.

19. Ibid., xvii–xxv.

20. The full name of the Dodd-Frank Act is the Dodd-Frank Wall Street Reform and Consumer Protection Act, and it was signed into law in 2010.

21. Ian Hathaway and Robert E. Litan, "Declining Business Dynamism in the United States: A Look at States and Metros," Brookings Institution, May 2014, www.brookings.edu/~/media/research/files/papers/2014/05/declining% 20business%20dynamism%20litan/declining_business_dynamism_hathaway _litan.pdf.

22. Joseph Stiglitz, *The Price of Inequality: How Today's Divided Society Endangers Our Future* (New York: W. W. Norton, 2013). In addition, see Harold Meyerson, "The Myth of Maximizing Shareholder Value," *Washington Post*, February 11, 2014, for a quick description of the issue. For a deeper, academic discussion, see William Lazonick, "From Innovation to Financialization: How Shareholder Value Ideology Is Destroying the US Economy," in Martin H. Wolfson and Gerald A. Epstein, eds., *The Handbook of the Political Economy of Financial Crises* (Oxford, UK: Oxford University Press, 2013).

23. On China's advances in the world economy, see the following: World Steel Association, "Crude Steel Production," n.d., www.worldsteel.org/statistics /crude-steel-production.html; European Cement Association, "Key Facts & Figures," n.d., www.cembureau.eu/about-cement/key-facts-figures; US Energy Information Administration (EIA), "International Energy Statistics," n.d., www .eia.gov/cfapps/ipdbproject/IEDIndex3.cfm?tid=2&pid=2&aid=12; Kathleen Caulderwood, "What a Chinese Railway System Means for Africa," *Interna-*

tional Business Times, May 12, 2014, Investing.com, www.investing.com/news /economy-news/what-a-chinese-railway-system-means-for-africa-283756; Jamil Anderlini and Lucy Hornby, "China Overtakes US as World's Largest Goods Trader," *Financial Times*, January 10, 2014, www.ft.com/intl/cms/s/0/7c2dbd70 -79a6-11e3-b381-00144feabdc0.html?siteedition=intl#axzz3243fMhujst; "China Ends U.S.'s Reign as Largest Auto Market (Update 2), Bloomberg News, January 11, 2010, www.bloomberg.com/apps/news?pid=newsarchive&sid=aE .x_r_l9NZE; China Law & Practice, "China: The World's Largest Mobile Phone Market," September 2006, www.chinalawandpractice.com/Article/1692039 /Channel/9951/China-the-worlds-largest-mobile-phone-market.html; "China to Become World's Largest Luxury Goods Market by 2020," RBR: Markets & Regulations, Markets, February 2, 2011, http://markets.retail-business-review .com/news/china-to-become-worlds-largest-luxury-goods-market-by-2020 _020211; "China to Become World's Largest Consumer Market in 2015: Commerce Minister," Xinhua, May 28, 2012, http://news.xinhuanet.com/english /china/2012-05/28/c_131615744.htm; Brad Plumer, "How China's Appetite for Raw Materials Is Changing the World," *Washington Post*, February 13, 2014, www.washingtonpost.com/blogs/wonkblog/wp/2014/02/13/how-chinas-hunt -for-raw-materials-is-changing-the-world/; US Energy Information Administration (EIA), "Today in Energy: China Dominates Global Coal Production," October 4, 2011, www.eia.gov/todayinenergy/detail.cfm?id=3350; World Aluminum, "Primary Aluminum Production," April 22, 2014, www.world-aluminium.org /statistics/primary-aluminium-production/; Index Mundi, "Titanium: World Production of Mineral Concentrates, by Country," n.d., www.indexmundi.com/en /commodities/minerals/titanium/titanium_t14.html (all accessed May 19, 2014).

24. See, for example, Richard McGregor, *The Party: The Secret World of China's Communist Rulers* (New York: HarperCollins, 2010), for a full discussion of the party's leading role.

25. See, for example, Michael Schuman, "The Real Reason to Worry About China," *Time*, April 28, 2013.

26. Meng Lu, "China's Anticorruption Crusade Is Reaching a Turning Point," GAB/The Global Anticorruption Blog, April 28, 2014, http://globalanti corruptionblog.com/2014/04/28/how-serious-is-xi-jinxing-about-his-anti corruption-crusade/. See also John Sudworth, "The Real Costs of China's Anti-Corruption Crackdown," BBC News China Blog, April 3, 2014, for a discussion of economic impact. Sudworth cites a Bank of America / Merrill Lynch report estimating that the anticorruption drive will cut China's GDP by $135 billion. See also Minxin Pei, "Corruption Threatens China's Growth," Policy Brief 55, Carnegie Endowment for International Peace, October 2007.

27. US Energy Information Administration (EIA), "International Energy Statistics," www.eia.gov/cfapps/ipdbproject/IEDindex3.cfm.

28. Zhao Xinying, "Numbers of US-China Exchange Students Ever Rising," China Daily, last updated March 24, 2014, www.chinadaily.com.cn/china /2014-03/24/content_17373789.htm.

29. Deng Xiaoping, "24 Character Strategy," quoted in US Department of Defense, *Annual Report to Congress: Military Power of the People's Republic of China, 2008,* www.defense.gov/pubs/pdfs/china_military_report_08 .pdf, 8.

30. See Chris Buckley, "China Takes Aim at Western Ideas," *New York Times,* August 19, 2013.

31. US Department of Defense, *Annual Report to Congress: Military and Security Developments Involving the People's Republic of China, 2013,* www .defense.gov/pubs/2013_china_report_final.pdf, 15.

32. Munk Debates, "China: Will the 21st Century Belong to China?" June 17, 2011, 19, transcript available at www.munkdebates.com/debates/china.

33. Radio Australia, "Member Nations of Western Pacific Naval Symposium in China Agree to Maritime Code of Conduct," Radio Australia, April 23, 2014, www.radioaustralia.net.au. See Elizabeth C. Economy and Michael Levi, *By All Means Necessary: How China's Resource Quest Is Changing the World* (New York: Oxford University Press, 2014), Chapter 3, for a perspective of China's resource game.

34. See, for example, Junheng Li, "Highs and Lows from China's Third Plenum," *Forbes,* November 24, 2013, www.forbes.com/sites/junhli/2013/11/24 /highs-and-lows-from-chinas-third-plenum/.

35. International Panel on Climate Change, *Climate Change 2013: The Physical Science Basis,* available at www.climatechange2013.org/.

36. Nicholas Stern, *Economics of Climate Change: The Stern Review* (London: HM Treasury, 2007).

37. CNA Corporation, *National Security and the Threat of Climate Change,* 2007, available at https://www.cna.org/reports/climate.

38. See William Nordhaus, *The Climate Casino: Risk, Uncertainty, and Economics for a Warming World* (New Haven, CT: Yale University Press, 2013).

39. Ibid., but this is mentioned everywhere in climate studies. See, for example, "Methane Hydrates and Global Warming," Phys.org, January 2, 2014, http://phys.org/news/2014-01-methane-hydrates-global.html; Carolyn D. Ruppel, "Methane Hydrates and Contemporary Climate Change," *Nature Education Knowledge* 3, no. 10 (2011): 29, www.nature.com/scitable/knowledge/library /methane-hydrates-and-contemporary-climate-change-24314790. See also Darryl Fears, "Collapse of the Antarctic Ice Sheet Is Underwater," *Washington Post,* May 12, 2014.

40. See, for example, Andrew Glikson "Methane and the Risk of Runaway Global Warming," The Conversation, July 26, 2013, www.theconversation.com /methane-and-the-risk-of-runaway-global-warming-16275.

CHAPTER 4

1. Zbigniew Brzezinski, *Strategic Vision: America and the Crisis of Global Power* (New York: Basic Books, 2011), 46.

2. National Intelligence Council, *Global Trends 2030: Alternative Worlds*, December 2012, available at www.dni.gov/index.php/about/organization/national -intelligence-council-global-trends, 98.

3. The Concord Coalition, "National Debt," www.concordcoalition.org/node /58.

4. See, for example, International Monetary Fund, "World Economic Outlook Update: Is the Tide Rising?" January 2014, www.imf.org/external/pubs/ft /weo/2014/update/01/; Robert Kagan, *The World America Made* (New York: Knopf, 2012), Chapter 4, 99–107, for a discussion of relative US economic strength.

5. Paul Kennedy, *The Rise and Fall of the Great Powers* (New York: Random House, 1987).

6. Vaclav Smil, *Why America Is Not a New Rome* (Cambridge, MA: MIT Press, 2010), 66; Niall Ferguson, *The Great Degeneration: How Institutions Decay and Economies Die* (New York: Penguin, 2013).

7. World Intellectual Property Organization (WIPO), *World Intellectual Property Indicators 2013*, Summary Highlights, available at www.wipo.int/ipstats /en/wipi/.

8. See, for example, Martin West, "Global Lessons for Improving US Education," Issues in Science and Technology, November 27, 2013, www.issues.org/28-3 /west/, for a good discussion of relative education levels and implications.

9. See Al Gore, *The Future: Six Drivers of Global Change* (New York: Random House, 2013), Chapter 3, for a good discussion of the rise of corporate power and its impact.

10. John Maynard Keynes, *The General Theory of Employment, Interest and Money* (New York: Harcourt Brace, 1936).

11. US Government Accountability Office, *2013 Annual Report: Actions Needed to Reduce Fragmentation, Overlap, and Duplication and Achieve Other Financial Benefits*, GAO-13-279SP, April 9, 2013, http://gao.gov/products /GAO-13-279SP.

12. See, for example, Thomas E. Mann and Norman J. Ornstein, *It's Even Worse than It Looks: How the American Constitutional System Collided with the New Politics of Extremism* (New York: Basic Books, 2012), 31–80, for a full discussion of the impact of money and media on modern US political culture.

13. Pew Research Center, in association with the Council on Foreign Relations, "Public Sees U.S. Power Declining as Support for Global Engagement Slips: America's Place in the World 2013," December 3, 2013, www.people -press.org/files/legacy-pdf/12-3-2013%20APW%20VI.pdf; Frank Bruni, "America the Shrunken," *New York Times*, May 3, 2014.

14. BBC, "BBC Poll: Germany Most Popular Country in the World," May 23, 2013, www.bbc.com/news/world-europe-22624104; Pew Research Center for the People & the Press, "Public Sees U.S. Power Declining as Support for Global Engagement Slips," "Section 5: Public Views of Selected Countries,"

December 3, 2013, www.people-press.org/2013/12/03/section-5-public-views-of
-selected-countries/; Pew Research Global Attitudes Project, "Global Image of
the United States and China," July 18, 2013, www.pewglobal.org/2013/07/18
/global-image-of-the-united-states-and-china/; "Commentary: U.S. Fiscal Failure
Warrants a De-Americanized World," Xinhua, Global Edition, October 13, 2013,
http://news.xinhuanet.com/english/indepth/2013-10/13/c_132794246.htm.

15. US Department of Commerce, Bureau of Economic Analysis (BEA), National Economic Accounts, "GDP: Percent Change from Preceding Period,"
www.bea.gov/national/index.htm#gdp; William A. Link and Arthur Stanley
Link, *American Epoch: A History of the United States Since 1900*, 7th ed., vol.
1 (New York: McGraw-Hill, 1992), 524; US Department of Labor, Bureau of
Labor Statistics, "Labor Force Statistics from the Current Population Survey,"
www.bls.gov/cps/cpsaat01.htm.

16. Board of Governors of the Federal Reserve System, Economic Research
and Data, www.federalreserve.gov/econresdata/default.htm; US Department of
Commerce, Bureau of Economic Analysis (BEA), www.bea.gov; Bain & Company, *Global Private Equity Report 2013*, www.bain.com/publications/articles
/global-private-equity-report-2013.aspx; BarclayHedge Hedge Fund Database,
2013, www.barclayhedge.com/.

17. US Department of Labor, Bureau of Labor Statistics, "The Employment
Situation—November 2013," news release, December 6, 2013, www.bls.gov
/news.release/archives/empsit_12062013.pdf; Board of Governors of the Federal Reserve System, Economic Research and Data, "Industrial Production and
Capacity Utilization," G.17 report released December 16, 2013, www.federal
reserve.gov/releases/g17/releases_2013.htm.

18. Juan M. Sánchez and Emircan Yurdagul, "Why Are Corporations Holding So Much Cash?" *Regional Economist*, January 2013, Federal Reserve Bank
of St. Louis, https://www.stlouisfed.org/publications/re/articles/?id=2314; Robin
Harding, "Corporate Investment: A Mysterious Divergence," *Financial Times*,
July 25, 2013, 5.

19. See, for example, "Market Is Still Missing Full-Blown 'Animal Spirits,'
Wells Fargo's Paulsen Says," The Tell, January 3, 2014, Wall Street Journal
Market Watch, http://blogs.marketwatch.com/thetell/2014/01/03/market-is
-still-missing-full-blown-animal-spirits-wells-fargos-paulsen-says/. Wells Capital Management's chief investment strategist is quoted as saying, "If real GDP
growth finally this year sustains 3%, corporate animal spirits should begin to
awaken."

20. Patrick Clark, "Why Small Business Bank Lending Won't Rebound
Soon," Bloomberg Businessweek, *The New Entrepreneur*, August 15, 2013.

21. See, for example, Nelson D. Schwartz, "Recovery in US Is Lifting Profits
But Not Adding Jobs," *New York Times*, March 3, 2013; Federal Reserve
Chairman Ben Bernanke, statement at the Annual Meeting of the American
Economic Association, Philadelphia, January 3, 2014, www.federalreserve.gov
/newsevents/speech/bernanke20140103a.htm.

CHAPTER 5

1. US Department of Energy, Office of Transportation and Air Quality, "Reduce Oil Dependence Costs," n.d., www.fueleconomy.gov/feg/oildep.shtml.

2. President Obama in 2011 called for the United States to become one-third less dependent on foreign oil over the next decade. Republican presidential nominee Mitt Romney in 2012 called for full North American energy independence (which some saw as a policy of "drill, baby, drill").

3. See, for example, Matthew DiLallo, "The World Needs 390 Billion Barrels of New Oil Production by 2035," The Motley Fool, September 22, 2013, www.fool.com/investing/general/2013/09/22/the-world-needs-390-billion-barrels-of-new-oil-pro.aspx.

4. US Energy Information Administration (EIA), *Annual Energy Outlook 2014, with Projections to 2040*, AEO2014 Early Release Overview, December 16, 2013, www.eia.gov/forecasts/aeo/er/.

5. White House, "Obama Administration Finalizes Historic 54.5 MPG Fuel Efficiency Standards," August 28, 2012, www.whitehouse.gov/the-press-office/2012/08/28/obama-administration-finalizes-historic-545-mpg-fuel-efficiency-standard; see also John Miller, "Can the New CAFE Standards Deliver (Promised Benefits)?" The Energy Collective, August 20, 2012, http://theenergycollective.com/jemillerep/104841/can-new-cafe-standards-deliver-promised-benefits.

6. Fred Lawrence, "The Imperishable Permian Basin," Master Resource, May 17, 2013, www.masterresource.org/2013/05/imperishable-permian-basin/; Jennifer Hiller, "Has the Eagle Ford Shale Crossed the 1 Million Barrel Mark?" Fuel Fix, October 24, 2013, http://fuelfix.com/blog/2013/10/24/has-the-eagle-ford-shale-crossed-the-1-million-barrel-mark/.

7. Marc Humphries, "US Crude Oil and Natural Gas Production in Federal and Non-Federal Areas," Congressional Research Service, March 7, 2013, http://energycommerce.house.gov/sites/republicans.energycommerce.house.gov/files/20130228CRSreport.pdf.

8. Wood Mackenzie, *Energy Policy at a Crossroads: An Assessment of the Impacts of Increased Access Versus Higher Taxes on U.S. Oil and Natural Gas Production, Government Revenue, and Employment*, revised June 24, 2011, www.api.org/news-and-media/news/newsitems/2014/mar-2014/~/media/Files/News/2011/SOAE_Wood_Mackenzie_Access_vs_Taxes.pdf; Congressional Budget Office, "Potential Budgetary Effects of Immediately Opening Most Federal Lands to Oil and Gas Leasing," August 2012, www.cbo.gov/sites/default/files/cbofiles/attachments/08-09-12_Oil-and-Gas_Leasing.pdf; Joseph R. Mason, "Beyond the Congressional Budget Office: The Additional Economic Effects of Immediately Opening Federal Lands to Oil and Gas Leasing," February 2013, Institute for Energy Research, www.instituteforenergyresearch.org/wp-content/uploads/2013/02/IER_Mason_Report_NoEMB.pdf.

9. See, for example, International Institute for Energy Research, "Oil Shale," 2012, www.instituteforenergyresearch.org/energy-overview/oil-shale/, for a quick review.

10. US Energy Information Administration (EIA), *Annual Energy Outlook 2013, with Projections to 2040*, April 2013, www.eia.gov/forecasts/aeo/pdf /0383(2013).pdf.

11. Susan Lund, James Manyika, Scott Nyquist, Lenny Mendonca, and Sreenivas Ramaswamy, "Game Changers: Five Opportunities for US Growth and Renewal," July 2013, McKinsey Global Institute, www.mckinsey.com/insights /americas/us_game_changers.

12. IHS, *America's New Energy Future: The Unconventional Oil & Gas Revolution and the US Economy*, Executive Summary, available at www.ihs .com/info/ecc/a/americas-new-energy-future-report-vol-3.aspx.

13. Ibid.; see also, for example, Michael Birnbaum, "European Industry Flocks to US to Take Advantage of Cheaper Gas," *Washington Post*, April 13, 2013.

14. Oil, gas, and coal come from plants and trees that grew hundreds of millions of years ago, whose residue has been compressed and recomposed by natural geologic processes into gas, oil, and coal; using these sources of energy releases into the atmosphere heat-trapping carbon previously safely sequestered deep underground. Biofuels, on the other hand, use as feedstock plants recently grown using atmospheric carbon dioxide; using these plants for fuel merely recirculates this carbon to the atmosphere.

15. For discussion of carbon-taxing schemes and alternatives, see Center for Climate and Energy Solutions, "Options and Considerations for a Federal Carbon Tax," February 2013, www.c2es.org/publications/options-considerations -federal-carbon-tax.

16. See Mack McLarty's opinion piece, "Time Is Right to Reset a Bipartisan Energy Policy," *Dallas Morning News*, April 8, 2014.

CHAPTER 6

1. See, for example, the testimony from US Senate, Committee on Foreign Relations, Subcommittee on International Development and Foreign Assistance, Economic Affairs, International Environmental Protection, and Peace Corps, "Different Perspectives on International Development," 113th Cong., 1st sess., May 22, 2013, www.gpo.gov/fdsys/pkg/CHRG-113shrg86151/html/CHRG-113 shrg86151.htm.

2. Ibid., statement by Todd J. Moss, vice president and Senior Fellow, Center for Global Development.

3. A full description and analysis of the Millennium Challenge Corporation can be found at Curt Tarnoff, *Millennium Challenge Corporation*, Congressional Research Service, April 8, 2014, www.fas.org/sgp/crs/row/RL32427.pdf.

4. World Bank, *The Growth Report: Strategies for Sustained Growth and Inclusive Development*, http://web.worldbank.org/WBSITE/EXTERNAL/EXT ABOUTUS/ORGANIZATION/EXTPREMNET/0,,contentMDK:2322 5680~pagePK:64159605~piPK:64157667~theSitePK:489961,00.html; Michael

Spence, *The Next Convergence: The Future of Economic Growth in a Multispeed World* (New York: Farrar, Straus and Giroux, 2011), 95.

CHAPTER 7

1. White House, *National Strategy for Counterterrorism*, June 2011, www .whitehouse.gov/sites/default/files/counterterrorism_strategy.pdf.

2. "Interview with Gerald Epstein," n.d., Political Economy Research Institute, University of Massachusetts at Amherst, www.peri.umass.edu/341/.

3. See, for example, Tom Conley, "Financialisation and Globalisation: Permanent Reverse or Cyclical Downturn," Big P Political Economy, April 2, 2013, http://tomjconley.blogspot.com/2013/04/financialisation-and-globalisation .html.

4. See, for example, Andrew Nathan and Andrew Scobel, "How China Sees America," *Foreign Affairs*, September-October 2012.

5. Gordon G. Chang, "China Now Claims Japan's Okinawa," *World Affairs*, July 25, 2012, www.worldaffairsjournal.org/blog/gordon-g-chang/china-now -claims-japan%E2%80%99s-okinawa.

6. Quoted in Ely Ratner, "Rebalancing Toward Asia with an Insecure China," *Washington Quarterly*, Spring 2013, 28.

7. United Nations, Economic Commission for Africa, *Making the Most of Africa's Commodities: Industrializing for Growth, Jobs and Economic Transformation*, Economic Report on Africa 2013 (Addis Ababa: Economic Commission for Africa, 2013), www.uneca.org/sites/default/files/publications/era2013 _eng_fin_low.pdf, 6.

8. Statement by Zhang Changhui, chief country risk analyst at Export-Import Bank of China, at the Africa Investment Summit in Hong Kong, November 2013, quoted by ECNS.cn in "Symbiotic China-Africa Relationship Expected to Grow," January 29, 2014, www.ecns.cn/2014/01-29/99328.shtml.

INDEX

Photo courtesy of the author

General (ret.) Wesley K. Clark is a distinguished fellow at UCLA's Burkle Center and a retired four-star general in the United States Army. He served as Supreme Allied Commander Europe, where he led NATO forces to victory in Operation Allied Force, the war in Kosovo. He is chairman and CEO of Wesley K. Clark & Associates, a strategic consulting firm, and is the author of *Winning Modern Wars, Waging Modern War*, and *A Time to Lead*. He serves as a member of the Clinton Global Initiative's Energy & Climate Change Advisory Board, and is the recipient of many awards, including the Purple Heart and the Presidential Medal of Freedom.

PublicAffairs is a publishing house founded in 1997. It is a tribute to the standards, values, and flair of three persons who have served as mentors to countless reporters, writers, editors, and book people of all kinds, including me.

I. F. STONE, proprietor of *I. F. Stone's Weekly*, combined a commitment to the First Amendment with entrepreneurial zeal and reporting skill and became one of the great independent journalists in American history. At the age of eighty, Izzy published *The Trial of Socrates*, which was a national bestseller. He wrote the book after he taught himself ancient Greek.

BENJAMIN C. BRADLEE was for nearly thirty years the charismatic editorial leader of *The Washington Post*. It was Ben who gave the *Post* the range and courage to pursue such historic issues as Watergate. He supported his reporters with a tenacity that made them fearless and it is no accident that so many became authors of influential, best-selling books.

ROBERT L. BERNSTEIN, the chief executive of Random House for more than a quarter century, guided one of the nation's premier publishing houses. Bob was personally responsible for many books of political dissent and argument that challenged tyranny around the globe. He is also the founder and longtime chair of Human Rights Watch, one of the most respected human rights organizations in the world.

·　　·　　·

For fifty years, the banner of Public Affairs Press was carried by its owner Morris B. Schnapper, who published Gandhi, Nasser, Toynbee, Truman, and about 1,500 other authors. In 1983, Schnapper was described by *The Washington Post* as "a redoubtable gadfly." His legacy will endure in the books to come.

Peter Osnos, *Founder and Editor-at-Large*